HEAVEN UPON EARTH

HEAVEN UPON EARTH
JESUS, THE BEST FRIEND
IN THE WORST TIMES

JAMES JANEWAY

SOLID GROUND CHRISTIAN BOOKS
BIRMINGHAM, ALABAMA USA

Solid Ground Christian Books
2090 Columbiana Rd, Suite 2000
Birmingham, AL 35216
205-443-0311
sgcb@charter.net
http://solid-ground-books.com

HEAVEN UPON EARTH
Jesus, the Best Friend in the Worst Times

James Janeway (1636-1674)

Taken from 1847 edition by Thomas Nelson Publishers

Solid Ground Puritan Classic Reprints

First printing of new edition April 2006

Cover work by Borgo Design, Tuscaloosa, AL
Contact them at nelbrown@comcast.net

Cover image is a painting of the Great Fire of London, of 1666 which was one of the main incidents of God's providence which prompted Janeway to write this book. (Read pages 21f. to see the impact of this terrible fire.)

ISBN: 1-59925-067-5

TABLE OF CONTENTS

New Introduction by Dr. Joel Beeke   1

Introductory Essay by Rev. F.A. Cox   5
The Family of the Janeways and the Times they Lived

HEAVEN UPON EARTH   37
"Acquaint now thyself with him, and be at peace; thereby good shall come unto thee." – Job 22:21

  DOCTRINE - ACQUAINTANCE WITH GOD   40
    1- A knowledge of God
    2- Nigh access to God
    3- Familiar converse with God
    4- Mutual communication between us and God
    5- An affectionate love towards God

  DUTY - TO ACQUAINT ONESELF WITH GOD   51
    1- Because this is the great design of the work of Christ
    2- Because therein is the improvement of man's highest excellency
    3- To refuse is to slight the greatest mercy God can show
    4- For without it we are in a necessity of sin and misery
    5- Because God himself doth acquaint himself with man

  USES OF THIS DOCTRINE   61
    1- Let us stand and wonder at the great condescension of God
    2- Let us judge ourselves to be too high for this world
    3- Let us inquire whether we are acquainted with him

  EXHORTATION   82

  MOTIVES   83
  First, the Nature of the Person I would have you acquainted with   84
    1- He is a most loving and kind Friend   84
    2- He is a most comfortable Friend   89
    3- He is a most able and powerful Friend   96
    4- He is a most active Friend   97
    5- He is a most humble and condescending Friend   98
    6- He is a most faithful Friend   101
    7- He is a rich Friend   105
    8- He is a sympathizing Friend   114
    9- He is a most patient Friend   116
    10- He is a most honorable Friend   118
    11- He is a suitable Friend   124
    12- He is a wise Friend   128
    13- He is an immortal Friend   131
    14- He is a present Friend   133
    15- He is a soul-Friend   137
    16- He is a necessary Friend   141
    17- He is a tried Friend   145
    18- He is an everlasting Friend   145
    19- He is a Friend who is willing to be acquainted with you   149
    20- He is a Friend who is altogether lovely   156

MOTIVES (continued)

Second, the Glorious Effects of being Acquainted with God 162
1- It makes the soul humble 162
2- It makes a man fall upon sin in earnest 166
3- It makes one have low thoughts of the world 174
4- It will ease us of all sorrows, or cure them 179
5- It honors him more highly 187
6- It puts abundance of life and vigour into the soul 190
7- It will make a man patient under God's providence 193
8- It makes all enjoyments doubly sweet 194
9- It makes a man wise 195
10- It makes a man rich 198
11- It makes a man like God 200
12- It makes a man better in all stations and relations 201

Third, the Grave Danger of not being acquainted with God 204

Fourth, the examples of others who made all the friends
they could get acquainted with God 211

Fifth, Acquaintance with God leads to Peace 215

Sixth, thereby good will come to you 217

QUESTIONS 226
1- Are these things you have heard true? 226
2- Are these things of weight and importance? 228
3- Why do you treat these things with such indifference? 229
4- Can you find a better friend than God? 230
5- Do you think this world will last always with you? 231
6- What will happen if you go on in your old ways? 231
7- Are you willing to bear the displeasure of God? 232
8- Are you contented to lose everlasting happiness? 232
9- How would you accept the service you give to God? 233
10- And now, what will you do? 235

DIRECTIONS 239
1- Get a thorough sense of your estrangement from God 239
2- Get a humble heart 245
3- Visit him often in meditation, prayer, fasting... 250
4- Get Christ along with you when you go to God 264
5- Come much where he is wont to be 267
6- Get acquainted with his friends 269
7- Entertain all messengers he sends you 274
8- Seek his acquaintance most earnestly 275
9- Be much in expostulating your case with God 280
10- Look after this speedily, do not delay 282

QUESTIONS 286
1- Are these things necessary or not? 286
2- Do you expect to look after these things later in life? 286
3- When would you get acquainted with God? 287
4- Who deserves your best, the world, flesh, the devil or God? 287
5- How would you take it if others served you the same way you serve God? 287
6- Do you think you can make too much haste? 287
7- Are you sure you will live an hour longer? 287
8- What will become of you if you put it off too long? 288
9- What would you do if you were sure you would die or the judgment would come before week's end? 288
10- Do you think you will get acquainted with God in another world when you neglect him here? 288

DIRECTIONS (continued) 288
11- Take heed of those things that keep God and man at a distance 288
12- Give yourself to God in a most solemn covenant 295

THE CONCLUSION 298

New Introduction

James Janeway (1636-1674) was born in Lilley, Hertfordshire. He was the fourth of nine sons of a minister, William Janeway, and the younger brother of John, who also became a Puritan minister. He was educated at Christ's Church, Oxford, where he earned a bachelor's degree in 1659. He then spent some time tutoring at Windsor.

Ordained a deacon in 1661, Janeway was ejected in 1662 for Nonconformity. He ministered on in conventicles, however, through national disasters such as the plague and the great fire of London in 1666. After Charles II issued his Declaration of Indulgence, Janeway was licensed as a Presbyterian minister in 1672.

Janeway's last years as preacher in Rotherhithe were his most fruitful and yet most difficult. In 1672, his supporters built a large meetinghouse for him in Jamaica Row, Rotherhithe, Surrey. Janeway's popularity so enraged Anglicans that several times they threatened to shoot him and actually attempted to do so twice. One time, a bullet pierced his hat. Another time, soldiers destroyed Janeway's church building. His congregation replaced it with a larger building.

After struggling several years with depression, Janeway contracted tuberculosis. He died when he was thirty-eight. At least five of his brothers also died of tuberculosis before reaching the age of forty.

Janeway's experience with suffering, persecution, and death is reflected in much of his work. His acute awareness of the mortality of man charges his work with spiritual intensity and eternal focus. This is particularly true of this welcome reprint, *Heaven upon Earth, or Jesus, the Best Friend, in the Worst Times* (1667). In this little masterpiece based on Job 22:21, Janeway earnestly exhorts us to a real, growing, and varied acquaintance with God, so that we might be at peace with Him. He argues for a real, vital, experiential knowledge of God by which a believer, like Moses, might "speak with God face to face, as a man speaketh to his friend" (1847 reprint, p. 56). Calling attention to the recent plague and fire in London, Janeway warns of the importance of befriending God before it is too late. In typical Puritan fashion, the book is packed with practical uses, exhortations, and motives that flow out of acquainting one's self with God.

Janeway's motives, especially those rooted in Jesus' friendship, are the cream of the book. Jesus, he says, is the most loving and kind Friend, the most comfortable Friend, the most able and powerful Friend, the most active Friend, the most humble and condescending Friend, the most faithful and richest Friend, the most sympathizing and patient Friend, and the most honorable and suitable Friend. He is a wise, immortal, present, necessary, soul-Friend. He is a tried and afflicted Friend, who desires to be acquainted with sinners. He is an altogether lovely Friend (pp.84-162). After expounding additional reasons for sinners to be motivated to seek acquaintance with God, Janeway concludes by providing twelve practical ways— most of which focus on a diligent use of various spiritual disciplines—by which a seeking soul may grow in acquaintance with God. This book is a masterful treatment of spiritual divinity—an invaluable handbook on how to grow in intimacy with God through His Son (pp. 239-298).

Two other titles of Janeway have been reprinted in recent years: Based on 2 Peter 1:11, *The Saints' Encouragement to Diligence in Christ's Service* (1674; reprinted by Soli Deo Gloria in 1994) is "an admonition to sinners to reform and an exhortation to zealous conscientiousness in the converted, in their performance of duties, in introspective scrutiny of their spiritual condition, and in meditation upon God's providences" (*Oxford DNB*, 29:782). This book powerfully exhorts believers not to grow weary in pursuing good, but to be diligent in the service of Christ. It is full of practical suggestions and applications. "Time is short," writes Janeway. "Our work, our Master, our wages are great, and, not to mince the matter, we have yet done little. Instead of creeping, let us run; instead of sleeping and dreaming, let us awake and work diligently."

An appendix to the book describes the Christ-centered deathbed experiences of a godly woman (named Mrs. B.) to enrich the book's theme of persevering in Christian diligence. In his preface, Richard Baxter says that such testimonies "help to confirm the reader's faith."

In *A Token for Children* (reprinted by Soli Deo Gloria in 2001), Janeway compiled numerous accounts of the conversions of young children and their testimonies prior to their early deaths in order to rescue children from their "miserable condition by nature" and "from falling into everlasting fire" (preface). Next to the Scriptures and Bunyan's *Pilgrim's Progress*, Janeway's book was the most widely read children's book in the seventeenth century.

HEAVEN UPON EARTH

Cotton Mather, a Puritan pastor in New England, wrote his own account of children converted by God and called it *A Token for the Children of New England*. That book plus Janeway's are printed together in this volume. They are most effective in showing how Puritan parents evangelized their children in the home.

John Gerstner says in the foreword to this book, "If we contemporary 'Christians' want to know what Christian experience is, we can do no better than to let these little children of centuries ago teach us. Every modern Christian parent ought to buy and study this book before making it required reading for all his/her offspring."

Janeway wrote two other popular books that have not been reprinted. His most popular book in his own day, *Invisibles, Realities, Demonstrated in the Holy Life and Triumphant Death of John Janeway* (1673, and reprinted eighteen in the next two centuries), expounds the spiritual joys that his older brother experienced prior to his untimely death at age twenty-four. Janeway wrote this biography as an antidote against atheists and those who opposed experiential piety. *Mr. James Janeway's Legacy to His Friends: Containing Twenty-seven Famous Instances of God's Providences in and about Sea-Dangers and Deliverances*, published shortly after his death in 1674, has similar goals in mind.

Dr. Joel R. Beeke
Puritan Reformed Theological Seminary,
Grand Rapids, Michigan

INTRODUCTORY ESSAY

ON

THE FAMILY OF THE JANEWAYS AND THE TIMES IN

WHICH THEY LIVED.

BY THE

REV. F. A. COX, D.D. LL.D.

~~~~~~

THE family of the Janeways is greatly distinguished in the annals of nonconformity for the number of its members who were devoted to the Christian ministry. Nearly all of them were eminent on account of their piety, zeal, and usefulness; and though we have reason to regret the scantiness of the materials which furnish information respecting their lives and habits, enough has been spared by time to supply a few interesting details, and to suggest important lessons to posterity. Of such men the fragments should be gathered, that nothing be lost.

The father of the more celebrated individuals, to whom we refer, was William Janeway, originally of Lilley, in Hertfordshire, but afterwards a resident in the village of Aspeden, or, as it is now called, Harpenden, to which place he removed about the year 1644. At length he became minister of Kelshall, where, after a severe spiritual conflict, he died in holy triumph, leaving a widow and eleven children. As we have not the means of tracing the particulars of his life and labours, a valuable page from the record of his dying hours, in the biography of his son John, may be introduced with advantage, and will be appreciated by the pious reader. Being under dark apprehensions of mind in his last illness, he expressed himself in the following manner to his son:—
" Oh, John! this passing into eternity is a great thing; this dying is a solemn business, and enough to make any one's heart ache, that hath not his pardon sealed and his evidences for

heaven clear. And truly, son, I am under no small fears as to my own estate for another world. Oh that God would clear his love! Oh that I could say cheerfully, I can die; and upon good grounds be able to look death in the face, and venture upon eternity with well-grounded peace and comfort!" His son, after making a suitable reply, which, however, did not restore his peace, retired to solitary prayer, earnestly imploring that his beloved father might be filled with joy in believing, as a token for good in leaving the world. These intercessions were manifestly heard and answered by a very bright beam of the divine countenance. Upon returning to his father, the son inquired how he felt himself. No answer was given; but the departing saint, though little subject to such emotions, wept for a long time, in an extraordinary manner, till at last he broke forth in the language of impassioned exultation—" Oh, son! now it is come, it is come, it is come. I bless God I can die: the Spirit of God hath witnessed with my spirit that I am his child. Now I can look upon God as my dear Father, and Christ as my Redeemer: I can now say, This is my Friend, and this is my Beloved! My heart is full; it is brim full; I can hold no more. I know now what that sentence means, ' The peace of God which passeth understanding.' I know now what that white stone is, whereon a new name is written, which none know but they who have it. And that fit of weeping which you saw me in was a fit of overpowering love and joy, so great, that I could not for my heart contain myself; neither can I express what glorious discoveries God hath made of himself unto me. And had that joy been greater, I question whether I could have borne it, and whether it would not have separated soul and body. Bless the Lord, O my soul, and all that is within me bless his holy name, that hath pardoned all my sins, and sealed the pardon. He hath healed my wounds, and caused the bones which he had broken to rejoice. O help me to bless the Lord! He hath put a new song into my mouth. O bless the Lord for his infinite goodness and mercy! Oh, now I can die! it is nothing; I bless God I can die. I desire to be dissolved, and to be with Christ."

The eldest son was also named William Janeway. He was admitted to the university of Cambridge about 1650, and in all probability succeeded his father at Kelshall, as he resided there, and was a preacher, in 1657. He does not appear to have possessed the rectory; if he did, it was only for a short time.

John Janeway, the next brother, was a most remarkable man. A tolerably full account of his life, and the circumstances of his death, written by his brother James, was some years ago republished, with a preface by the Rev. Robert Hall. He was born October 27, 1633, at Lilley, and was successively educated at Paul's School, Eton College, and King's College, Cambridge, of which he afterwards became a fellow. His reputation was so great at the period of his admission, though only seventeen years of age, that the electors contended for the honour of being his patron. Greatly advanced, however, as he was in literature, and equally distinguished for the modesty and courteousness of his deportment, the crowning excellence of his character, decided religion, was not attained till the following year. "The Lord was pleased," says his fraternal biographer, "sweetly to unlock his heart, by the exemplary life and heavenly and powerful discourse of a young man in the college, whose heart God had inflamed with love to his soul. He quickly made an attempt upon this hopeful young man, and the Spirit of God did set home his counsels with such power, that they proved effectual for his awakening, being accompanied with the preaching of those two famous worthies, Dr. Hill and Dr. Arrowsmith, together with the reading of several parts of Mr. Baxter's "Saints' Everlasting Rest."

No sooner did he become converted to God than he manifested the deepest interest in the spiritual condition of his brethren and friends, speaking and writing to them in terms of extraordinary urgency and power. As a fellow of a college, he used his utmost efforts to promote religion in the minds of all with whom he came in contact, and over whom he could exert the influence of a natural or official superiority. One who was intimately acquainted with him was accustomed to say that he was like deep waters that were most still—a man of hidden excellency.

Upon the recommendation of the provost of his college, he engaged for a time in the service of a family as private tutor, but ill health compelled him to relinquish his situation, and he retired to live in the country with his mother and brother. Many apprehensions were entertained that he would not live;

but not only did he enjoy a perfect peace himself, he was the consoler and instructor of others around him, and of some at a distance, by his fervent pen, winged with holy words and heavenly pleadings. After he had in some measure recovered, the author of the following treatise states his renewed earnestness in the discharge of every duty, especially prayer and meditation. " His time," says he, " for that was commonly in the evening, when he usually walked into the field, if the weather would permit; if not, he retired into the church, or any empty solitary room, where (observing his constant practice, that, if possible, I might be acquainted with the reason of his retiredness) I once hid myself, that I might take the more exact notice of the intercourse that I judged was kept up between him and God. But, oh! what a spectacle did I see! Surely a man walking with God, conversing intimately with his Maker, and maintaining a holy familiarity with the great Jehovah. Methought I saw one talking with God;—methought I saw a spiritual merchant in a heavenly exchange, driving a rich trade for the treasures of another world. Oh, what a glorious sight it was! Methinks I see him still. How sweetly did his face shine! Oh, with what a lovely countenance did he walk up and down; his lips going, his body oft reaching up, as if he would have taken his flight into heaven! His looks, smiles, and every motion spake him to be upon the very confines of glory. Oh, had one but known what he was then feeding on! Sure he had meat to eat which the world knew not of! Did we but know how welcome God made him when he brought him into his banqueting-house. That which one might easily perceive his heart to be most fixed upon, was the infinite love of God in Christ to the poor lost sons and daughters of Adam. What else meant his high expressions? What else did his own words to a dear friend signify, but an extraordinary sense of the freeness, fulness, and duration of that love? To use his own words:—' God,' said he, ' holds mine eyes most upon his goodness, and the promises which are most sure and firm in Christ. His love to us is greater, surer, fuller, than ours to ourselves. For when we loved ourselves so as to destroy ourselves, he loved us so as to save us.' "

At the age of twenty-two, he devoted himself to the Christian ministry; a work for which he was eminently qualified, not only by his intellectual attainments, but more especially by the depth of his religious experience, and the ardour of his love for souls. It is remarkable, however, that he lived to preach only two sermons, the subject of which was—both being from the same text—on communion with God. But in reality, almost every day was with him a Sabbath, and every conversation a sermon. The intensity of his sympathy with the spiritual condition of others, and the moral courage which impelled him onward in the path of duty and devotedness, were such, that he never hesitated to avow whatever he deemed right, or to rebuke whatever he considered wrong. He exhibited those extremes of excellence in character which, to men of the world, appear paradoxical, but which Christianity is fully capable of displaying in perfection; the lamb-like grace of humility, with the lion-like virtue of fearlessness.

That dreadful scourge of humanity, consumption, which had been long insidiously undermining his constitution, at length brought him to the grave in June 1657, at the early age of twenty-three. His last sickness brought out in rich and beautiful manifestation those heavenly graces that adorned his character. His death-bed was a field of triumph; and as his ardent soul approached eternity, it seemed to catch the splendours of the invisible world, and reflect their glories around the dark valley, and upon every spectator of the rapturous scene. Never, perhaps, was piety more exalted, or victory over death more complete. He could not rein in the unwonted vehemence of his affections and joy as his race was terminating, and the chariot wheels seemed, as it were, to burn for the goal.

"When one came to visit him,* and told him that he hoped it might please God to raise him again, and that he had seen many a weaker man restored to health, and that lived many a good year after: 'And do you think to please me,' said he, "by such discourse as this? No, friend, you are much mistaken in me, if you think that the thoughts of life, and health, and the world, are pleasing to me. The world hath quite lost its excellency in my judgment. Oh, how contemptible a thing is it in all its glory, compared with the glory of that invisible world which I now live in the sight of! And as for life, Christ

* The quotations are from his brother James's narrative.

is my life, health, and strength; and I know I shall have another kind of life when I leave this. I tell you it would incomparably more please me, if you should say to me, You are no man of this world: you cannot possibly hold out long: before to-morrow you will be in eternity. I tell you I do so long to be with Christ, that I could be content to be cut in pieces, and to be put to the most exquisite torments, so I might but die and be with Christ. Oh, how sweet is Jesus! Come Lord Jesus, come quickly. Death, do thy worst! Death hath lost its terribleness. Death; it is nothing. I say, death is nothing, through grace, to me. I can as easily die as shut my eyes, or turn my head and sleep: I long to be with Christ: I long to die.'

* * * "I verily believe that it exceeds the highest rhetoric to set out to the life what this heavenly creature did then deliver. I say again, I want words to speak, and so did he, for he said things unutterable; but yet, so much he spake, as justly drew the admiration of all that saw him; and I heard an old experienced Christian minister say it again and again, that he never saw, nor read, nor heard, the like. Neither could we ever expect to see the glories of heaven more demonstrated to sense in this world. He talked as if he had been in the third heavens."

After introducing several impassioned expressions and sentences, the biographer proceeds:—" About eight-and-forty hours before his death, his eyes were dim, and his sight much failed; his jaws shook and trembled, and his feet were cold, and all the symptoms of death were upon him, and his extreme parts were already almost dead and senseless; and yet, even then, his joys were, if possible, greater still. He had so many fits of joy unspeakable, that he seemed to be in one continued act of seraphic love and praise. He spake like one that was just entering into the gates of the new Jerusalem; the greatest part of him was now in heaven; not a word dropped trom his mouth but it breathed Christ and heaven. O what encouragements did he give to them which did stand by, to follow hard after God, and to follow Christ in a humble, believing, zealous course of life, and adding all diligence to make their calling and election sure, and that when they also should find that they should have a glorious passage into a blessed eternity!

* * * "One rare passage I cannot omit, which was this: that when ministers or Christians came to him, he would beg of them to spend all the time they had with him in praise. 'O help me to praise God; I have now nothing else to do, from this time to eternity, but to praise and love God. I have what my soul desires upon earth. I cannot tell what to pray for, but what I have graciously given in. The wants that are capable of supplying in this world are supplied. I want but one thing, and that is, a speedy lift to heaven. I expect no more here, I cannot desire more, I cannot hear more. Oh, praise, praise, praise that infinite, boundless love, that hath, to a wonder, looked upon my soul, and done more for me than thousands of his dear children. Oh, bless the Lord, O my soul, and all that is within me, bless his holy name. Oh, help me, help me, O my friends, to praise and admire him that hath done such astonishing wonders for my soul; he hath pardoned all my sins, he hath filled me with his goodness, he hath given me grace and glory, and no good thing hath he withheld from me.'

"'Come, help me with praises, all that's little; come, help me, O ye glorious and mighty angels, who are so well skilled in this heavenly work of praise! Praise him, all ye creatures upon the earth; let everything that hath being help me to praise him! Hallelujah, hallelujah, hallelujah! Praise is now my work, and I shall be engaged in that sweet employment for ever. Bring the Bible; turn to David's Psalms, and let us sing a psalm of praise. Come, let us lift up our voice in the praise of the Most High; I with you as long as my breath doth last, and when I have none, I shall do it better.'"

He took leave of the several members of his family, one by one, in affectionate addresses. "Then," adds his brother and biographer, "that godly minister came to give him his last visit, and to do the office of an inferior angel—to help to convey his blessed soul to glory, who was now even upon Mount Pisgah, and had a full sight of that goodly land at a little distance. When this minister spoke to him, his heart was in a mighty flame of love and joy, which drew tears of joy from that precious minister, being almost amazed to hear a man just a-dying talk as if he had been with Jesus, and come from the immediate presence of God. Oh, the smiles that were then in his face, and the unspeakable joy that was in his heart! One might have read grace and glory in such a man's countenance. Oh, the praise, the triumphant praises, that he put up! And every one must speak praise about him, or else they did make some jar in his harmony. And indeed most did, as well as they could, help him in praise; so that I never heard nor knew any more praise given to God in one room than in his chamber.

"A little before he died, in the prayer, or rather praises, he was so wrapt up with admiration and joy, that he could scarce forbear shouting for joy. In the conclusion of the duty, with abundance of faith and fervency, he said aloud, Amen, amen!"

After contemplating such a scene of elevation and rapture, it is not easy at once to descend to the commonplaces of chronological detail, or a scanty memorial of kindred worth; but the next brother, James, the recorder of these affecting scenes, was himself a large partaker of the character of him on whose excellence he expatiates, and greatly assimilated in the joys and triumphs of his departure. Passing his name for a moment, we will refer to the next in order, Abraham Janeway. He was a preacher in London, previous to the period of the plague; but being of a contemplative turn of mind, which somewhat unfitted him for very active or public exertions, he retired with his wife to live with his mother or mother-in-law at Buntingford, in Huntingdonshire. His Presbyterian principles, however, being notorious, he was seized by Justice Crouch, under a pretence of friendship; but having made his escape from the grasp of the persecutor, he sunk under the family complaint of consumption, in September 1665. "Though he died that very week in which the plague was at the highest, (there being no fewer than 7165 persons who died of the sickness in that one week,) yet he did not die of that distemper, for which his brother and other relations were very thankful. Mr. Vincent says of him, ' He was a righteous person, a righteous minister, a dear brother, taken away in the flower of his years. He was a merciful man, and showed great pity and compassion to souls; was earnest with them to leave their sins and close with Christ. He spent himself, and hastened his own death, to keep others from perishing everlastingly.

He was an upright man, a true-hearted Nathanael, and one of very promising hopes for very considerable usefulness.' "*

Joseph Janeway was the youngest of the fraternal band, and a Conformist. In this only, we believe, did he essentially differ from the rest. It is a striking fact that all of them were consumptive, all died under the age of forty, and all were pious men.

James Janeway, to whom we cursorily referred as next in chronological order to John, and an account of whom we reserved, as being more especially connected with the present publication, was born at Lilley. He became a student in Christ-church, Oxford, in 1655, where he took the degrees in arts in due time. At the close of his pursuits in the university, he went to reside in his mother's house at Windsor, and devoted himself to private tuition. It is probable he had no benefice, but, as a Nonconformist, was silenced by the act of 1662. During the plague he was indefatigable in preaching the gospel, but escaped the contagion. As soon as he supposed the persecuting spirit of the age allowed, a chapel, or meeting-house as it was then termed, was erected for him in Jamaica Row, Rotherhithe. It was, however, pulled down by the soldiers; but the people built another on the same spot upon a larger scale. He had numerous and respectable audiences, and was the honoured instrument of effecting a great reformation in the neighbourhood.†

The high party, being exceedingly exasperated at his popularity and success, made several attempts on his life. On one occasion, as he was walking along the wall at Rotherhithe, he had a narrow escape from a shot. The bullet went through his hat, but inflicted no personal injury. At another time, the soldiers broke into his meeting-house, exclaiming, as they pressed through the crowd, " Down with him! down with him !" They jumped upon a form or bench, with the view of pulling him out of the pulpit, but providentially the bench

* Calamy's continuation of his account of Ejected Ministers. The Rev. Nathanael Vincent referred to, preached his funeral sermon, which is published at the end of a tract, entitled, " God's Terrible Voice in the City."

† This congregation gradually declined during many years, till scarcely any hearers were left. This induced the new pastor, Dr. Flaxman, to resign in 1783, when the people dispersed. See Wilson's Hist. and Antiq. of Dissenting Churches, vol. 4.

gave way. The confusion which ensued afforded an opportunity of escape; for some of his friends threw a coloured coat over him, and put a white hat on his head. The mob, however, probably misled as to his person by the clever deception, seized upon one of his people, Mr. Kentish, and carried him away to the Marshalsea prison, where he was confined for a considerable time. It is supposed this was Mr. Richard Kentish, who had been ejected from St. Katherine's, in the Tower.* A farther attempt was made to secure him when engaged in preaching at a gardener's house. The troopers, having dismounted, rushed into the premises, but he had time to throw himself upon the ground, where his friends, intercepting the soldiers, concealed him so effectually from them, by covering him with cabbage-leaves, that he again escaped. He died in the prime of life, on March 16th, 1674, in the thirty-eighth year of his age, and was buried in St. Mary's Church, Aldermanbury, near his father.†

The Rev. Nathanael Vincent, before mentioned, who appears to have been intimately acquainted with the Janeway family, preached a funeral sermon for him, entitled, "The Saint's Triumph over the last Enemy;" to which he prefixed an address to the congregation, expressive of the highest estimate of his character. "Oh," he exclaims, "what a friend did you lose when your pastor was snatched from you! You were as dear as his own soul! How did he pray, and weep, and preach, and labour, and all to this end, that you might be sincere converts, and work out your own salvation. Very few could match my brother Janeway in zeal, in compassion, in holy activity, in affection, in sincerity. He sought not yours, but you, and desired ten thousand times more to gain souls than ought beside. He endeavoured to debase the world in your esteem, and it was low in his own; he strived to raise your affections heavenward, and there was his heart and treasure. Christ he loved, in Christ he believed; Christ he preach-

* Palmer's Noncon. Memorial.

† It is perhaps scarcely worth while, even in a note, to cite the characteristic scurrility of Anthony Wood; yet it is instructive. "He set up a conventicle," says he, "at Redrift, near London, where, to the time of his death, he was much resorted to by those of his persuasion, and admired as a forward and precious young man, especially by those of the female sex." Wood's Ath. Oxon.

ed, Christ he commended. And how did he rejoice when any that before rejected the Lord Jesus were persuaded to give their consents to him." The discourse itself is throughout an excellent specimen of Puritanic simplicity and power. It displays, moreover, a great deal of ingenuity. At the close of it he enters into considerable detail respecting his character and the circumstances of his death, the fidelity of which we cannot question. These sketches are fraught with an interest that will more than justify their transcription.

" What I have to say concerning my dear deceased brother, I shall speak in this order. I shall tell you wherein the Lord made him to excel in his lifetime, and what his carriage was at his departure.

" For the first there are those following particulars very remarkable.

" 1. *Great was the sweetness of his natural temper and disposition.* And his excellence of nature was very much heightened and ennobled by the grace of God. He was far from moroseness and bitterness of spirit; candour was to be discerned in his very countenance, and by conversing with him it was much more apparent; and in his kindness and affability, and proneness to oblige, he had a design of good upon souls, for he knew he could not more oblige any than to endeavour their eternal welfare.

" 2. *He made it his business to be religious.* He practised himself what he preached to others, and was a follower of Christ, as he exhorted others to follow him His works were good as well as his words; and oh, how oft and seriously did he lift up his soul to God, desiring nothing more than to be a man and pastor after the heart of the Lord!

" 3. *He was a serious mourner for the decays of godliness in this backsliding age.* How would he mention the old Puritan strictness and circumspection, and bewail the excesses and licentiousness of professors!

" 4. *His heart was inflamed with love to Christ.* And though his affections were so strong and vehement, yet they were still aspiring higher. His expressions sometimes showed unusual raptures and ecstacies of love. He would beg that he might equal Paul or John, nay, the very seraphims, in loving, that he might be sick and die of love. Blessed soul, thou hast now thy fill! Thou lovest thy Lord now, and enjoyest this love to the uttermost of thy capacity!

"5. *His bowels of compassion yearned towards immortal souls.* He knew the worth of his own, and the souls of others; and as he was acquainted with the value of souls, so he was sensible of their danger. How earnestly would he warn them to flee from future wrath! How eagerly and sweetly would he woo them to give their consents to be espoused to Christ! How admirably would he expostulate with them concerning their egregious folly in refusing! He pitied the souls of all,— old and young; nay, he was deeply concerned for little children: witness those books which he styles *tokens* for them.

"6 *He laboured abundantly, spending himself in his Master's work.* If he had wrought less, he might in all probability have lived longer; but he chose rather, like the candle, to consume, that he might give light to others. He preached, he visited, he catechised; he was instant in season, out of season; and truly the Lord honoured him exceedingly in making him instrumental to convert the profane, to strengthen the weak in grace, to speak comfortable and healing words to the distressed and wounded in their spirits.

"7. *He was a man mighty in prayer.* There was an elegant (eloquent?) fluency in his expression, both when he prayed and preached; but, oh, the spiritual and heavenly matter was most to be admired. Augustine tells us of a certain person who prayed as if he would *expirare orando*—breathe out his very soul and life in prayer, and adds, *quas tuorum preces si non has exandis.* What supplications will be prevalent if not such as these? This may be applied to my brother Janeway. He was a mighty wrestler with God, and would not be put off without a blessing.

"8. *He was much for unity and love.* Though, according as it was foretold, love is grown so cold in most, it was warm in him. He followed peace as well as holiness, and was of a most yielding spirit, ready, as far as he might, to comply with any, rather than a breach should be or be continued.

"9. *He abounded in works of charity*, having seriously pondered that saying of our Lord, 'It is more blessed to give than to receive.' As he was liberal in imparting the treasure of the gospel, so of his own substance which God had given him. It was his constant course, whatever he received, to give two shillings in the pound, that is, the tenth, unto good uses. He endeavoured to persuade others to be charitable. The widows and the fatherless had a great interest in his compassions, and may well bewail his departure, by whom now they can be no more relieved.

"10. Which crowned all his other excellences, *he was exceeding humble.* He was much in praising, admiring, and adoring God, and had very low thoughts of himself, and in honour preferred others before himself. He would say he was the least of ministers, less than the least of all saints.

"In these particulars you have something of his character, but the half has not been told you; yet enough has been said to make you sensible how heavy the stroke was which took him away. The loss of him is not only his relations' loss, but Redriff's (Rotherhithe's) loss, London's loss, England's loss, the church's loss; for he was of such a public spirit that all are like to miss him.

"In the next place, I am to speak of his carriage at his death.

"He had a great conflict with Satan somewhile before his leaving the world; and truly I do not wonder that the devil should buffet him who had with such vigour and success endeavoured to overthrow his kingdom. To prepare him for the encounter, the Lord at first did shine upon his soul, and gave him some assurance that heaven was his inheritance. But afterwards there intervened a cloud, and Satan's chain was lengthened. That lion roared upon him, and endeavoured to disturb his peace. The great thing he blamed himself for was his aptness to slubber over private duties, since he was so much engaged in public work. The accuser of the brethren was very fierce in his accusations, and so far prevailed, that Mr. Janeway cried out, *I am at infinite uncertainties as to my future state. I thought I had been sincere, but Satan tells me I have been a hypocrite;* and then added, *Whatever you do, do not dally in religion; it is only godliness in the power of it that can strengthen against the fear of death.* Satan would not yet give over, but having begun to batter his faith, gives a fresh assault; then, with a mournful voice, he cried out, *Eternity! Eternity! Eternity! Infinite! Infinite!*

Infinite! Everlasting! Everlasting! Everlasting! A relation that stood by added, *An eternity of glory!* To which he replied, *Of horror! of horror! unspeakable horror!*

"This was his conflict, and truly it was a sore one. But after this blackest darkness followed the break of day. Satan prevailed so far, that he might be the more remarkably foiled, for the God of peace did 'tread the evil one under his feet.' The Comforter, even the Spirit of Truth, did visit him, and bare witness with his spirit that he was a child of God, and helped him to discern and look back upon the uprightness of his heart with satisfaction.

"Not long before he died, he blessed God for the assurance of his love, and said, *He could now as easily die as shut his eyes;* and added, *Here am I longing to be silent in the dust, and enjoying Christ in glory. I long to be in the arms of Jesus. It is not worth while to weep for me.* Then, remembering how busy the devil had been about him, he was exceeding thankful to God for his goodness in rebuking him.

"Afterwards, he brake forth, saying, though so weak, with a loud voice, *Amen! Hallelujah! Hallelujah!* and desired others to join with him; which they not presently doing, he added, *James Janeway is the only singer.* He was quickly seized upon with another rapture of joy, and thus expressed it, *Millions of praises to the most high Jehovah! Heaven and earth praise him! Ye mountains and hills praise him! All his hosts praise him! All ye saints bless him, who hath visited us in our low estate, and redeemed us unto himself! All must be ascribed to free grace, from the beginning to the end.*

"Then he begged of God that *he would bless his people, and take away animosities and names of division from among them.* These were the last words which he was heard to speak distinctly.

"Thus triumphantly he went to glory. Thus an abundant entrance was administered to him into the everlasting kingdom! But if his joy and praises were such before he was got quite thither, when he was actually come within heaven's gate, and first saw the Lord face to face, oh, who can conceive his joy and wonder!"

To some persons it may seem mysterious that so eminent a servant of Jesus Christ should have been so agonized, as the previous account represents him to have been, with apprehensions of an awful eternity, and with suspicions of his own sincerity in religion. But all Christians are more or less subjected to the temptations of Satan, and often the more exalted the character, the more severe is the trial. In general this may have a tendency to produce beneficial searchings of heart, and to perfect piety, by inducing watchfulness, increasing diligence and prayer. It is part of that parental discipline by which our heavenly Father trains his children for heaven, and detaches their too deeply rooted affections from the soil of earth. Rough is the instrument indeed, but kind the purpose, that plucks them up, for their predestined transplantation to a better place and more congenial skies. And they learn not to repine, and not to mistake his gracious dealings, when they realize the effects in their happy experience. Consistently with the same principle in the divine proceedings, he suffers Satan to molest, in some instances, their dying hours—it may be, to exterminate some latent evil, to subdue yet unextinguished pride, to conquer some self-seeking passion, or to give an intensity of feeling to the hour of final triumph, which shall clear the mind of every past apprehension, every recent consideration, and tend to the confirmation of religion in surviving friends and a distant posterity.

But we have not unfrequently to encounter an objection of a different kind, when the world, or even professing Christians insinuate the charge of enthusiasm against the sublime ardour of an impassioned religion. On this subject we may quote the observations of a distinguished writer, in his brief preface to the modern edition of John Janeway's life, as equally applicable to the closing scene of James, as just narrated. "I am aware that some will object to the strain of devout ecstacy which characterizes the sentiments and language of Mr. Janeway in his dying moments; but I am persuaded they will meet with nothing, however ecstatic and elevated, but what corresponds to the dictates of Scripture and the analogy of faith. He who recollects that the Scriptures speak of a *peace which passeth all understanding*, and of *a joy unspeakable and full of glory*, will not be offended at the lively expressions of those contained in this narrative; he will be more disposed to lament the low state of his own religious feeling, than to suspect the propriety of sentiments the most rational and scriptural, merely because they rise to a pitch that he has never reached. The sacred oracles afford no countenance to the supposition that devotional feelings are to be condemned as visionary and enthusiastic, merely on account of their intenseness and elevation: provided they be of a right kind, and spring from legitimate sources, they never teach us to expect they can be carried too far. David *danced before the Lord with all his might*, and when he was reproached for degrading himself in the eyes of the people, by indulging these transports, he replied, " If this be to be vile, *I will yet make myself more vile.*" That the objects which interest the heart in religion are infinitely more durable and important than all others, will not be disputed; and why should it be deemed irrational to be affected by them in a degree somewhat suitable to their value, especially in the near prospect of their full and perfect possession? Why should it be deemed strange or irrational for a dying saint, who has spent his life in the pursuit of immortal good, to feel an unspeakable ecstacy at finding he has just touched the goal, finished his course, and in a few moments is to be crowned with life everlasting? While he dwells on the inconceiveably glorious prospect before him, and feels himself lost in wonder and gratitude, and almost oppressed with a sense of his unutterable obligations to the love of his Creator and Redeemer nothing can be more natural and proper than his sentiments and conduct. While the Scriptures retain their rank as the only rule of faith and practice; while there are those who feel the power of true religion, such death-bed scenes as Mr. Janeway's will be contemplated with veneration and delight. It affords no inconsiderable confirmation of the truth of Christianity, that the most celebrated sages of Pagan antiquity, whose last moments have been exhibited with inimitable propriety and beauty, present nothing similar nor equal, nothing of that singular combination of humility and devotion, that self-renouncing greatness, in which the creature appears annihilated, and God all in all. . . . .

" Let me be permitted, however, to observe, that the experience of Mr. Janeway in his last moments, while it developes the native tendency of Christianity, is not to be considered as a standard to ordinary Christians. He affords a great example of what is attainable in religion, and not of what is indispensably necessary to salvation. Thousands die in the Lord, who are not indulged with the privilege of dying in triumph. His extraordinary diligence in the whole of his Christian career, his tenderness of conscience, his constant vigilance, his vehement hunger and thirst after righteousness, met with a signal reward, intended, probably, not more for his own personal advantage, than as a persuasion to others to walk in his steps. As he was incessantly solicitous to improve his graces, purify his principles, and perfect holiness in the fear of the Lord, no wonder he was favoured with an abundant entrance into the joy of his Lord. *He which soweth sparingly shall reap also sparingly; and he which soweth bountifully shall reap also bountifully.*"*

Of the various publications issued by Mr. Janeway,† the most celebrated are the "Token for Children," and "Heaven upon Earth." The former obtained a wide circulation during the author's lifetime, and has ever since continued to interest and benefit our juvenile population. With the latter we have now more immediate concern, as being republished in the present volume. It is not free from the defects which characterize the writings of that age; but though somewhat quaint, immethodical, and prolix, it is replete with sterling sense and powerful appeal. Few pious persons can read it without benefit; and could the irreligious be persuaded to peruse its pages, we should anticipate a happy result. He who could have written thus must have been an excellent Christian and a sound divine.

It appears from the epistle to the reader, that the events which most deeply impressed Mr. Janeway's mind, and were the immediate occasion of his composing this treatise, were *the*

---

* Robert Hall.

† 1. Heaven upon Earth. 2. Token for Children; in two parts. 3. Death Unstung; a Funeral Sermon for Thomas Mousley, an Apothecary. 4. Invisible Realities, demonstrated in the holy Life and Death of Mr. John Janeway, 1673. 5. The Saints' Encouragement to Diligence in Christ's Service, 1673. 6. Legacy to his Friends; containing 27 famous Instances of God's providence in and about sea dangers and deliverances, 1674. 7. Saints' Memorials, 1674. 8. The Duties of Masters and Servants; a Sermon in supplement to Morning Exercises, 1674. 9. Man's last End; a Funeral Sermon on Ps. lxxxiv. 8, 1676. 10. The Murderer punished and pardoned; with the Life and Death of T. Savage.

Plague and *the Great Fire of London*. The former took place in 1665; the latter in the autumn of 1666. These domestic incidents were accompanied by others of a calamitous nature, affecting the social condition of the people, and the political welfare of the empire. Seldom, indeed, have the clouds gathered more thickly over the land, or burst in more alarming tempests. Political misrule, ecclesiastical oppression, and court profligacy, darkened the whole scene; while Providence spoke in accents of thunder to a nation that seemed to be doomed to destruction.

The times of Charles the Second were replete with manifold evidences of the great mistake of the Restoration, while the Church of God, though at first filled with dismay, soon found occasion to display the sublimity of her character, in consequence of the Act of Uniformity in 1662. Never was there a severer attack upon conscience, and never a nobler victory achieved, without a battle or a sword. Persecution issued her edict, and Christianity went forth armed with glory and honour, in the persons of her two thousand self-denying heroes, who, like their renowned predecessors, "rejoiced that they were counted worthy to suffer shame for the name of Jesus."

Some time afterwards, the Conventicle Act was passed, by which the Nonconformists were prohibited from attending any places of worship excepting those of the established religion, without incurring, by a graduated scale of punishment, various and monstrous penalties. The execution of this edict having been committed to the King's forces, as well as the civil authorities, the prisons soon became crowded with the victims of fanatical intolerance and military despotism. In Scotland, its atrocious oppressiveness chiefly affected the Presbyterians.* "Invigorated," says an able historian, "by the Scotch Conventicle Act, Archbishop Sharp 'drove very violently,' establishing what proved to be a high commission court,—one of the worst tyrannies cast down by the civil war,—and persecuting his former brethren of the kirk without pity, and without calculation of the personal danger he was thereby incurring. The aspiring churchman, not satisfied with his immense and unconstitutional ecclesiastical powers, attempted to get himself made the head of the law in Scotland; and though he failed in this,

his creature, the Lord Rothes, was made Chancellor; and Rothes browbeat the magistrates and lawyers, and twisted the law as Sharp thought fit. The prisons in Scotland were soon crammed like those of England, the prisoners meeting with still worse usage. Sometimes they were fined, and the younger sort whipped about the streets. Troops were quartered throughout the country to force the people to respect the bishops, the liturgy, and the new-imposed Episcopalian preachers. These troops were commanded by Sir James Turner, 'who was naturally fierce, but he was mad when he was drunk, and that was very often.' He scoured the country, and received such lists as the new ministers brought him of those who would not go to church, and use the Book of Common Prayer; and then, without any proof or legal conviction, he fined them according to their substance or his own caprice, and sent soldiers to live upon them till the fines were paid."*

At this crisis a Dutch war commenced, in consequence of the seizure of some of their settlements on the coast of Africa. The commercial jealousy of the merchants of England, the mercenary spirit of the king, and the pride of the people, conspired to stimulate this hostility; supplies were voted, and fleets prepared. But this direful moment of a nation's fury was signalised by a nation's humiliation; for what has been emphatically termed *the Plague of London* broke out, by which calamity thousands and tens of thousands perished. Thus were the circumstances analagous to those of Greece, when, about four hundred and thirty years before the Christian era, a plague raged at Athens, the most dreadful perhaps recorded in history, while the Peloponnesians, under the command of Archidamus, laid waste the surrounding territory.

It appears from authentic documents, that the plague was imported from Holland, the prohibition of parliament to introduce merchandise from that then infected country having been in some instances disregarded. The evil was small in its commencement, but rapid in its diffusion. At the close of 1664, two or three persons died suddenly in Westminster, and upon examination, it proved to have been occasioned by this fearful malady. Many of their neighbours, seized with alarm, instantly removed into the city; but instead of escaping from

* Pict. Hist. of England, vol. iii. p. 694.

the calamity, carried it with them, and multiplied its horrors by spreading it on every hand. Though somewhat checked for a season by measures taken to prevent intercommunication as far as possible, and by the severities of a hard winter, it re-appeared in the middle of February 1665, when it was a second time checked; but in the ensuing April, it broke out with renewed power and malignity. A very large proportion of the houses in the city were shut up, having this deprecating inscription, in conspicuous letters, on their walls, " The Lord have mercy upon us!" But the plague-monster heeded not these precautions, or these ominous tablets; on the contrary, he continued to slay his thousands, and achieved his direful conquests by the pent-up air generating the contagion, or imparting to it an unwonted intensity of destructive strength. While many perished, others, forcing their way out in utter despair, spread abroad the virus, and scattered mischief, misery, and death wherever they flew. At the height of the disorder, the carts moved about, creaking and rumbling through every part of the metropolis, with each its melancholy tinkling death-bell, while the grave-diggers uttered, in sepulchral tone,—" Bring out your dead!" Where the feet of many generations had multitudinously and joyously pressed the ground, for business, for mirth, or the thousand purposes of life, the grass grew in the untrodden street; the clergy forsook their pulpits, and desolation and ghastly horror sat enthroned amidst the moanings of living agony, and the awful silence of the piled-up monumental dead. All men became naturally anxious to escape from this region of woe; merchants and owners of ships sought a refuge on board their respective vessels in the river, at Greenwich, Woolwich, and other places, while others rushed to distant parts of the country, to find a secure asylum.

It is observable that while the pulpits of the regular clergy were vacated, and their usual sphere of labours entirely abandoned, the persecuted Nonconformists re-entered the very churches from which they had been driven, and, inspired with the love of souls, hesitated not to face the formidable danger and to administer spiritual instruction to the sick and dying. " Knowing the terrors of the Lord," they sought even then " to persuade men;" and with a moral heroism that brightly displayed the character of true Christianity, they stood in the very territories of the pale monarch with his spectral terrors, to exhibit the Cross and proclaim the great salvation.

At this very moment, incredible as it may seem, the King of England, having with his minions removed to Oxford from dread of the plague, not only continued his dissolute course of life, but devised, with the aid of his court, clergy, and parliament, another scheme of vengeance against the very men who had been expelled from their benefices, and were now acting as the ministering angels of heaven's beneficence to the perishing subjects of the realm, by enacting the Five Mile Act, the object of which was to make it penal for any Nonconformist minister to teach in a school, or come within five miles (except as a traveller) of any city, borough, or corporate town, or any place whatever in which he had preached or taught since the passing of the Act of Uniformity, unless he had previously taken the oath of non-residence. Not satisfied with this, a bill was brought into the House of Commons, for imposing the oath of non-resistance upon the whole nation, which the Oxford parliament would have passed, but for the remarkable circumstance of Peregrine Bertrie being that morning only introduced into the House by his brother, made Earl of Lindsay, and Sir Thomas Osborne, then created Lord Treasurer Danby, who gave their votes against it: thus, as it has been said, "three voices had the merit of saving their country from the greatest ignominy that could have befallen it—that of riveting as well as forging its own chains." In reference to this melancholy state of affairs, Baxter exclaims, " So little did the sense of God's terrible judgments, or of the necessities of many hundred thousand ignorant souls, or the groans of the poor people for the teaching which they had lost, or the fear of the great and final reckoning, affect the hearts of the prelatists, or stop them in their way."

The Dutch war was not only prolonged, at this crisis, but attended by a new calamity to England, the junction of the French with their enemies. Fleets were prepared on either side, and met in hostile array. The Duke of Albemarle and Prince Rupert were the British commanders, and the celebrated De Ruyter and Van Tromp headed the antagonist force. A sea-fight ensued of four days; one of the most memorable engagements in English history. Two circumstances sufficiently elucidate the madness of the individuals in these national struggles. When, on the third morning, the English fleet was retreating towards the Dutch coast, Albemarle declared to the Earl of Ossory, one of the undaunted devotees of human glory, then on board with the admiral, that he was resolved rather to blow up the ship and perish gloriously, as he termed it, than yield to the enemy. Lord Ossory fully concurred in this desperate purpose! Subsequently, when De Ruyter was worsted, and the Dutch fleet scattered, he exclaimed, with burning indignation, as he yielded, " My God! what a wretch am I! Among so many thousand bullets, is there not one to put an end to my miserable life?" Here are sayings and doings considered worthy of celebration by the political historians of mankind, and which will ever be lauded by those who coalesce with the spirit of the world, by confounding glory with pride, and greatness with ambition; but bring into comparison the character and conduct of those who, with a courage as undaunted, but a principle more godlike, rushed from safety to peril, on the noble enterprize of saving the plague-smitten population of the metropolis, though denounced and insulted by a nation's monarch and a nation's parliament for their heretical benevolence; and the zeal of the piety will appear as superior to the heroism of war, as that which is divine and immortal surpasses that which is earthly and vanishing away.

While this miserable contest continued with various success, another awful visitation of Providence took place, to which Janeway solemnly refers in his epistle to the reader:—" The voice of the Lord was not heard, the language of the plague was not understood; wherefore the dreadful Jehovah spake louder and louder, as he did once from Mount Sinai, in fire, flame, and smoke;—he rode in a chariot of flaming fire, whilst the bells did ring their own knells as they were tumbling; and it is to be feared, were more melted at the anger of the mighty God, than thousands of hard-hearted men and women were. The leads of the churches were dissolved into showers more easily far than stupid professors that were wont to sit under them. That was a black cloud indeed which no wind could blow over till it fell in such scalding drops."

The *fire of London* broke out in the night, between the

second and third of September, at a baker's shop, near London Bridge. The summer had been intensely hot, and the city being chiefly constructed of timber, the fire, aided by a violent wind, spread with irresistible rapidity, till four hundred streets, comprising thirteen thousand houses, became one vast heap of ruin. It was only at last arrested by the blowing-up of houses. "The fire and the wind," says Clarendon, " continued in the same excess all Monday, Tuesday, and Wednesday, till afternoon, and flung and scattered brands burning into all quarters; the nights more terrible than the days, and the light the same,—the light of the fire supplying that of the sun." He observes, moreover, " let the cause be what it would, the effect was very terrible; for above two parts of three of that great city were burned to ashes, and those the most rich and wealthy parts of the city, where the greatest warehouses and the best shops stood. The Royal Exchange, with all the streets about it, Lombard Street, Cheapside, Paternoster Row, St. Paul's Church, and almost all the other churches in the city, with the Old Bailey, Ludgate, all Paul's Churchyard, even to the Thames, and the greatest part of Fleet Street, all which were places the best inhabited, were all burned, without one house remaining. The value or estimate of what that devouring fire consumed, over and above the houses, could never be computed in any degree." It is not easy to conceive the sublime aspect of such a conflagration, although we may imagine a circumference of several miles blazing with flame and smothered with smoke, so dense and voluminous, as to render every object frightful, with a lurid glare, and every moving inhabitant a spectre. The orb of day appeared like a fiery Mars, and the stars of night were darkened. One of the great city buildings, Guildhall, is represented as having exhibited a curious and magnificent spectacle. The oak of which it was built was too solid to be enflamed, but burnt like charcoal; so that for several hours the whole edifice seemed like an enchanted palace of gold or burnished brass.

As the mind is naturally more impressed with particular statements than general descriptions, it may be desirable to furnish the reader with some particulars of the damage that ensued.

Thirteen thousand two hundred houses, at twelve years' purchase, supposing the rent of each L.25 sterling,	L.3,960,000	0	0
Eighty-seven parish churches, at L.8000,	696,000	0	0
Six consecrated chapels, at L.2000,	12,000	0	0
The Royal Exchange,	50,000	0	0
The Custom House,	10,000	0	0
Fifty-two Halls of Companies at L.1500 each,	78,000	0	0
Three City Gates, at L.3000 each,	9,000	0	0
Jail of Newgate,	15,000	0	0
Four stone Bridges,	6,000	0	0
Sessions House,	7,000	0	0
Guildhall, with the Courts and Offices belonging to it,	40,000	0	0
Blackwall Hall,	3,000	0	0
Bridewell,	5,000	0	0
Poultry Compter,	5,000	0	0
Wood Street Compter,	3,000	0	0
St. Paul's Church,	2,000,000	0	0
Wares, household stuff, money, and moveable goods lost or spoiled,	2,000,000	0	0
Hire of porters, carts, waggons, barges, boats, &c., for removing goods,	200,000	0	0
Printed books and paper in shops and warehouses,	150,000	0	0
Wine, tobacco, sugar, &c., of which the town was at that time very full,	1,500,000	0	0
	L.10,689,000	0	0*

If ever a nation were addressed by the Invisible God, it was surely at that period; and if ever a nation disregarded the appeal, it was then, when plague, and war, and conflagration failed to turn them from their iniquities. Notwithstanding the enkindled zeal and the pious activity of a few of the consecrated children of God, irreligion continued its unimpeded progress among the people, and that, too, under the very forms of sanctity; and profligacy maintained its triumph-

* Ency. Brit. *Art.* London.

ant sway among the great. The court renewed, if, indeed, it had ever suspended, its revels; the king and parliament pursued their domestic warfare, the multitude hurried again to the indulgence of their religious prejudices, their political subserviency, and their personal vices. He who had spoken from heaven was not heard; and in refusing to speak again, his silence seemed to indicate they were to be abandoned to the most awful of destinies, to be providentially " let alone." All were frightened by the tempest; but when it had passed, few appeared to be benefited. It is no wonder, therefore, that these should have been characterized by our author, in connection with his own sufferings, as " the worst of times."

In reviewing the history of the two disastrous events which have been noticed—the plague and the fire—we are aware that many might be disposed to contend the point of their being judicial or providential visitations, and to maintain that the manner of their origin in either case proves them to have been accidental. And this is their favourite method of interpreting occurrences which they find recorded in past ages, as well as others with which their own experience has rendered them conversant. For their sakes, therefore, and equally for the confirmation of believers, it may be well to devote a few words to the subject.

An accurate use of terms is essential to correct ideas. On this account we would distinguish between *accidental* and *fortuitous* circumstances. The former term may not be, as Christians often deem it, objectionable, when we attach to the use of it that restricted view of its meaning which it may fairly claim. Let it be understood to designate an occurrence, simply sudden, unexpected, and unforeseen, or unavoidable by calculation. This, it will be seen, has relation strictly to human agency or human anticipation. In this sense, it does not in the least interfere with any notion we may entertain of a divine superintendence and appointment. What may be accidental to our ignorance, is perfectly in the order of a fixed providential law to His wisdom. But when fate or chance is involved in the use of any expression or word, another and objectionable sentiment is introduced. This enters into the conception of an event as fortuitous. It takes it out of the system of order, and puts it into the chaos of casualties. It denies the regularity of an infinitely extended and perfect disposition of the universe. If, therefore, by saying that an occurrence was accidental, it be simply meant—as we think the term may properly mean—that it was beyond the power of man to prevent, or out of the reach of his sagacity to foresee, no reflection is cast upon that great Being who "orders all things according to the counsel of his own will;" but if, by affirming it to have been fortuitous, it is intended to detach it from the immediate hand and direction of God, from his premeditative plan, the notion is plainly false and atheistical. Under this impression, we should say that the communication of the plague by a bale of goods or other trifling importation, or the setting fire to London by the ignition of a little combustible matter in a baker's shop, by the flame of a candle or the spark from an oven, was in either instance accidental, but not fortuitous; there was in it much of the uncalculating carelessness of man, but nothing, as it regards the Supreme Disposer, of uncertainty, unexpectedness, and chance.

Our weak minds are apt to view things which are essentially, that is, providentially the same, in a different manner, according to their comparative magnitude. It seems to us as if that which was small and insignificant in itself were less the object of attention to the universal Ruler, than that which is apparently and imposingly great. The fall of a sparrow and the rise of an empire are two events which, as to their importance, seem to be in striking contrast; and while many a mind is ready to admit the theory of a providence in relation to the latter, on account of its vastness, its complicated relations, and its mighty influence upon the affairs of mankind, the sense of littleness in the former instance induces the presumption that it must of necessity be overlooked as nothing in the government of Omniscience. But this is neither a scriptural nor a rational conclusion.

Admitting that the world is not abandoned by its Creator, it is as conceivable that he should exercise the most minute and detailed inspection as the most general. We are indeed soon perplexed by multiplicity, and confused by number; the power of combination is in us extremely imperfect, and hence we acquire knowledge by very slow degrees; it is only step by step that we ascend, and owing to the obstacles that occur, the misconceptions to which we are ever liable, the prejudices we have to surmount, the intricacies of error we have to disentangle, and the brevity of human life, it is not possible even for the greatest genius to attain to any considerable elevation, before the shadows of the last evening overtake him. But since everything is fully known, and known at once, by the Divine mind, it cannot be more difficult, consequently is not less probable, that all the separate points in universal nature should be carefully observed, all the movements and changes that spring from material combinations, and all the proceedings of intelligent beings should be regulated, than that any *one* point is seen, any *one* movement ordered, any *one* proceeding directed. It is no greater exertion of mind to Omniscience to superintend each subdivision of existence than to direct the whole; nor can any confusion arise from such an observance to perplex an Infinite Intelligence.

Unquestionably too, an equal *necessity* is apparent in either case. General harmony must result from particular order: the machine cannot produce the expected result, unless the intermediate movements are correct; the chorus will not be complete if the separate parts be ill adjusted, or any one be entirely omitted. Supposing a general providence to superintend the universe at large in such a manner as to effect the happiest final issue, such a termination can only be secured by "making ALL THINGS work together" for the ultimate "good." Disarrangement in the least thing must be prevented, or the mighty thread of events would soon become entangled, and disastrous consequences ensue; but such mischief can only be avoided by the unsleeping vigilance of an all-seeing eye, watching the minutest circumstance, and the perpetual control of an omnipotent arm, regulating the most insignificant event. We are therefore compelled to the conclusion that either God is in all things, or there is no God.

It may be said that this or that evil results immediately from the folly, incaution, or passion of an individual, as we see in tracing the origin of the plague and conflagration in 1666. It may be said—and analogous questionings are frequently indulged—*if* some careless man in Holland, evading law and seeking to gratify his mercenary spirit, had not contrived to transmit infected goods to London, the plague would not have existed ; *if* something inflammatory had not caught in the baker's premises, perhaps by a puff of air upon a spark or an incipient flame, the great fire would not have happened: be it so; admit these suppositions, and the consequences they imply; we maintain there is nothing in them fairly to impugn the doctrine of providential superintendence, which is the doctrine of divine foresight and moral government.

The Supreme Intelligence must necessarily know the future actions of men, the train of causes which lead to them, and the manner in which their passions, with their seemingly contingent effects, will, under all imaginable circumstances, operate. That which to the view of a finite mind is future, is to the infinite one perfectly and fully present; since past, present, and future, are terms expressive simply of our ignorance or imperfection of knowledge: and this supposition does by no means interfere with the freedom of human action; for the nature of an action as morally good or bad, or only neutral, can suffer no alteration through being foreknown.

There is besides no difficulty in the supposition, that men may be placed in the world successively in such situations in point of time, connexions, and other circumstances, that their whole conduct may coincide with the minutest arrangements of that foresight which is attributable to the Deity, and that order which he has established. It is reasonable to imagine this without supposing any infringement of human liberty, because the very carelessness of human inconsideration, and the very excesses of the passions may be made to subserve the purposes of God, as well as the diversified capacities, rank, possessions, and influence of individuals; so that there may be good instead of evil, even in what we deem simply evil, by the counter-workings of unthought-of agencies, still specially designed,—as the very plague of London itself became the means of calling into operation a ministerial instrumentality, not otherwise likely, or perhaps possible, to have been employed, which, in the conversion of many souls, produced results the most glorious, and having their far-reaching influences beyond all calculation into eternity. Thus, as the contrary movements of a machine, though confusing to the eye of an unskilled spectator, are prepared for by the contriver to promote the ultimate effect so each material change;

or, if you will, accidental occurrence, every action, with all its tendencies and consequences, every passion, with all its irregularities, constitute together the several parts of a complex but harmonious system. It may be assumed, therefore, as essential to the perfection of the great economy of the universe, that, while every person, in every age, is fulfilling, or aiming to fulfil, his own wishes, the MIND that rules over all is limiting to its proper sphere the exertions of the individual by invisible agencies, without interfering with his volitions; and every particular aim and effort is so ordered, as to render its occurrence an indispensable link in the chain of events.

The suggestions of reason are substantiated by the declarations of Scripture. The whole volume is, in fact, a history of providence, unfolding its evidences and characteristics in the phenomena of nature and the affairs of the church—in the walking pestilence, the exterminating war, the prevailing prayer, the progression of things in revolving ages. The doctrine of providence—a providence at once powerful, boundless, and gracious—has been written in the arrested sun of Gibeon and the awe-stricken moon of the valley of Ajalon, in the bright stars that fought against Sisera, in the commissioned stone that flew from the sling of David to the head of the giant of Philistia, in the edicts that dismissed Vashti and called Esther to the court of Ahasuerus, in multiplied and ever-multiplying events, great and small, and especially and above all, in the birth, life, death, and triumphs of Him in whom was revealed the great mystery of ages and the mercy of Heaven. This providence is represented in the dream of Jacob, in the wheels of Ezekiel, in the language alike of the Old Testament and the New; and, with its attendant constellations of grace and promise, is the pole-star of the believer across the deeps of life, till he obtain "an abundant entrance into the everlasting kingdom of our Lord and Saviour Jesus Christ."

HEAVEN UPON EARTH;

OR,

JESUS THE BEST FRIEND OF MAN.

HEAVEN UPON EARTH;

OR,

JESUS THE BEST FRIEND OF MAN.

"Acquaint now thyself with him, and be at peace; thereby good shall come unto thee."—Job xxii. 21.

THEY who have improved their experience of things by wisdom, and gathered up the value of man's life, by comparing his desire with his enjoyments, his troubles and sorrows with his content and joy, have concluded the worth of the life of man to be below nothing; they have drawn a black line upon the whole, and shut up all in darkness. Thus Jacob of old, in the account which he gives of his life to Pharaoh, Gen. xlvii. 9; Job v. 7; and also Solomon, who had an extraordinary measure of wisdom by divine dispensation, who had a large spirit like the sand of the sea-shore, he gave himself great liberty in trying what that good under the sun for the sons of men was, Eccl. ii. 1. When he had taken a taste of all the world's contents, yet he finds a bitterness mixed in all delights, which abideth no longer than the pleasure, ver. 11, 17. And whosoever shall enter into himself, and feel the workings of his own mind, shall be able to read over the transcript of the same in his own conscience. Who is he among the sons of men, that in his natural life hath attained to a state wherein he was able to say, Here I will stay, it is now well with me, I desire no addition to my present condition? If there be any such, I dare undertake to prove him unacquainted with himself. Where now shall I fasten the blame of this universal evil? Shall we fall out with our life, as a thing not worth the having? Shall we shrink into our former nothing, and cast up our being and life into the hands of God, as that out of which we gathered nothing but bitterness and disquiet? Far be this from us; this were to justify that evil and wicked servant, who said of God, that "he knew he was a hard Master, reaping where he had not sown, and gathering where he had not strawed." This would be to accuse God of having made us to an unavoidable necessity of misery. How then comes it to pass, that we are all held fast in this common calamity? It is from thyself, O man, it is from thyself; this evil is because of our falling from God. It is a righteous thing with God, that when man departed from him, he should reap the fruit of his own doings; and indeed it is impossible for a creature of our composure and constitution, but to feel itself dissatisfied with all worldly material employments, and to find trouble and disquiet in itself, while it is deprived of its true good. If we would have a true account of our disquiet and dissatisfaction, this is it. God made man, of all the works of his hands, to be the nearest to himself, and hath fitted his principles for a higher life than that which hath the things of this world for its object; but man hath made himself like the beasts that perish. We have given our souls into captivity to our bodies, or rather, we are fallen from our union with God, and are gathered up into ourselves, and become deprived of a sufficiency in separation from God; then it must needs be, that we, being gone down into a lower state than that which we were made to, should find nothing but dissatisfaction and emptiness: here we are by nature, and hitherto we have brought ourselves by forsaking God.

Now the great inquiry will be, what remedy there is for this our woful condition; is there any way whereby we may be delivered from this misery? If there be, what way is it? These words which I have chosen to speak to, do contain the answer to this inquiry.

"Acquaint now thyself with him, and be at peace; thereby good shall come unto thee." This is the counsel of one of Job's three friends to him in the time of his great affliction. You have heard of the affliction of Job, and how his three friends came to relieve him with their counsel; but the devil, who had a commission from God to try his utmost with Job, yet sparing his life, made use of his friends, who are to be a comfort in the hour of adversity, to be a great means of his disquiet, so that he cries out of them, "Miserable comforters are ye all," ch. xvi. 2. And the great way of their troubling him was, by misapplying, by making false application of true principles. In their discourses there are many excellent truths; yet, by their hard construing, and ungrounded condemning of him, they by God are reproved, as not having spoken the thing that was right, ch. xlii. 7; yet in many things their counsel was suitable and seasonable; of which sort the words in the text may be accounted. In this chapter Eliphaz had been inquiring into the cause of Job's great affliction; and holding this for an undeniable principle, that the righteous God, being the great disposer of affliction, did bring this evil upon him because of his sin, he measured the greatness of his sins by the greatness of afflictions; he made account, because God's hand was gone forth in an extraordinary manner against Job, therefore there was some extraordinary guilt upon him: "And thou sayest, How doth God judge through the dark clouds?" ver. 5, 13. Thus we have this apprehension of Job, as one under great affliction because of his great sins; and the text is Eliphaz's counsel to Job under this character; and so is suitable advice to those that are under sickness or great afflictions, and that are under the guilt of great sin.

"Acquaint thyself with him, and be at peace; thereby good shall come unto thee." The words are a doctrine for the soul under a sense of its lost condition, with a promise very comfortable upon the embracing thereof.

The doctrine is, "Acquaint thyself with him, and be at peace."

The promise, "Thereby good shall come unto thee."

These words, "Be at peace," may be referred either to the former, as an addition to the doctrine, "Be at peace;" that is, keep yourselves in a quiet submission to the hand of God; or to the latter; and so, "Be at peace," is as much as, "Peace shall be to thee."

In the doctrine we are to consider the act and object.

The act, Acquaint.
The object is God.

DOCTRINE.

So that the doctrine is, to enter into acquaintance with God. This proposition stands forth to the view of every eye, and it is the duty of man to be acquainted with God.

Now the first thing that is before us to inquire after, is, what this acquaintance with God is.

Secondly, To evidence and clear it to be the duty of man to acquaint himself with God. Acquaintance with God implies several things.

1. It signifies a full and determinate knowledge of this truth, that there is a God, and so to know him, as to his nature, distinct from all other beings.

There is a three-fold knowledge of God.
    1. A rational.
    2. A natural.
    3. A supernatural.

First, There is a rational knowledge of God, which is a clear discovery of an almighty, all-sufficient Cause of all things, which is attained by a reasonable discussing power of the soul, which argueth from things that are visible and sensible to an invisible and self-principled Cause of all things. Man found himself brought into the world furnished with an innumerable variety of creatures, and none of these having power to make itself; we see likewise such an accurate order in every particular creature, and in all the creatures one with another, that we cannot but see clearly that there is a supreme almighty Cause of all things, who hath by his power brought forth all things into being; who is likewise the most wise Agent, who, by his unsearchable wisdom, hath curiously framed every creature, and by his wonderful counsel hath set them in such an order, that they all serve one another, till at length they all meet in man, as in the common centre.

Secondly, There is a natural knowledge of God, which is the inward touch and mental sensation of a supreme righteous Judge, to whose trial we feel ourselves under an unavoidable bond, in doing good and evil. This is that which is commonly called conscience; this a man finds in himself, if at any time he have committed any secret sin whatsoever, which none in the world knows but himself, he feels it to be a pressure upon his spirit, as being under the examination of a power superior to himself. Now this is nothing else but a secret impression that God hath made or himself upon the minds of men, by which man is bound to stand before the tribunal of God. These two ways of knowing God were very clear to man in his perfect state, but since the fall of man they are much weakened and decayed. But,

Thirdly, There is a supernatural way whereby we come to know God, which hath repaired our loss by Adam's sin, and that is by God's extraordinary revelation of himself in his holy Scriptures: by these we may come to have a more clear, distinct knowledge of God, both that he is, and what he is. To these three ways of letting the knowledge of God into the soul, three mental acts of the soul do answer.

First, A rational discourse, by which we find out God by the creatures.

Secondly, An inward sensation, which feels God as just in good and evil.

The third mental act is faith, which for its foundation hath the word of God.

There is a fourth way of knowing God, which is by experiment; which is when God manifests himself to his peculiar ones, and lets out the knowledge of himself to their souls; as when the sun breaks forth with a bright shining in a cloudy day: but this belongeth rather to another head.

Thus you see the first thing employed in this acquaintance with God, which is the lowest.

Yet how many are there that have little acquaintance with God in these signs! May we not come to many who profess they know God, and yet among all their thoughts they have had few or none to satisfy themselves concerning him? How gross are the apprehensions of some concerning God! Some men resist and stifle that natural knowledge that they have of God, such as those, Rom. i. 28; they did not like to retain God in their knowledge, and God gave them over to a reprobate mind, or a mind void of judgment, as the word signifies. Others have lived all their days upon the bounty and goodness of God, and yet have not been led by the streams to the fountain from which all hath flowed. Others can busy themselves all their time in other things, and little inquire into the word of God, by which they may be led to the knowledge of him. But woe to those on whom the fury of the Lord shall be poured out, because they know not God, Jer. x. 25.

2. Acquaintance with God implies frequent access unto God. We do not usually reckon ourselves acquainted with any person, by a bare knowledge that such a person there is, and that we are able to give some general description of him; but when we say we are acquainted with any, it is understood that we have been in such a one's company, we have come to him, and been with him: such is our acquaintance to be with God.

Under this head I shall speak,

First, Of that separation that is of the soul from God.

Secondly, Of the return of the soul to God.

Thirdly, Of the abiding of the soul with God.

First, Of the separation and distance of the soul from God. That corrupted estate in which every man comes into the world, is a state of separation from God. This distance is not to be understood as a physical natural distance, for so God is near to every one of us by his omnipresence, and by his infinite power, sustaining us in our being and actions. "Though he be not far from every one of us: for in him we live, and move, and have our being," Acts xvii. 27, 28. But this is to be understood.

First, Of a moral separation from God. There is a great strangeness between our souls and God: we reckon ourselves to have little to do with him, and to be very remotely concerned in him, we reckon that God takes very little regard of us, we look upon God as far from us, and we think God looks upon us as at a great distance; we love not God, and think that God loves not us.

Secondly, This separation may be understood of a judicial

distance, at which God hath set sinful man from himself. Man is kept out from God, as being unfit to approach to him in his sinfulness and impurities, and that is either in this life, in which condition every one is, till he be made nigh by Christ, and set before the Father without sin in him; till they are born again of the Spirit, and justified and sanctified by Christ: "Ye that sometimes were afar off, were made near by the blood of Christ," Eph. ii. 13. Here this judicial separation is the execution of that terrible sentence, "Depart from me, ye cursed, into everlasting fire, prepared for the devil and his angels," Matt. xxv. 41. Thus ye see the distance at which man is from God, which is not physical, but either moral or judicial.

Secondly, When we are thus separated from God, if we will be acquainted with him, there is required a returning to God. Acquaintance doth necessarily imply a union. Now where there was a former separation and distance, there is required a motion to compliance, and a return either in both parties, or in one at least: so that before ever we can be acquainted with God, there must be a forsaking our former distance, the separation must be removed. Now God hath done what could be conceived, and beyond what could be expected, towards the reducing of us to a union with himself; whereas, he might justly have thrust us away from him for ever, and never have given us liberty to come near him more, as being so filthy by sin, that his holiness cannot endure us, yet he hath freely set open a door of hope for our return. He did not come thus nigh to angels when they fell, but they were turned away from him, and are bound in chains of darkness to the judgment of the great day; it is impossible for them to return any more. And so it would have been for us, had not God made it possible by an act of free love; and he hath likewise revealed his willingness to receive us if we return, yea, his earnest desire: "Turn ye, why will ye die?" Yea, his rejoicing in our return, as a father rejoiceth to receive a prodigal son that hath departed from him. But that God should go further, to close with us while we retain our impurities and remain at a distance from him, it is impossible, because of the unchangeableness and simplicity of his nature, and because of the purity and exactness of his holiness; it must therefore necessarily follow that a yielding and return must be on our parts, or else there is no possibility of compliance between God and us, after that we have forsaken him by sin. And this is most righteous and equal, for man did forsake God, God did not forsake man; man made the difference, man ran away from God. God follows man as far as his holiness and unchangeable nature will permit him; he calls to us to return, he is ready to meet and embrace us in the arms of his love, and to receive us into acquaintance with himself, as the father in the parable met his prodigal son, Luke xv. 20, "He saw him afar off, and had compassion on him, and ran, and fell on his neck, and kissed him." Herein have we shadowed out to us the great readiness of God to receive returning sinful man; but as the prodigal son must return to his father, so man must return to God. Now it is sin that separates between us and God, and keeps good things from us: "Your iniquities have separated between you and your God, and your sins have hid his face from you," Isa. lix. 2. Therefore, while we cleave to our sins, we are separated from God; till we are separated from our sins, we cannot be united to God. Thus ye see our separation from God, and our necessity of returning to God, before there can be any acquaintance with him.

Thirdly, To our acquaintance with God is required an abiding with God. We reckon not ourselves acquainted with any person upon the first meeting, or when there hath passed but a word or two between us, but it is supposed to acquaintance, that we have made a considerable stay with him, and have had frequent access to him. Thus it is between God and us; we must not only come to him but abide with him, or else we shall never be acquainted with him: "If ye continue in my word, then are ye my disciples," John viii. 31. So I say, if you return to God, and continue with God, then shall ye be acquainted with him indeed. Acquaintance signifies not a bare act, but a state or habit. Now this is the difference between an act and a state; that an act is passing and is gone, but a state signifies an abiding and continuance. There may be a drawing nigh to God, without abiding and continuing with God, upon some deep conviction, or strange providence, or eminent danger; as it is said, "In their affliction they will seek me early," yet they may soon forget and forsake God. This is but a seeming and partial approaching to God, a drawing nigh in appearance, when the heart is far from God; but that approaching to God which makes acquaintance with God, is abiding with him. Those that are acquainted with a spiritual life know these things what they are, and that they are the greatest realities in the world; they know that sometimes there is a greater nearness of their souls to God; they are sensible of the approaches of their heart to God, and of the withdrawing of their souls from God; they know what it is for the soul to feel the approaches of God, and his smiles fill their souls with unspeakable comfort; and to feel God withdrawing from the soul, this clouds their joy and makes them go mourning. They can tell you at such a time they were brought unto his banqueting house, and his banner over them was love. They can tell you at such a time Christ came into his garden to eat his pleasant fruits; at such a time they heard the voice of their beloved, saying, "Open to me, my sister, my spouse, my love, my dove, my undefiled." And when the soul hath neglected this knock of Christ to open to him, that then he hath withdrawn; "I opened to my beloved, but my beloved had withdrawn himself, and was gone." These things are the experiences of a precious child of God, which I fear are little felt and little known amongst us; but where these things are not there is no acquaintance with God. For,

First, They do know him.

Secondly, They draw nigh to him, they have near access to him.

Thirdly, They have intimate converse with him. This is another thing required to acquaintance. We are not said to be acquainted with any person, unless we have had intimate converse with him. We may be next neighbours, and yet have no acquaintance, unless our conversation hath been mutual. So it is between God and us; there may be a nighness between the soul and God, and yet no acquaintance between the soul and God. We are nigh to God in our dependence upon him, we are near to God by his immediate providence and sustentation of us, and by his omnipotence. There is a nearness to God by way of dedication. As God set apart the children of Israel to be a people near unto himself, so the visible church of God is nearer to him than those that are not of the church. There is a nearness of dedication among us by baptism. But all this may be without acquaintance. There is, therefore, required to our acquaintance with God, an intimate converse with God. We have great converse with those who are of the family or society with us: now such is our acquaintance with God, as those who are of his family. God is called the Father of the families of all the earth; and the visible church is reckoned as God's family: but in a great family there may be little acquaintance with those persons which be of remote employments; but to acquaintance with God there must be such a relation as implies familiar converse. This intimacy that the people of God have to him is expressed by the nearest relations in Scripture: as, Abraham is called the friend of God: Jehoshaphat prays unto God, and saith, "Art not thou our God, who didst drive out the inhabitants of this land before thy people Israel, and gavest it to the seed of Abraham thy friend for ever?" 2 Chron. xx. 7. "And the Lord spake unto Moses face to face, as a man speaketh to his friend," Exod. xxxiii. 11. "Henceforth I call you not servants; for the servant knoweth not what his Lord doeth: but I have called you friends; for all things that I have heard of my Father I have made known unto you," John xv. 15. Now by *friend* is commonly understood a state of converse and society one with another. And this intimacy is expressed likewise by the relation of husband and wife: "For thy Maker is thy husband," Isa. liv. 5. "Then shall she say, I will go and return to my first husband; for then was it better with me than now," Hos. ii. 7. By husband there is meant God. And the whole Book of the Canticles is a relation of the mutual converse betwixt God and his people, betwixt Christ and his church, under the relation of a bridegroom and his spouse. Now what converse more intimate than between husband and wife? such is that between a soul acquainted with God. Again, this is shadowed out to us under the relation of a father and his children: "Behold what manner of love the Father hath bestowed upon us, that we should be called his sons!" 1 John iii. 1. And the Holy Spirit is given to be the spirit of adoption in the hearts of God's people: "Ye have received the spirit of adoption, whereby ye cry, Abba, Father. The Spirit itself beareth witness with our spirit, that we are the children of God," Rom. viii. 15, 16. What is signified by this relation, but a nigh union and intimate converse between the soul and God? And this is necessary to our acquaintance with God, even intimate converse with God. By this I mean a nearness of employment, when the objects of our employments are the same, then are we said to converse with God, when we are employed about those things wherein God is most. When there is, as it were, a mutual commerce and trading between the soul and God; man giving himself up to God, and God giving himself out to man; man taking up the interest of God, and God undertaking for the interest of man; these and such like actings are the converse which the soul hath with God. I speak of things which the men of the world are not acquainted with; but those that are acquainted with God know these things, and upon the mention of them, their hearts leap within them. As face answereth to face in a glass, so experience answereth these things. When this string is struck, their hearts do harmonize; as when a lute string is struck, the other strings of nighest concord with it move also. But these things are a mystery to the world, and they say, as those of Christ's word, "We know not what he saith." And it is no wonder, for they are the actings of a divine life, to which all are naturally dead, till they are raised to newness of life by the quickening of the Spirit of God. But I proceed to show what is meant by this acquaintance with God.

Fourthly, To this acquaintance with God there is required a mutual communication. Where there is acquaintance between man and man, there hath been a mutual interchange of conference and discourses. Thus when the soul is acquainted with God, there is an interchange of conference between God and the soul. The soul openeth its wants, breathes out its complaints, spreadeth its necessities before God; God openeth the treasures of his love in his Son, the rich mines of his precious promises, and the secrets of his good will to the soul. Thus, Ps. xxv. 14, "The secret of the Lord is with them that fear him, and he will show them his covenant." "The Lord said, Shall I hide from Abraham the thing that I do?" Gen. xviii. 17. Those that are friends and acquaintance, they will let out their thoughts and purposes one to another, and they give out themselves mutually into communion one with another. Thus Christ knocks at the door of the soul: "Behold, I stand at the door and knock: if any man hear my voice and open the door, I will come in and sup with him, and he with me," Rev. iii. 20. Here is Christ offering himself to the soul, and the soul is to entertain him: at another time the soul goes to God, and God entertains it; God hath promised that he will open: "Knock, and it shall be opened unto you," Matt. vii. 7; and to him that knocks it shall be opened. There are frequent actions among those that are acquainted. and by these are expressed to us the acquaintance of the soul with God.

Now, the communications that are between the soul and God are exceeding transcending all communications that are between men's acquaintance. Men may communicate their thoughts, their estates, their assistance to one another; but they cannot communicate their life, nor their nature, nor their likeness; but such communications there are between God and the soul that is acquainted with him. All being is a communication from God, the first Being: nay, the several degrees of being have several communications from God, some greater and some lesser; spiritual beings have a higher communication than natural; but God's highest communications have been to man in that mystical union of the divine nature to the human nature in Christ, and next in the mystical union of the sons of God to Christ, and in him to the Father. Thus Christ is said to live in us. "I live," saith Paul; "yet not I, but Christ liveth in me," Gal. ii. 20. Thus Christ prays the Father for his children, that they may be one, "as thou Father art in me, and I in thee; that they may be one in us," John xvii. 11, 21; "Whosoever shall confess that Jesus is the Son of God, God dwelleth in him, and he in God. He that dwelleth in love dwelleth in God," 1 John iv. 15, 16. We are said to be "partakers of the divine nature," 2 Pet. i. 4. This expression implies high communication of God to man. Again, there are high acts of communication from man to God, (for though God receives not from man, yet man is to act as giving out himself to God;) such as to give up the will to God's will. As that of Eli: "It is the Lord, let him do what seemeth him good." And that of David: "If he thus say, I have no delight in thee; behold, here am I, let him do with me as seemeth good unto him," 2 Sam. xv. 26.

Another act of high communication of a man's self to God, is parting with present enjoyments for future hopes, in confidence of God's promise. Thus the spirit of God works in the children of God a readiness to forsake father or mother, and brethren and sisters, and life itself, for the cause of God. Thus John Baptist was willing to become nothing, that Christ might become all, to be cast down, that Christ might be lifted up; John iii. 30, "He must increase, but I must decrease." Thus Abraham gives his Isaac to die when God calls for him. Thus Moses esteemed the reproach of Christ greater riches than the treasures of Egypt, Heb. xi. 26. Paul counted not his life dear for Christ, Acts xx. 24. These have been the actings of the souls of those that have been acquainted with God, and such workings as these are the feeling of a child of God.

I have showed you four things which are requisite to acquaintance with God,

First, Knowledge of God.

Secondly, Access to him.

Thirdly, Converse with him.

Fourthly, Communication to him, and from him.

Fifthly, There is likewise required to acquaintance, a loving compliance. Amongst men acquaintance implies affection. And so it is between God and man. Never any soul was acquainted with God, that did not love God; and such a soul is an enemy to God; therefore, very few are acquainted with God; but all that are not acquainted with God are enemies to God. If we should come to a person that is not acquainted with God, and say, Thou art an enemy to God; this would seem a heavy imputation: but I speak it freely; thou, whosoever thou art, that art not acquainted with God, thou art an enemy to God; for thou art still as thou wert born: but we are all enemies to God according to our corrupt nature, and abide enemies till we come to be acquainted with God. Love to God, and acquaintance with God go together, are heightened by one another. First, God lets into the soul by his Spirit a partial discovery of himself, and by this with the working of his Spirit, he inclines the heart in love to him. Then on the first working of the soul towards God, he lets in a clear light, whereby he draweth the soul to a further degree of love. A clear place for this, Eph. iii. 17–20, "And that being rooted and grounded in love, ye may be able to comprehend with all saints, what is the length, and breadth, and depth, and height; and to know the love of God, which passeth knowledge: that ye might be filled with all the fulness of God." The love of God fits the soul to comprehend the glorious discoveries of God; and the discoveries of God doth heighten our love to God. Acquaintance with God makes us like unto God; as in 1 John iii. 2, "We shall see him as he is." And our likeness to God, as it makes us the delight of God, so it makes us delight in God; for the cause of complacency and love is a likeness between the lover and beloved. God doth not love us with a love of complacency, till we are like him, nor do we love God, till we are made like God. Now our beholding God, and being acquainted with him, is a great way to our being made like God: "We all, with open face beholding as in a glass the glory of the Lord, are changed into the same image, from glory to glory, even as by the Spirit of the Lord," 2 Cor. iii. 18. Thus you see that love is likewise required to our acquaintance with God; without it no acquaintance.

I have in the first part spoken of the nature of acquaintance with God in five particulars. There must be,

First, A knowledge of God.
Secondly, Nigh access to God.
Thirdly, Familiar converse with God.
Fourthly, Mutual communication between us and God.
Fifthly, An affectionate love towards God.

The next thing should be to show that man is to be acquainted with God; but we will first take a review of these things. We have taken these things into our understandings; now let us set our hearts to these things, for in these things is the life of religion. If there be acquaintance with God, then gross wickedness drops off, as scales from an ulcerated body, when the constitution of the body is mended. In acquaintance with God will be your only true comfort in this life; and the perfection of it is the very happiness of heaven. Let us then behold, till our hearts earnestly desire, till our souls be drawn out after acquaintance with God. If God be to be known, to be approached unto, to be conversed with by me, will he communicate himself to me, and I myself to him? Oh that he would love me, that I might love him! Oh, blessed are they that know him, as they are known of him! It is good for me to draw nigh to him. "A day in his court is better than a thousand elsewhere. My soul longeth, yea, fainteth for the courts of the Lord. My heart and my flesh crieth out for the living God." Oh that I were received into converse with God! that I might hear his voice, and see his countenance, for his voice is sweet, and his countenance comely! Oh that I might communicate myself to God, and that he would give himself to me! Oh that I might love him! that I were sick of love! that I might die in love! that I might lose myself in his love, as a small drop in the unfathomless depth of his love! that I might dwell in the eternal love of him! This is acquaintance with God.

"Acquaint now therefore thyself with God, and be at peace; so shall good come unto thee." We now proceed to the next thing, which is to evidence it to be the duty of man to acquaint himself with God. This then is that into which the whole Scripture runs, as into a common channel. The Scriptures are a discovery of God's proceedings with man under a double covenant, and this is the great design of God in both covenants. The first covenant was, "That while man did remain in obedience to God, God would give man free and intimate acquaintance with himself." But if man became disobedient, then he should be dispossessed of an interest in God, and of communion with him; which was that death threatened upon the eating the forbidden fruit. The death of the body is its being separated from the soul, but the death of the soul is in separation from God. Now immediately upon Adam's transgression, man becomes unacquainted with God; so that upon the hearing of the voice of the Lord, "they hid themselves from the presence of the Lord, among the trees of the garden." What a woful case is man naturally in! He hath lost his acquaintance with God, and was in a way, never, never to recover it: upon God's approach he flees. And such is the nature of all sin, it puts a man into a disposition to greater sins. Every departure from God inclines towards a greater. In the first covenant this is the whole of it; it is both a command to keep nigh to God, and a promise of God's being nigh to them, and a threatening of God's putting them away far from him, man breaking the first covenant. The immediate effect of it was the sin of fleeing from God, quite contrary to that acquaintance. Instead of their former apprehensions of God, they seem to have forgotten his omnipresence; instead of peace with God, they have nothing but dread and torment in the thoughts of God; instead of drawing nigh to God, they run away from him; instead of converse with God, they choose never to have to do with him more; instead of giving themselves up to God, they, if it had been possible, would have hid themselves from God. Acquaintance with God is the sum of the first covenant; unacquaintance with God is the misery of the breach of the covenant. This is likewise the great design and purpose of God in the second covenant. The second covenant is this: When God beheld man in a miserable condition, by reason of the breach of the first covenant, in the unsearchable riches of his goodness, according to the eternal purpose of his good will towards man, he made an agreement with his Son to send him amongst a generation of sinful men, that if he would undertake to bring them back into acquaintance with the Father, he was willing and ready to receive them again into acquaintance with him; the Son, being the express image of his Father's will and person, hath the same good will to man with the Father, and is ready to close with his Father's proposals; and so enters into a covenant with the Father to satisfy divine justice, and to take away sin, and to take away the middle wall of separation, to recover a chosen generation, and to bring them back again to God. Thus he became the head of another covenant between God and man. And as the first covenant was made with Adam for him and his seed, so the second covenant is made with Jesus Christ for him and his seed. Because the first covenant was broken in Adam, therefore the second covenant was put into surer hands; into the hands of the Son, the second Adam, the Lord from heaven. Now I say that the great design and purpose of this second covenant is in reference to man's acquaintance with God, is clear. This is held forth to us in that parable of the lost sheep, Luke xv. 4, 5, "When the shepherd had lost one sheep, he leaves the flock and seeks for that which was lost." So when man was lost by sin, Jesus Christ leaves all, to recover and fetch home that which was lost. "We are all gone astray like lost sheep," as David saith of himself, Ps. cxix. 176. "Christ is come to seek and to save that which was lost." "But now in Christ Jesus they who sometimes were afar off are made nigh by the blood of Christ; for he is our peace who hath made both one," Luke xix. 10; Eph. ii. 13, 14. In ver. 12 is a description of our state without Christ, "being aliens from the commonwealth of Israel, being strangers from the covenant of promise, and having no hope and without God in the world." This is a description of our unacquaintance with God. But Christ makes up the breach, and that by a double act.

First, By covenant with the Father, to make man fit for communion with him.

Secondly, His giving man assurance that the Father will receive him upon his return.

This then is the great design in all those glorious accomplishments of Christ; for this he left his Father's bosom, that he might bring us into acquaintance with the Father; for this end did he who thought it no robbery to be equal with the Father, make himself of no reputation, and took upon him the form of a servant, and was made in the likeness of man; and being found in fashion of a man, he humbled himself, and became obedient unto death, even the death of the cross, that he might bring man into a re-union with God; for this end did Christ live a wearisome troublesome life among a company of rebels and enemies, as if a man should live among toads and serpents. So that he cried out, as weary of any longer abiding with them, " O, faithless generation! How long shall I be with you? How long shall I suffer you?" For this did he make himself an offering for sin, that by taking away sin, he might bring men to God. This is the great purpose of Christ in all his offices. Ye have heard of the three offices of the Mediator, that he is a Priest, a Prophet, and a King. This is the end of the priestly office. The purpose of Christ's offering up himself a sacrifice was, by satisfying the justice of God, to make way for sinners' return to God. This is the end of his prophetical office, to lead men into knowledge and acquaintance with God. This is the end of his kingly office; that governing them, and ruling their hearts by his Spirit, he might effectually bring men to God, to acquaintance with him. Now, then, since this is the great design of God in his great dispensation towards man, to keep man in acquaintance with himself, and to reduce him when he had lost it; doth it not concern us to do our part for the bringing to pass this great work? Shall God lose his end in making us, and in setting man in the world every way furnished for his service? and shall God lose his end in sending his Son to receive us, when we had forsaken him? Shall Christ leave his Father's bosom to bring us home to the Father, and shall we refuse to return? Shall he pour out his soul an offering for sin, that he might make way for our access to God,

"That we who were far off might be made nigh by the blood of Christ?" and shall we frustrate all by our refusing to go to him? Shall Christ come and offer us his help and direction to come to the Father, and shall we abide still strangers? Shall the King's Son come into our cottages to invite us to dwell with his Father at court, and shall we shut the door upon him, esteeming our cottages better than his palace?

Secondly, It is the duty of man to acquaint himself with God, because therein is the improvement of his highest excellency. Every one acknowledgeth an excellency in man, above all the rest of this lower world. Now what is this excellency of man? Is it not that he is made in a capacity of knowing God, and enjoying God, and having communion with God? This is the height of his glory. "Thus saith the Lord, Let not the wise man glory in his wisdom, let not the mighty man glory in his might, nor the rich man in his riches; but let him that glorieth glory in this, that he understandeth and knoweth me, that I am the Lord that exercise loving-kindness, judgment, and righteousness in the earth, for in these things I delight, saith the Lord," Jer. ix. 23, 24. Ye see here wherein man is to glory, for which he may value himself as truly glorious. In his understanding and knowing of God, man standeth above the rest of the creatures, in that he is a rational intellectual agent. This is part of the image of God, even knowledge, "which is renewed in knowledge after the image of him that created him," Col. iii. 10. The nigher anything resembleth God, the greater is the excellency of that thing: now in this we resemble God more than any other creature, in that we are knowing understanding agents; and the highest improvement of this excellency of man is in the knowledge of God and acquaintance with God: "The spirit of a man is the candle of the Lord," Prov. xx. 27; that is, it is a light set up in the soul, to direct the soul to a discovery of God. This is the highest improvement of our greatest excellency, and this is the excellency of man above other creatures: this is that whereby one man excels another. Who are those whose names are as precious ointment poured forth?

who are those which have obtained a good report? Are not they those who were most acquainted with God? Enoch is said to walk with God; an expression which signifies intimate acquaintance with God; and therefore was "translated that he should not see death." And Noah, whose family alone was preserved when God destroyed the old world by water, he was said to walk with God, Gen. vi. 9. Among all the sons of men he kept close to God; and God took care of him alone. Abraham, who was the father of the faithful, he was called the friend of God. Moses, who was the mediator of the old covenant, he was said to "speak with God face to face, as a man speaketh to his friend." I might make mention of many more, who were the excellent ones of the earth; because they did delight in God, and God delighted in them. "They that feared the Lord spake often one to another; and the Lord hearkened and heard: and the book of remembrance was written for them that fear the Lord, and that thought upon his name: And they shall be mine, saith the Lord of Hosts, in the day when I make up my jewels," Mal. iii. 16, 17. Ye see how God accounts of those that are of his acquaintance, that met together and spake of God, and that thought upon his name; he reckons them amongst his jewels, his peculiar treasure. Such honour have all those that are acquainted with God. Ye see then the excellency of man above all the rest of the other creatures. Now if man fail in this which is his highest excellency, he will become the vilest of creatures. Everything, if it fail in its chiefest end and purpose, and highest excellency, becomes base and of no account. "If salt lose its savour," saith our Saviour, "it is good for nothing." If man have lost his acquaintance with God, he is henceforth good for nothing. The mind of man is his eye, by which he is to behold God; now if this eye be blind, if the light be darkness, how great is that darkness! The Jews, in Ezek. xv. 3, are likened to a vine, which, if it be barren, is good for no use: "Shall wood be taken thereof for any work?" It is fit for nothing but to burn. So it is in man, his great use and excellency is his acquaintance with God: now if he fails in this, he is good for nothing. Verily, man is a base, vile, worthless thing, without acquaintance with God. None are less esteemed among men than they that want wisdom to converse among men. None are less esteemed before God than they that know him not, that have not acquaintance with him, to converse with him. Ye see wherein the excellency and worth of man consisteth, and that if there be a deformity where ought to be our chiefest beauty, the whole is accounted as a deformed piece. It concerns us then to look that we keep our glory unspotted, our excellency in its due value; that we do not degrade ourselves below what God hath placed us in. If we are not acquainted with God, our souls serve us to little purpose: it is causing the soul [the prince] to go on foot, and to serve the body, which should be as servant; it is to let the candle of the Lord burn out in waste.

Thirdly, Another enforcement of this duty of acquaintance with God, is this: If we refuse acquaintance with God, it is a slighting the greatest of all the mercies that God bestows. Favours are to be valued, either by their proper excellencies, or according to the good will of him that bestows them; both these ways this is to be accounted the greatest of mercies. In God's giving us leave to be acquainted with him, he gives out himself to be known, to be loved, to be conversed with, to be enjoyed. What greater gift can God give than himself? God is the portion of his people, he is the greatest portion, the surest, the most suitable, and the only durable portion. Thus they that know him esteem him. "My flesh and my heart faileth; but God is the strength of my heart, and my portion for ever," Ps. lxxiii. 26; "The Lord is the portion of mine inheritance: the lines are fallen to me in pleasant places; yea, I have a goodly heritage," Ps. xvi. 5, 6. "Blessed are the people that are in such a case; yea, blessed are the people whose God is the Lord." No greater mercy can be bestowed upon any people, family, or person, than this, for God to dwell among them. If we value this mercy according to the excellency and worth of that which is bestowed, it is the greatest; if we value it according to the good will of him that gives it, it will appear likewise to be the greatest favour. The greatness of the good will of God in giving himself to be our acquaintance, is evident in the nature of the gift. A man may give his estate to them to whom his love is not very large, but he never gives himself but upon strong affection. God gives abundantly to all the works of his hands; he causeth the sun to shine upon the evil and upon the good, and the rain to descend upon the just and the unjust; but it cannot be conceived that he should give himself to be a portion, a friend, father, husband, but in abundance of love. Whosoever therefore shall refuse acquaintance with God, slighteth the greatest favour that ever God did bestow upon man. Now consider what a high charge this is; to abuse such a kindness from God is an act of the greatest vileness. David was never so provoked as when the King of Ammon abused his kindness in his ambassadors, after his father's death. And God is highly provoked when his greatest mercies, bestowed in the greatest love, are rejected and cast away. What could God give more and better than himself? And how heavy will this imputation be! These are those that look upon God as not worth being acquainted with. Let us therefore consider how we shall be able to stand to these accusations. Shall we not be speechless when these things shall be charged upon us? Shall we not be confounded when we stand to the trial of Him to whom we had offered these great indignities? How shall we escape if we neglect so great salvation, so great a mercy.

Fourthly, It concerns us to acquaint ourselves with God, for without it we are in a necessity of sin and misery.

1. The soul unacquainted with God is in a necessity of sinning: "Having their understanding darkened, alienated from the life of God through the ignorance that is in them, because of the blindness of their hearts," Eph. iv. 18. For want of acquaintance with God, every thought and imagination of their heart is evil continually. "There is none righteous, no not one. There is none that understands, there is none that seeketh after God," Rom. iii. 10, 11. Not understanding, nor seeking after God, is the necessary cause that there is none doeth good. The soul of man is an active being, which is continually in motion; if it be not in

motion to God and in God, it will be in motion from God. Hence it is that the prayer of the wicked is an abomination: that which goes for prayer, God abhors, because they are not acquainted with him: "The ox knoweth his owner, and the ass his master's crib, but Israel doth not know me," Isa. i. 3. To this, saith he, "your incense is abomination unto me, the new moons and sabbaths, the calling of assemblies, I cannot away with; it is iniquity, even your solemn meetings." ver. 13, 14. Now the reason why there is a necessity of sin without acquaintance with God, is, because whatsoever is not done with a good heart is not good: "A good man, out of the good treasure of his heart, bringeth forth good fruit; and an evil man, out of the evil treasure of his heart, bringeth forth evil fruit: for of the abundance of the heart his mouth speaketh," Luke vi. 45. As an evil tree cannot bring forth good fruit, so an evil heart cannot bring forth a good action. Now without knowledge the heart is not good. "That the soul be without knowledge, it is not good," Prov. xix. 2. And there is no knowledge like the knowledge of God, and acquaintance with him, to make the heart good: "Because there is no truth, nor mercy, nor knowledge of God in the land; therefore by swearing, and lying, and killing, and stealing, and committing adultery, they break out," Hosea iv. 1, 2. Thus, want of knowledge of God and acquaintance with God, we may plainly see, is the necessary cause of sin. Now there is no greater evil on this side hell, than that of a necessity of sinning. Those of whom it is said "they cannot cease from sinning," are called "cursed children," 2 Pet. ii. 14. He that chooseth any sin rather than affliction, doth it through the blindness of his mind. This is laid as a heavy accusation: "For this hast thou chosen rather than affliction," Job xxxvi. 21. To choose iniquity rather than affliction is the greatest folly imaginable. It is one great part of the misery of hell, that they never cease from sinning; and this is the greatest misery on earth, our being so much under the power of sin. I appeal to any gracious soul that hath the feeling of the burden of sin; what is its great trouble and sorrow? Is it not because of sin? What are his secret moans to God? Is it not the sense of corruption? "O wretched man that I am! who shall deliver me from the body of this death?" saith Paul, Rom. vii. 24. He had been complaining of the mass of corruption that did still press hard upon him, and in the strong workings of his spirit against it, he calls it the body of death. It was as grievous to him as if he had been bound to a stinking rotten carcass. How wretched then is the state of every soul unacquainted with God; who can do nothing but sin, because they want the right rule of action, a right pattern of imitation, a right principle for action, a right object for action, a right end for action, the only assistance of action. It concerns us then, as we make any difference between good and evil, if we have any respect unto holiness and purity before sin and iniquity, to see to get acquaintance with God; because without acquaintance with God, we are in a woful necessity of sinning.

2. Without acquaintance with God we are in a necessity of misery. Indeed sin is a great misery; and to be in a necessity of sinning is part of the necessity of misery. But besides that, there is a necessity of misery of another kind. What is the great employment of men unacquainted with God? "Men labour in the very fire, and weary themselves for very vanity," Hab. ii. 13. This was the misery of men, because they know not God. But in ver. 14 there is a promise of better days: "When the earth shall be filled with the knowledge of the glory of the Lord, as the waters cover the sea." Then, and not till then, will there be a deliverance from labouring in the fire when there is the knowledge of God. The reason of it is, because true satisfaction and peace cannot be till our desires and enjoyments are alike; and this cannot be till the soul is acquainted with God; for nothing can fill up the desires of the soul but God. The soul of man is mighty spacious, so that it cannot be filled with the world; and while it feels an emptiness, it still cries out for more, and cannot be filled till it be filled with the fulness of God, Eph. iii. 19. The prodigal son had nothing but husks to feed upon, when he was gone from his father's house; he would fain have filled his belly with the husks, but could not; they were not food for the soul. When we

are departed from God, we have nothing to feed on but the world, and we would fill our souls with the world, but cannot; for it is not food for the soul. Acquaintance with God is the food of the soul: "I have esteemed the words of his mouth more than my necessary food," Job xxiii. 12. So that a soul that is not acquainted with God is famished for want of food; "My soul thirsteth for God, for the living God: when shall I come and appear before God?" Ps. xlii. 2. David was acquainted with God, but for want of an actual enjoyment, how doth he here breathe out the trouble of his spirit! "As the hart panteth after the water-brooks, so panteth my soul after thee, O God," ver. 1. The soul is still panting. "Some pant after the dust of the earth," Amos ii. 7. These were of the serpent's seed, whose curse from God was, "Dust shalt thou eat:" but the seed of Christ, they pant for God, and they that pant after God shall be filled with the fulness of God: but he that panteth after anything besides God will never find any fulness: he will feed as upon the dust of the earth. And what can follow but dissatisfaction and misery? Acquaintance with God is the only way to be freed from a necessity of sin and misery.

Fifthly, Acquaintance with God is the duty of man, because God himself doth acquaint himself with man. Shall the king seek after acquaintance with the meanest of his subjects, and he refuse acquaintance with his sovereign? Shall God acquaint himself with man, and shall not man acquaint himself with God? It is expected among men, that the inferior should seek for acquaintance with the superior, and not the superior to the inferior; but yet God, out of his wonderful love, hath sought first to man for acquaintance. Thus, Prov. viii. 31, it is said concerning the Son of God, who is meant by the Eternal Wisdom of the Father, that he "rejoiced in the habitable parts of the earth, and his delight was with the sons of men." If God thus delights in converse and acquaintance with the sons of men, how much more ought men to rejoice in converse and acquaintance with God! God saith, "I am found of them that sought me not," Isa. lxv. 1. All men were departed from God, and not a man that did seek after God; there is none that understands or seeks after God, yet God is found of them. The good Shepherd seeks his lost sheep, before the sheep sought him. When the soul is asleep, it hears the voice of its Beloved that knocks, saying, "Open to me, my sister, my love, my dove, my undefiled," Cant. v. 2. Christ saith to the revolting church, that he was ready to spue them out of his mouth. "Behold I stand at the door and knock: if any man will hear me, and open the door, I will come in and sup with him, and he with me," Rev. iii. 20. "Thou hast ascended on high, thou hast led captivity captive: thou hast received gifts for men; yea, for the rebellious also, that the Lord God might dwell among them," Ps. lxviii. 18. Is it not becoming, then, that man should open when God knocks? He seeks to dwell among the rebellious; is it not fit that man should enter into acquaintance with God, when God doth thus acquaint himself with man? Thus I have opened to you the nature of acquaintance with God, and evidenced it to be the duty of man to acquaint himself with God; let us now make some improvements of this truth.

USE I.

First, Is there to be an acquaintance between the soul and God? Let us then stand and wonder at the great condescension of God! This may surprise our souls with an ecstacy of admiration, that God should dwell with man; that the mighty Jehovah should have such respect to the work of his hands. "Who is like unto the Lord, who dwelleth on high, who humbleth himself to behold the things that are in heaven and in earth?" Ps. cxiii. 5, 6. The Psalmist admired God, that he humbled himself to behold things that are in heaven; and how much more then is he to be admired that he humbled himself to acquaint himself with man? Let us then be filled with admiration, that God should take us so nigh unto himself. As, Ps. viii. 4, "What is man, that thou art mindful of him? or the son of man, that thou shouldst visit him?" And Job vii. 17, 18, "What is man, that thou shouldst magnify him? and that thou shouldst set thy heart upon him? and that thou shouldst visit him every morning?" Man in the pride of his heart seeth no such great matter in it, but a humble soul is filled with astonishment. "Thus saith the high and lofty One that inhabiteth eternity, whose name is Holy; I dwell in the high and holy place, with him also that is of a contrite and humble spirit, to revive the spirit of the humble, and to revive the heart of the contrite ones," Isa. lvii. 15. Oh, saith the humble soul, will the Lord have respect unto such a vile worm as I am? Will the Lord acquaint himself with such a sinful wretch as I am? Will the Lord open his arms, his bosom, his heart to me? Shall such a loathsome creature as I find favour in his eyes? In Ezek. xvi. 1-5, we have a relation of the wonderful condescension of God to man, who is there resembled to a wretched infant cast out in the day of its birth in its blood and filthiness, no eye pitying it; such loathsome creatures are we before God, and yet when he passed by, and saw us polluted in our blood, he said unto us, Live. It is doubled, because of the strength of its nature; it was "the time of love," ver. 8. This was love indeed, that God should take a filthly wretched thing, and spread his skirts over it, and cover its nakedness, and swear unto it, and enter into a covenant with it, and make it his; that is, that he should espouse this loathsome thing to himself, that he would be a husband to it; this is love unfathomable, love inconceivable, self-principle love; this is the love of God to man, for God is love. Oh the depth of the riches of the bounty and goodness of God! How is his love wonderful, and his grace past finding out! How do you find and feel your hearts affected upon the report of these things? Do you not see matter of admiration, and cause of wonder? Are you not as it were launched forth into an ocean of goodness, where you can see no shore, nor feel no bottom? Ye may make a judgment of yourselves by the motions and affections that ye feel in yourselves at the mention of this. For thus Christ judged of the faith of the centurion that said unto him, "Lord, I am not worthy that thou shouldst come under my roof. When Jesus heard this, he marvelled, and said to them that followed him, I say unto you, I have not found so great faith, no, not in Israel," Matt. viii. 8, 10. If, then, you feel not your souls mightily affected with this condescension of

God, say thus unto your souls, What aileth thee, O my soul, that thou art no more affected with the goodness of God? Art thou dead, that thou canst not feel? Or art thou blind, that thou canst not see thyself compassed about with astonishing goodness? Behold the King of glory descending from the habitation of his majesty, and coming to visit thee! Hearest not thou his voice, saying, "Open to me, my sister: behold, I stand at the door and knock. Lift up yourselves, O ye gates, and be ye lifted up, ye everlasting doors, that the King of glory may come in. Behold, O my soul, how he waits still while thou hast refused to open to him! Oh the wonder of his goodness! Oh the condescension of his love, to visit me, to sue unto me, to wait upon me, to be acquainted with me! Thus work up your souls into an astonishment at the condescension of God.

USE II.

Secondly, Is there to be acquaintance between the soul and God? Then let us learn to make a right judgment of our own excellency; let us judge of ourselves as too high and noble to converse with this base and beggarly world. I am of a nobler original than to debase myself to such mean things. I am the offspring of God, and shall I acquaint myself with earth? I am of the family of God, and shall I converse with Satan? Is there bread enough in my Father's house, and shall I perish for hunger? Lift up thyself, O my soul, shake off the entanglements of the flesh, break out of that bondage of the devil, trample upon the glory of the world, and scorn to let out thy precious desires upon dung and dross; get the moon under thy feet, clothe thyself with the sun, put on the Sun of righteousness, come into the palace of God, and acquaint thyself with him; for this is thy glory, this is thy excellency. You precious ones, who can call God Father, and the Son Brother, who have fellowship with the Father and the Son, who may have communion with the Holy Ghost, what do you lying among the pots? What do you raking in dunghills? What do you conversing with the world? Have a holy scorn of these things as below the dignity of your souls: know your worth; esteem yourselves as of more value than all these lower treasures. This is your glory and your excellency, that ye are of God's acquaintance, that ye are sons of God, heirs of God, and joint heirs with Christ, that ye understand and know God.

There are two things wherein most men are mistaken.

First, In the nature of pride. Some look upon that only as pride which manifesteth itself in costly apparel and bodily ornaments beyond the degree and rank of the person. Some look no farther than the carriage of one man towards another. Now favourably consider with me, that the greatest pride in the world is man's undue esteem of himself toward God; and this is in the heart of every one by nature. Every one by nature doth lift up himself against God, goes about to dethrone God, and to crown himself: every one takes counsel in his heart against the Lord, saying, "Let us break his bands asunder, and cast his cords from us." This is the voice of every one that dares wilfully to sin: "We will not have God to rule over us." Yet this is the working of the pride of a man against God, to thrust God out of the throne of his majesty, and to set himself in. For what is God's glory and respect among his creatures? Is it not this; that he being the beginning and Author of all, should be likewise the end of all? And this is the very purpose of God in making man, that having received himself from God, he should have what he might freely give up to God; so that all man is, and all that he hath, is to be offered to God, as the end and centre of all. Now a sinning creature brings God under to serve him, to provide for him. Now though this pride of man against God be not so much taken notice of, yet it is the very daring sin of the world. It is indeed to be wondered at, that ever creature did cast out the first thoughts of such an attempt. Now consider how far man's pride is from his true excellency in his union with God. We are therefore to distinguish between that high esteem that man is to have of himself, and pride. For man to look upon himself as a noble being, and of rank above all the natural world, it is not pride, for thus he is (being a spiritual understanding agent) in a capacity of being acquainted with God, of being united to God, and as I may say, of exchanging himself with God.

Secondly, Another mistake of most men is, concerning their dignity and excellency, and in the rule and measure of their excellency. Most measure their dignity by the advantage which they have over others in this world: as some in their power and authority; some in their friends and relations; some in their riches and estates; some in their wisdom and faculties; some in their strength and power. And what more universal evil is there than this, for every one into something or other to lift himself up in his own esteem, and in his thoughts to tread upon others, as something inferior to himself? But men lie blinded in their own delusions, not considering what is the true excellency of man; nor know the right rule by which man's worth is to be judged of. The way for us to judge rightly concerning ourselves, is to see how we stand towards God. God is the perfection of excellency; and the nigher we are to God, the greater is our excellency. This is the greatness of a nation, to be nigh to God. "What nation is there so great, which hath God so nigh unto them?" Deut. iv. 7. And Amos viii. 7, God is called the excellency of Jacob. God sweareth not by anything below himself; therefore God is here meant. God is called the Glory of his people. "The Lord shall be to thee an everlasting light, and thy God thy glory," Isa. lx. 19. Now God is the glory of those that are acquainted with him.

First, By virtue of the relation wherein God stands towards them. An intimate relation to those that are persons of dignity and worth doth communicate worth and dignity to those who are so related to them. Thus the son of a mean man is not so highly valued and esteemed as the son of a prince. David reckoned it to be a great thing to be son-in-law to a king: "Who am I, and what is my life, or my father's family in Israel, that I should be son-in-law to the king?" 1 Sam. xviii. 18. Thus are we to reckon it our dignity and excellency to be in nigh relation to God, to be sons of God, to be heirs of God, and to be the friends of God; what greater honour than this, to be in such a nigh relation to the God of glory? Now the excellency that we have from this relation ariseth from the excellency of that act which is the foundation of this relation, and that is our being born of God, as we are sons, John i. 12, 13. God marrying us to himself, as he is our Husband; "Turn, O backsliding children, saith the Lord, for I am married unto you," Jer. iii. 14. God takes us into fellowship and communion and acquaintance with himself, as he makes us his friends and his acquaintance. This act of God doth instamp a worth and excellency upon man, as the impression of the king's seal upon wax, and makes it of value. It is spoken as the glory of the servants of God. Those that follow the Lamb, "they shall see his face, and his name shall be in their foreheads," Rev. xxii. 4; that is, God hath chosen, and, as it were, marked them out for his own: and this marking them and owning them sets a high dignity upon them, such as secures them from the curse that is to be upon all besides; as, Rev. ix. 4, they are commanded to hurt none " but those who have not the seal of God on their foreheads." This relation of the soul to God gives the soul an excellency, as it doth interest the soul in the glory and excellency of God himself; they are God's, and God is theirs; "I will dwell in them, and walk with them, and I will be their God, and they shall be my people," 2 Cor. vi. 16. He argues, from the dignity of this relation, that they should count themselves too good to converse with the world; "Wherefore, come out from among them, and be ye separate, saith the Lord, and touch not the unclean thing; and I will receive you, and be a Father unto you, and ye shall be my sons and daughters, saith the Lord," ver. 17. Thus you see the dignity that is upon the soul by its acquaintance with God. Our relation to God in our acquaintance with him, doth ennoble us, lift us above the world, make us that we are too good for the company of those that are not acquainted with God. It is then no pride in us thus to esteem ourselves, to have high thoughts of ourselves, because of that acquaintance which our souls are to have with God. It is pride to think too highly of ourselves: but it is sobriety to think of ourselves according to that acquaintance which we have with God. "I say, through the grace of God given to me, to every man that is among you, not to think of himself more highly than he ought to think; but to think soberly, according as God hath dealt to every man the measure of faith," Rom. xii. 3. Here the apostle commands them to measure the esteem which they have of themselves by the measure of faith which they have from God; because by faith they come to be valued excellent in the eye of God. So likewise we are to measure our esteem which we have of ourselves by the measure of our acquaintance which we have with God; because by acquaintance with him, we come to be truly excellent. And while we do thus, we shall not think more highly of ourselves than we ought to think: for while we account ourselves excellent because of our acquaintance with God, we, in lifting up ourselves, magnify God; and while we thus glory, we glory in the Lord, 1 Cor. i. 31. But now herein we are to beware of two things.

First, That we distinguish carefully between our capacity of being acquainted with God, and our being actually acquainted with him; for our capacity, or being so as that we may be acquainted with God, is of no worth, unless we be actually acquainted with him. We are in a remote capacity naturally as men, and we are in a more nigh capacity by the mercy and covenant of God; but this adds no true worth to the soul, without the actual acquaintance of the soul with God. Yea, man is the worse for this, if he be without the other; for if man, being made fit for enjoyment of God and communion with him, and never attain to an enjoyment of him, he becomes more vile than those things whose nature is inferior, if they attain to the perfection of that nature. And it is like to fare worse with man, if he fall short of the glory of God, because he was capable of the glory of God, than with beasts which are not capable of it. And again, in regard of that more nigh capacity wherein we are by Jesus Christ of acquaintance with God, if we are not really acquainted with God, we shall thereby not only have no addition of excellency, but thereby we shall be more vile and miserable: and therefore those who through the mercy of God have been in the visible church, and have heard of the good will of God to man through Christ, and know that God is ready to entertain them into acquaintance with himself; if they shall fall short of this, their condemnation will be greater than that of those who never heard of God's invitation and his grace in Jesus Christ. If we therefore shall glory in our capacity of being of the acquaintance of God, and neglect to be really acquainted with him, we do but as the Jews of old, who cried out, "The temple of the Lord are these," Jer. vii. 4. And the nigher we are to God, if we do not come to a thorough closure with him, the nigher we are to the stroke of his wrath: as the nigher any is to a musket-shot, the greater will the force of it be upon him. Distinguish, therefore, between our capacity of being acquainted with God, and our actual acquaintance with him.

Secondly, We must beware lest in our esteem of ourselves we lay the foundation of our glory in ourselves. There is that in every one's corrupt nature which doth provoke him to it: so that I dare boldly say that there is not a man in his corrupt natural state who doth not, some way or other, lift up himself in his own esteem for something of his own. And we are apt to make every spiritual excellency to be matter for pride and self-conceitedness. We do not sufficiently eye God as the fountain, the author, the foundation, the rule, and pattern of all our excellency. Such is the way wherein God receiveth man to acquaintance with himself, that he might hide pride from his eyes, and that no flesh might glory in his presence, 1 Cor. i. 29. If we therefore lay the foundation of our glory in ourselves, and please ourselves in the sparks that we have kindled, we shall glory in our shame, and lie down in sorrow. This high esteem which we are to have of ourselves, because of our acquaintance with God, doth not at all contradict that precious grace of humility, but they rather help forward one another; for the more any esteems himself, because of that relation which he hath to God, the less is the esteem of himself, because of anything of his own; the more we make God the matter of our glory, the less do we glory in ourselves; the more we apprehend of our excellency being from God, the less account do we make of all other seeming excellencies. When the light of the sun ariseth, then all star-light disappears.

First, All dignity we have seems to arise from that relation which we have to God in acquaintance with him.

Secondly, By acquaintance with God, we come to have an absolute positive dignity, which is real in our persons, yet still depending upon God. As by our union with Christ, we come to have a righteousness imputed, which is our justification, and a righteousness likewise inherent, which is our sanctification; so, by our acquaintance with God, we have a dignity, as it were, imputed by our relation to God, and a dignity real, which is that excellency whereby we are made absolutely better. By acquaintance with God we come to be like God; and the image of God in us is the greatest excellency that we are capable of. When Moses had been forty days in the mount with God, his face did shine with such a brightness, that the people could not behold him: so those that converse with God retain a lustre which shines in their converse with men. The image or picture of any worthy person is esteemed by them that esteem the person, and this esteem of it is from a relation which it hath to that person; but now the children of any person whom we love, being a lively image of their father's person, have another value upon them, having not only a relation worthy, because of their resemblance in the outward lineament, but a real participation of nature and disposition, which they receive from their father: so there is an excellency in those that are acquainted with God, not only as being in relation to him, but as receiving, and being partakers of the divine nature. As children learn to pronounce their words according to the pronunciation of the mother or nurse with whom they converse, (as every one is apt to be formed unto the manner and disposition of the company wherein they most usually are;) thus those who converse with God become in some measure like unto God; and this is positive personal excellency which those have which converse with God. Thus the Apostle John urgeth concerning that perfection of glory and excellency, which hereafter is to be upon those that are the sons of God: "But it doth not yet appear what we shall be, but we know that when he shall appear, we shall be like him, for we shall see him as he is." In heaven we shall be like God, because we shall see God; and on earth, those that converse with God shall in some measure be like God, according to their measure of acquaintance with him. And so Paul argues concerning this present life: "But we all, with open face beholding as in a glass the glory of the Lord, are changed into the same image, from glory to glory, even as by the Spirit of the Lord," 2 Cor. iii. 18. Here we see clearly, that beholding the glory of the Lord doth change into the same image of God, and likewise that this image of God only is the glory of man; for that is meant by "from glory to glory;" that is, from one degree of glorious similitude to another degree of glorious resemblance and likeness to God. Thus ye have seen that the excellency of man consisteth in his acquaintance with God; and that, by the virtue of his relation to God, he hath an imputed excellency; and an excellency by his propriety in God, in whom is all excellency: and that by his converse with God, and acquaintance with him, he becomes really like God, which is his inherent excellency. Let us then reckon of ourselves as those who have their dignity and excellency from God, and in this let us glory, that we know God, and are acquainted with God. This is the second use of this proposition.

USE III.

First, If man ought to be acquainted with God, then let us all inquire into ourselves, whether we are acquainted with him or no. Let us every one turn into our own bosoms, and ask ourselves this question; Thou hast heard, O my soul, that which is thy great duty, that which is the very end of thy creation and thy redemption, and that the highest perfection of thy noblest faculty consists in knowing God, and being acquainted with him, which contains a nigh union to him, and intimate converse with him, and mutual communion to God, and from God, and radicated unmoveable love to God; these are excellent things, O my soul: what is thy case? Art thou one of those precious ones, who converse oft with God, and talk oft of God, whom he will make up with his jewels? Or art thou one of those wretched creatures, who are alienated from the life of God by reason of the ignorance that is in them? Or art thou one of those who, having been sometimes afar off, are now made nigh to God by the blood of Christ, and so are led into fellowship and communion with the Father and the Son by the Spirit? Or art thou one of those who look upon God afar off, and whom God looks upon afar off? I beseech you, every one of you, deal seriously and accurately with yourselves in this inquiry; for it is most certain that most men in the world, yea, in the visible church, are not acquainted with God. Thus it hath been in all generations from the beginning of the world, and thus it is at this day: the people of God have been like a little flock of sheep, while the rest are like locusts, covering the whole face of the earth. The people of God have still complained that they are but as the gleaning of the vintage, and as two or three olive-berries in the top of the utmost branches, when the rest have been gathered. The visible church of God, in respect of the rest of the world, how small a part is it! In the visible church how few live up to their religion, by any considerable profession! How little difference is there between most among us, and heathens! And of those that profess, and lay claim to something beyond others among whom they live, how many betray their profession by their wicked practice and worldly conversation! So that when we have made inquiry, there will remain very few of those that are really acquainted with God; it concerns us then to be very diligent in inquiring, what is our case?—how we stand towards God.

Secondly, I shall be the more earnest in pressing you upon a diligent search into what acquaintance you have gotten with God, because I know that those that have least acquaintance with God are most apt to neglect this inquiry. It may be, a tender soul that hath been much with God will be ready upon the first hint to enter into the secrets of his own heart, to look over his evidences, to call to mind, When have I drawn nigh to God? When have I conversed with God? When have I communion with God? Hath my life been a walking with God? Have I dwelt with God, and made my abode with him? Thus the soul that makes high account of its acquaintance with God will be trying and examining itself; and it may be, upon its more awakened signs of its sometimes departing from God, or feeling some present strangeness, it will be apt to conclude of itself, Surely I am none of those precious ones whose life is a converse with God. But the common generation of the world, oh, how hardly will they be brought to ask themselves this question, whether they are of the acquaintance of God or no! How often have they been urged with a great and vehement affection upon trial, how their souls stand towards God! and hitherto they have neglected it. Many are so inconsiderate as to think what is spoken is nothing to them: they come and sit in the congregation, but their hearts are out of reach, out of the shot of the word; so they go away, and the word to them is as if it had not been. Many are so light and vain, and frothy in their spirits, as that the streams will almost as soon return to their fountain, as they will be persuaded to turn in and inquire into their own souls. In all naturally there is an averseness to come to the light, that their works and hearts may be manifested. If I should come to you one by one, and beseech you with the greatest earnestness wherewith I were able, when you go from the congregation to take opportunity to go in secret, and enter upon trial with your hearts, and ask yourselves thoroughly this question, and let them not alone till you have a clear determinate answer, whether you are in a state of acquaintance with God; I fear you would go, one to his pleasures, another to this vanity, and another to this covetousness, and almost all of you neglect this work of so great concernment. Let me therefore urge you with all earnestness, that you will not account it a small matter, whether you be acquainted with God or not; and so neglect this trial of yourselves: but bring up your hearts roundly to the examination, yield not to their unreasonable withdrawings, force them to answer. If you make any account of the charge of God, if you make any account of the excellency of man, if you would not lose the highest privilege of the creature, if you have any esteem of the life of heaven, know yourselves in this, whether you are in a state of acquaintance with God, and be serious and diligent in this inquiry.

Thirdly, Because men are so exceeding apt to be mistaken, and to misapprehend concerning themselves, that they are in a state of acquaintance with God, while they are mere strangers unto him; such as those whom our Saviour speaks of, Matt. vii. 22, 23, "Many will say to me in that day, Lord Lord, have we not prophesied in thy name? and in thy name have cast out devils? and in thy name done many wonderful works?" and then he will profess unto them, "I never knew you: depart from me, ye workers of iniquity." They take it for granted, that because of such privileges, and gifts, and common graces which they had, therefore they were well acquainted with Christ; but our Saviour answereth, "I never knew you;" that is, I never had any acquaintance with you. Such are those who are resembled to us by five foolish virgins, Matt. xxv. 11, 12. The five foolish virgins come when the door is shut, and say, "Lord, Lord, open unto us;" but he answereth, "Verily I say unto you, I know you not;" that is, never had acquaintance with you: you never knew me in the time of your life, and I will not know you now: you were ashamed to own me before men, and I will be ashamed to own you before my Father. Men are so apt to be mistaken in judgment of themselves, that they think themselves rich and increasing with goods, and to have need of nothing, when they are wretched, miserable, and poor, and blind, and naked. And this made David to cry out, after he had been trying himself, "Search me, O God, and know my heart; try me, and know my thoughts; and see if there be any wicked way in me, and lead me in the way everlasting," Ps. cxxxix. 23, 24. This unaptness in us to make a right judgment of ourselves in our relation to God, ariseth,

First, From that deep root of self-love that is in us by nature, whereby we are apt to apprehend well of ourselves, and please ourselves with a good conceit of ourselves, though we are never so bad. And such is the nature of this affection, that it blinds our eyes, and prejudices the mind, that it cannot make a right judgment. As affection in some parents to their children makes them reckon that which is a blemish to be a beauty in their children; so doth inordinate self-love work in men, in the judgment of themselves. Men, when they judge themselves, look into a flattering glass, which presents them in greater beauty than that which is their own.

Secondly, We judge amiss of ourselves, because we take not a right rule for our judgments, as those of whom Paul speaks, 2 Cor. x. 12: "Some commend themselves: but they, measuring themselves by themselves, and comparing themselves with themselves, are not wise." If we take ourselves to be the rule and measure, then we cannot discern our own crookedness and irregularness.

Thirdly, We judge amiss of ourselves, because of the deceitfulness of our hearts. "The heart is deceitful above all things, and desperately wicked: who can know it? Jer. xvii. 9. Gross wickedness is apparent to the purblind eye; but where there is an abstaining from gross outward sins, there are special workings of corruption, such as pride, self-love, distrust of God, and love of the world; any of which shut up the soul against God, as with bolts and bars; and these lying inward are not discerned. Other accounts may be given of the unaptness to make a due judgment of ourselves. It concerns us, therefore, to be exact in our trial, and trust not to a sudden answer; for we are ready to make a short work of it, and to save ourselves the labour, and to sit down with charitable thoughts of ourselves. Whatsoever answer, therefore, our hearts give us, let us see cleared, and have such reason for it, that we may know how to proceed with ourselves, upon a right judgment of ourselves. The chief work of trial in this particular acquaintance with God will be from those particulars wherein I opened the nature of the soul's acquaintance with God. Let us, therefore, take those heads, and our own experience of ourselves, and by a rational deduction, let us find out our own estate.

As thus: 1. Those that are acquainted with God are brought

nigh to God. Whereas sometimes there was a strangeness and remoteness, a vast separation, now the partition is taken out of the way, and I am made one in Christ. I have taken God to be my portion and my Father; I have been a prodigal, and have departed from him; but I, finding myself lost and undone, and that nothing could satisfy my soul in the world, therefore I resolved I would return to my Father's house, and try if he would receive me again into his family. And so I have done: I have cast off my old converse with the world and with corruption; I have broken my league with hell, and have entered into a covenant with the Father, through his Son Jesus Christ; therefore I may comfortably conclude that I am now in a state of acquaintance with God.

But if, in the inquiry into myself, I find not these things, if I find that now I am as in former days; I have felt no such change in myself, and that all things are with me as they were of old; I never was sensible of any loss in myself; I never knew what strangeness and nighness to God meant; I never understood what union with God and distance from God was; this signifies ill, it is a symptom of a bad state, of a state of unacquaintance with God.

2. So again, for our converse with God. He that is acquainted with God hath had his converse with God, he hath dwelt with God, and God with him; he hath supped with Christ, and Christ with him; his great business and employment hath been nigh God, in those things wherein is most of God. If I find my soul much conversing with God, oft sending out breathings to heaven, oft casting my eye towards God; if I find the great work of my mind to be with God, my great business lies in heaven, my treasure is laid up there, and my thoughts, and desires, and joys, and delights, and meditations are there; I may comfortably conclude that I am in some measure acquainted with God. But if, in the inquiry into myself, I find that I have my whole converse with the world, that I can afford no time for prayer to God in my family and in secret; if I find all the day long my cares, and desires, and thoughts, run out most naturally and fully without control towards the things

of the world, or that I will mind myself in a natural carnal way, and mind not the things of God; this signifies to me my unacquaintance with God, and it will be an ungrounded presumption in me to reckon myself any other than a stranger to him.

3. So for communion and fellowship, which is in acquaintance. Those that are intimately acquainted, their communion in the way of discourse is very frequent, in making known their thoughts and apprehensions, their fears and wants; their minds are open one to another, and that which is the propriety of one is by their acquaintance communicated to the use of both. If, then, I can find, in reviewing the workings of my soul, that there hath been this sight of heaven, this spiritual communion between my soul and God; that my heart hath been open to God; that I have gone to God when my heart hath been burdened with sorrow, I have discharged it into the bosom of God, as into the bosom of a friend; that in my doubts I have betaken myself to him, expecting comfort from him; that upon hearing his voice, I have opened to him, and upon my opening he hath come in with smiles of love, and given me tokens of his favour; these things signify a state of acquaintance with God. But if I know not what it is to have given up my soul to God, to be his, and to have taken God to be mine; if I have had experience of receiving nothing else from God, but a partaking of the things of the world; if I have not been wont to communicate the workings of my mind to God, it betokeneth my unacquaintance with God.

4. And again, for that friendly working of love and affection in the soul towards God. Those that are in a state of acquaintance are supposed to comply with each other in kindness, and love, and good will, and affection. If, then, I can, upon search into myself, find that God hath the highest room in my affections, that my heart is his, that his love is prevailing with me above the love of all things besides, and that I love those that are his beloved for his sake, then I have in me a sign of real acquaintance with God; for love is the very quintessence of acquaintance: but if, in the search into the workings of my mind, I can find no

such friendly compliance, but that God was still thwarting and crossing my designs, that I should find myself better content if there were no God, and that those workings of my mind that are about God are sour, harsh, and tearing upon my spirit; then it is to be feared that I have no acquaintance with God.

And hast thou made an impartial inquiry into thy state? And how stand things between thy soul and God? Art thou acquainted with him, or art thou not? Consider seriously, O sinners, that this is one of the weightiest questions in the world; and if this question were but well resolved, it would put an end to a thousand other questions. He that can say of God and Christ, This is my Beloved, and this is my Friend, he need not very solicitously ask, what news? He hath heard good news from heaven, which will easily balance all; come what will come, he need not much pass, as long as there stands that one text in the Bible, that "all shall work together for good to them that love God." He hath no cause to go a-begging to the world, and to say, "Who will show me any good?" As long as the Lord hath shined upon him with the light of his countenance, he need not complain, What shall I do? I have lost this or that dear friend; when he hath found him who can make up all with one look, whom he can never lose. In a word, he need not ask, How shall I do to live? and what shall I eat, and what shall I drink, and wherewithal shall I be clothed? so long as he knows that he hath a noble Friend, who will ease him of all his care, and never see him want. Well then, hast thou answered this great question or not? Or wilt thou do with thy conscience as Felix, put it off, and say thou wilt hear of these matters at some more convenient season? and I wonder when that more convenient season will be; and why not now, I pray? What season more fit than the present? I am sure God saith, "Now is the acceptable time;" and do you know better than he? What hast thou to do that is more necessary? Speak out, I pray. Is the following of thy pleasures? Is the serving of Satan? Is the damning of thy soul more necessary than the saving of it? Is the life and death of a soul nothing? Are everlasting glory and misery small matters? Is the love or hatred of thy God so inconsiderable a thing? Awake, O sinner, what meanest thou? Arise speedily, and look about thee, man. Consider seriously, as thou valuest thy soul, what best becomes a sinner in thy condition. What answer shall I return to my Master? Are not these things worth the thinking of? Shall I say for all this, that thou art not at leisure to look after an interest in his favour, or anything that tends to it? Shall I tell him that thou hast something of greater weight and higher importance to trouble your head with? And do you in sober sadness think so? For you make account that excuse is sufficient? I pray, then, make use of it yourself; for I dare not. When God shall come to ask you, why you did no more vigorously mind the getting acquaintance with himself, tell him then, if you think that answer will serve your turn, that you were not at leisure, you had such urgent occasions which took up the whole of your time, such and such a friend you had, who sent for you to the tavern, and you could not possibly come when he invited you; tell him, if you believe that plea will hold water, that you would have been glad to have come upon his invitation, but that you were taken up with such good old friends, the world, the flesh, and the devil. How do you think such an answer will be taken? You may think to put us off with such kind of reasons as this: but do you hope by this answer to satisfy your Judge? Believe it, sinner, God will not thus be put off. Wherefore I do again, with all the earnestness I can for my soul, renew my suit to thee, that thou wouldst act like a man in his wits; make some serious inquiry into the state and condition of thy soul. And consider, for the Lord's sake, again and again, before you send me away thus, what errand I come to you on. It is to treat with you about a rich match for thy poor undone soul: therefore consider well what you do before you make light of this business, and know when you are well offered; believe it, God will not long send after you in this manner, and you are not like every day to have such proffers; divine patience and goodness will not always plead at this rate with you; God will ere long say, Let them alone: the Lord will ere long speak to scornful sinners in such language that will make their ears to tingle; he will despise and slight as well as they: and who is like to have the worst of it at last. I leave to any rational man to judge? The time is coming, when your ungodly hearts shall ache to see Him whom you might have had for your Husband; when you shall have him for your Judge, whom you might have had for your Advocate. And though we could not get you to be willing to be acquainted with him, no, not so much as to have any serious thoughts about it, or to make any inquiry after him, to inform yourself concerning him; yet you shall have him for your enemy whether you will or no. But, oh, let us not part thus! let me, a man like thyself, reason the case a little more with thee. Come, tell me, poor ignorant creature, thou that still standest demurring, and sayest, Shall I, shall I? what evil is there in thy God, that thou shouldst be thus hardly brought so much as to discourse this business with thy own soul? What is the reason that thou scarce thinkest it worth thy while to trouble thy head about anything that doth concern your interest in his love? Thou that mindest his love so little, tell me, what dost thou think had become of thee long before this, if God had regarded thee as little as thou dost him? What wouldst thou have done, had the Lord said to any disease, the least of his messengers, Fetch that rebel before me, that values not my favour; he shall know what my anger is, seeing he will not prize my love. Oh, what a lamentable case hadst thou been in had God but done by thee as thou hast by him? Acquaintance with God! Methinks sinful man should stand and wonder at such a word; methinks he should be even surprised with an ecstacy of admiration, and say, And will God indeed be acquainted with such a worm, such a dead dog, such a rebel as I? "Lord, what is man that thou art mindful of him; or the son of man, that thou shouldst make such an offer to him?" One would think thou shouldst no more dispute the matter than Esther did, when that great monarch made her his queen. Were it but in sensible things, that nothing near such an offer were made, (which is impossible,) man would think the very questioning in such a case a strange folly. One would think that every one of God's enemies that have been in open rebellion against him, and are utterly unable to make their part good against him, when they hear of such terms of mercy from their Prince, who hath all their lives in his hand, should rejoice at this news, and say, "How beautiful are the feet of them who bring such tidings!" How did Benhadad look, when instead of a halter he had a coach! when instead of Rebel, he heard, Brother! Whatever we may think of these things, David thought it high time for him to bid such a messenger welcome, and to open his heart for the receiving his God. Hear what he saith to his own heart and others: "Lift up your heads, O ye gates; and be ye lifted up, ye everlasting doors; and the King of glory shall come in," Ps. xxiv. 7. And because the door of men's hearts is locked, and barred, and bolted, and men are in a deep sleep, and will not hear the knocking that is at the gate, though it be loud, though it be a King; therefore David knocks again, "Lift up your heads, O ye gates, and be ye lifted up, ye everlasting doors." Why, what haste, saith the sinner? What haste? Why, here's the King at your gates; and that not an ordinary king neither; he is a glorious King, that will honour you so far, if you open quickly, as to lodge within, to take up his abode in your house, to dwell with you. But the soul for all this doth not yet open, but stands still questioning, as if it were an enemy rather than a friend that stood there, and asks, "Who is this King of glory?" Who? He answers again, "It is the Lord of hosts;" He that if you will not open quickly and thankfully too, can easily pull your house down about your ears; He is the Lord of hosts, that King who hath a mighty army always at his command, who stands ready for their commission, and then you should know who it is you might have had for your friend; "Lift up, therefore, your heads, O ye gates." Open quickly, ye that had rather have God for your friend than for your enemy. Oh, why should not the soul of every sinner cry out, Lord, the door is locked, and thou hast the key; I have been trying what I can do, but the wards are so rusty that I cannot possibly turn the key. But, Lord, throw the door off the hinges, anything in the world, so thou wilt but come in and dwell here. Come, O mighty God, break through doors of iron, and bars of brass, and make way for thyself by thy love and power. Come, Lord, and make thyself welcome; all that I have is at thy service: Oh fit my soul to entertain thee! But where is the sinner that is in this note? How seldom do poor creatures desire God's company, or bewail his absence! Where almost are the men and women to be found, that do in good earnest long to be acquainted with God? Men are naturally strangers to God, and it is a wonderful difficult thing to persuade men to enter into so much as a serious deliberate consideration of these things. Though it be so infinitely for their interest; though the God that made them, out of pity to their souls, desire it; though he send his ambassadors in his name to beseech them to be reconciled unto God, against whom they have been in open arms; though in infinite mercy he persuade them to lay down their weapons, and promise them free and general pardon, and to receive them into favour, and to forget and forgive; yet where is the sinner almost to be found that with any thankfulness doth close with these tenders? Now it being a business of such infinite concernment, and it being the very work and business of a minister of Christ to bring God and man into union, to get man acquainted with God, I shall, in the next place, labour to enforce this exhortation upon the hearts of sinners, and do what I possibly can to prevail with them that are as yet strangers, to get acquainted with God, that they may have peace, and that thereby good might come unto them.

EXHORTATION.

Once more, poor sinner, that God who can in a moment stop thy breath and send thee into hell, doth offer to be friends with thee. If thou wilt come upon his invitation, well and good, thou art a happy man for ever; if not, thou wilt rue the day that ever thou wert born: yet, through mercy, the matter is not gone so far, but that thou mayest, if thou wilt now at last in good earnest humble thyself to him, be received into favour. Behold, a pardon, mercy and grace.

Stand astonished, O ye heavens, at this infinite condescension! Wonder, O ye angels, and pry into this kindness! Was there ever such condescension, love, and goodness heard of? If thou didst but understand, O stupid sinner, what an offer is made to thee, thou couldst not but adore that goodness that can pardon and forget such offences, and receive such a creature into favour; thou wouldst also cry out with as great admiration as he did, What manner of love! you would think it a mercy not paralleled, a kindness never to be forgotten, a proposal by no means to be refused, Now that I may, if possible, prevail with some that are yet afar off, to come near, I shall enforce this exhortation with many powerful motives, the least of which (were men but well in their wits as to spiritual matters, were the world not to a wonder fools, in the great affairs of their souls and eternity) might easily prevail. Oh that I might prevail! Oh that some might be persuaded! Oh that God would put life and power into these words, that they might prove effectual to the intended ends! Oh that some rebellious sinner might be made to close with the most advantageous offers that ever were, or could be made to creatures in our condition!

MOTIVES.

The first head of motives that I shall insist upon to enforce this exhortation, shall be taken from the nature of the Person that I would have you acquainted with. Consider well what kind of Friend you are like to have of him; and if, after you have well weighed what I shall (with God's leave) say, you can find out any one in heaven or in earth that will be a better friend to you, and stand you in more stead; if in all the world you bring one that deserves better at your hands, and is more worthy of your choicest love and acquaintance; if I bid you to your loss, why then, let me bear the name of a cheater for ever. And if after trial, through trial, and intimate acquaintance, you find yourself deceived, and that it was not worth the while to give yourself so much trouble, why then let me be branded to eternity, for the veriest liar and impostor in the world. For my part, I envy not men their happiness; but I wish, with all my heart, that men would do that which may be most for their interest. It was the counsel of Epictetus, none of the weakest men, though a heathen: "Make choice of that which is really most excellent; and if there be a friend to be found better than thy God, the first thing thou dost, get an interest in him." But consider whether there be not a contradiction in the terms. Better than the best. It's perfect nonsense. I know it's impossible for any one that hath right apprehensions of God to undervalue him. Wherefore it is a grand piece of religion, to have clear apprehensions of God; such can't but believe him to be infinitely lovely, wise, and powerful, and to be obeyed in all things; and all the reason in the world to acquiesce in his will, who is so good and so wise; such will place happiness in nothing below his favour. Wherefore I think Plutarch was not mistaken, who affirmed that "man's life was given him of God, only to get the knowledge of God." But I shall be a little more particular in speaking to the excellent qualifications of Him whom I would fain get every poor sinner acquainted with.

First, He is the most loving and kind Friend. Poor ignorant creatures that are strangers to him, talk at a mad rate concerning him; those that know him not will be speaking bad and thinking worse of him; but, oh, did they but know what God is to them that are acquainted with him; had they but conversed with him themselves; did they but see what entertainment he gives; had they but been in his company, and experienced what some have experienced; had they but beheld how affectionately he embraces them who come to him; they would quickly say that it was a false report, and wicked scandal, that the devil and the world, which know not God, had raised of him; they would soon cry out, that they would not for a world but that they had been at his house, and that they have cause to bless God for the day that ever they knew such and such who brought them acquainted with such a Friend; they will never, while they live, for the future, believe anything that is spoken against God or Christ, let who will speak it. Is this the God they had such hard thoughts of? Is this the kindness that they did so slight? Is this the Friend that they were so loath to come to? And thus ingenuous souls will even be ashamed that they should ever harbour such low thoughts of Him whom now to their comfort they have found beyond apprehension kind. Believe it, sirs, you cannot conceive what a Friend you shall have of God, would you but be persuaded to enter into covenant with him, to be his, wholly his. I tell you, many that sometimes thought and did as you do now, that is, set light by Christ and hate God, and see no loveliness in him, are now quite of another mind; they would not for ten thousand worlds quit their interest in him. Oh, who dare say that he is a hard Master? Who that knows him will say that he is an unkind Friend? Oh, what do poor creatures all, that they do entertain such harsh sour thoughts of God? What, do they think that there is nothing in that scripture, Ps. xxxi. 19, "Oh, how great is thy goodness which thou hast laid up for them that fear thee!" Doth the Psalmist speak too largely? Doth he say more than he and others could prove? Ask him, and he will tell you in ver. 21, that he blesseth God. These were things he could speak to, from his own personal experience; and many thousands as well as he, to whom the Lord had showed his marvellous kindness, and therefore he doth very passionately plead with the people of God to love him, and more highly to express their sense of his goodness, that the world might be encouraged also to have good thoughts of him. What nation under heaven can say they have not tasted of his goodness? "All the earth is full of the goodness of the Lord," Ps. xxxiii. 5. Read over Ps. cxlv., and let us hear then what you have to say against God. Some indeed may speak of the might of God's terrible acts; some that have despised his love have felt his power and justice; as for these we cannot think them competent judges in this case; they will not, it may be, commend God's goodness: yet even they cannot, will not, condemn God of injustice, but exclaim against themselves for their unspeakable folly in slighting his kindness when it was tendered to them. But as for others, ask them, and they will declare the goodness of God, they will abundantly utter the memory of his great goodness, and sing of his righteousness. Do but try, poor sinners, do but try; come a little nearer, and believe your own experience; and if, after a thorough knowledge of God, and a real acquaintance with him, you can say that his favour is not to be sought after, his love not worth the desiring; why, then, I have done, I have no more to say. I am sure, if God were as the devil and the world represent him to be; in so many thousands of years, among so many thousands and millions that have been acquainted with him, and entertained by him, some of them would have complained before this; we should at one time or other have heard something against him. Now I challenge all the world to produce me but an experienced solid saint, that when he acted like himself, and after he had been in the company of God, and had been feasted by him, could say that he kept a short house; especially, could we but inquire of those that sit down at his table, and are always in his presence; which of them all have a word to say against him? But of that more hereafter. No, no, it is in sinners themselves, there lies the fault; they believe the malicious father of lies, they easily credit the inexperienced ignorant world: and how little reason you have to believe so malicious enemies before the word of truth, I leave yourselves to determine. Oh, why will you take up a standard against your Creator so easily? Why will you receive such great things, wherein your eternal welfare is concerned, upon trust? Do such search diligently, turn over the Bible, consult the experiences of wiser men, and see whether things be not as I tell you. And how doth the matter stand now, poor heart? What, must the devil be believed before God? What, is God a hard Master still? Of all the creatures in the world, some of you have little reason to say so. Hast thou not been fed, clothed, and delivered a thousand times by him? Who is it that provided so richly for you? Who filled your barns? Who restored your health at such and such a time, when the doctor gave you over? Was that one of his unkindnesses? Are these the things for which you slight him? God himself makes a challenge in Jer. ii. 5-8: " What iniquity have your fathers found in me, that they are gone far from me, and have walked after vanity, and become vain? Neither said they, Where is the God that brought us out of the land of Egypt, and led us through the wilderness; through a land of deserts and pits, through a land of drought, and of the shadow of death, where no man dwelt? And I brought you into a plentiful country, to eat the fruit thereof, and the goodness thereof; and yet you know not me, saith the Lord." Was there ever such ingratitude heard of! "Pass ye over the isles of Chittim, and send unto Kedar, and consider diligently, and see if there be such a thing. Hath a nation changed their gods? but my people hath changed their glory for that which doth not profit," ver. 10, 11. And what sayest thou, O ungrateful Israel? Have the heathens more reason to cleave to their idols? Are the pagans more beholden to their stocks and stones than thou art to the living God? And now, what hast thou got by all this? Hast thou increased thy riches? Are thy barns more full of corn? Are there ever the more cattle in thy pastures? Are thy presses more full of grapes? Art thou not now grown poor? Is not the heaven become as brass, and the earth as iron? Do not thy cattle groan for want of food? Are not thy vines and fields grown barren? Why, you may thank yourselves for all this; you did not know when you were well. Return, therefore, O backsliding Israel, and thou shalt know the difference between my service and the service of devils, Jer. iii. 12, &c. Let me therefore again plead with thee, O God-despising sinner. If for all this thou wilt not be persuaded, let me expostulate the case with thee, as God did with Israel. Did not God bring thee into a world every way furnished for thy use? Hath he not subjected the creatures of the world to thee? Who waters thy fields out of his treasuries? Who opens the clods of the earth, and sends thee out of his storehouse provisions year by year? What would quickly become of thee, if thou hadst not a fresh supply from him every year, nay, every moment? Oh, is this his unkindness for which thou hatest him? And is it for this that thou hast such sour thoughts of him? And if all this were too little, he would do greater things than these. Hath he not sent his Son out of his bosom? Doth he not offer thee heaven and glory? What canst thou in reason ask, that is good for thee, that he would deny thee, if thou wouldst but be acquainted with him? And if this be an unkind Friend, I do not know who is kind: if this be not love, I know not what is. What could he have done more to express his love to the world than he hath done? Isa. xliv. Ask David what he thinks of God; he was well acquainted with him; he dwelt in his house, and by his good will would be never out of his more immediate presence and company: inquire, I pray, what he found amiss in him? That you may know his mind the better, he hath left it upon record in more than one or two places, what a Friend he hath had of God. "The lines are fallen to me in pleasant places; yea, I have a goodly heritage," Ps. xvi. 6. Why, what is that you boast of so much, O David? Have not others had kingdoms as well as you? No, that's not the thing; a crown is one of the least jewels in my cabinet: "The Lord is the portion of mine inheritance, and of my cup," ver. 5. So in Ps. xxiii., quite through. Nay, doth he not sometimes come out and beckon to the poor, beggarly, starved world, to come and eat their fill of the same dish? "O taste and see that the Lord is good," Ps. xxxiv. 8. If you will give any credit to his word, he will tell you, "No friend like to God." "Whom have I in heaven but thee? and there is none upon earth that I desire besides thee. My flesh and my heart faileth: but God is the strength of my heart, and my portion for ever. For, lo, they that are far from thee shall perish: thou hast destroyed all them that go a-whoring from thee. But it is good for me to draw near to God," Ps. lxxiii. 25–28. Let others think or do as they please, as for him, he values the light of God's countenance above corn and wine and oil, Ps. iv. 6, 7. And what sayest thou now, poor creature? Art thou still of the same mind? Wilt thou have God for thy God and friend, or no? Is he good and kind, or not? Is his favour worth the desiring and seeking after? "Understand, oh ye brutish among the people; and ye fools, when will ye be wise?" Ps xciv. 8. If God himself may not be believed, if David his servant may not be credited, hear what one of your brethren—a heathen, I mean—saith in this case. I shall translate his words into English. They are as follows:—"The goodness and providence of God to man is so great, that if he were well in his wits, he would do nothing publicly or privately but praise God and speak well of his name." (Ar. Epic. l. i. c. 16.) Doth it not become man, while he is ploughing, and digging, and eating, &c., to be singing, "Great is that God who hath given us land to till, instruments to work with! Great is that God who hath given us hands and feet, and other members; above all, that he hath given us an understanding soul!" And seeing most men are blind in these things, is it not fit that some that are more wise and able should publicly praise God for all these things? And now I am a lame old man, but partaker of reason, God is to be praised by me; this is my work, and this I will do, and I will not leave this station as long as I live; and I wish that all the world would join with me in singing a song of thankfulness to this good God. Hear what a testimony he gives of the goodness of God! Hark how he invites you to join in that sweet consort of singing praises to your Maker! Hark at what a rate he talks, that never read a Bible, or heard of a Christ, or knew what this acquaintance with God that I am speaking of meant; how bravely doth he set out the goodness of God! What say you? Will you yet be persuaded to think well of God? Methinks I am loath to see my good Master thus slighted and undervalued. Methinks it grieves me to see thee too, so foolishly to refuse such an offer. I shall conclude what I have to say upon this head, with another notable expression of the same divine and God-admiring Stoic. (Idem. c. 6.) "If men would study the nature of things, and had but grateful minds, they might see cause sufficient to praise God from every creature in the world." It is not therefore because God hath no goodness or beauty in him, that men do not more earnestly desire acquaintance with him; but because their eyes are shut, or they look upon him through a wrong prospective. This is the first qualification of this Friend, which may commend his acquaintance to you, that he is the most loving and good Friend.

Secondly, He is a most comfortable Friend. It is a vulgar and yet a dangerous error, which the devil would fain keep up the credit of, that a religious life is a sad, melancholy, pensive life; and that, upon our acquaintance with God, we must bid an everlasting farewell to joy, pleasure, and comforts. And is it true that a Christian's life is so uncomfortable a life? What, then, doth David mean to take his harp so oft in his hand? What makes him so frequently to warble out those melodious notes? How seldom is his viol out of tune? Why is he so oft singing and rejoicing? Read the last Psalms at your leisure, and then tell me whether that be the language of a sad, mournful, melancholy man. Do you never hear him speak of God, his exceeding joy? Doth he not tell God plainly sometimes, that he can scarce relish anything but that which comes from his table? Nothing else can comfort him. Hence it is, in Psal. cxix. 76, 77, that he puts up this earnest request to God: "Let, I pray thee, thy merciful kindness be for my comfort." As for his part he could take comfort in nothing below that, and that was it that the Lord had graciously promised to feed his servant with, as long as he lived; whereupon he urges God with his promise, "According to thy word unto thy servant." And that none might think this to be only God's common kindness that he means, he adds, "Let thy tender mercies come unto me, that I may live." God's common mercies would not serve his turn, that was a dish that the world fed upon as well as he; if he might not have these sweet dainties, peculiar, spiritual, fatherly mercies, he could not live, he should even pine away for hunger. Wherefore he saith, a little after, that his soul did even faint for God's salvation. And the soul that hath not a full meal here; oh, how is it raised! How doth it cry, Roast meat! "The King hath brought me into his chambers," Cant. i. 4. And what had you there? Nay, that's more than the soul can express; only this she can say, "The taste of that mercy she hopes to keep in her mouth for ever; she shall remember his love more than wine." Nay, so comfortable a Friend is God, that those who have an interest in him can rejoice in such times, when others would be weeping and wringing their hands. God's company is so refreshing, that it turns a prison into a palace; it brings joy and pleasure into a dungeon. Stand forth, O ye suffering saints, and speak your experiences! The world objects to your state as a sad state, and they think you have good reason to accuse God, and if any have anything to say against the comfortableness of a religious life and this Friend, it is you. Well then, will you promise, O sinners, to stand to the judgment of the greatest sufferers? We will inquire of them that have been sawn asunder, tormented, roasted for God's sake. Look into that little "Book of Martyrs," and you shall find as uncomfortable as their state was, yet they would not accept of deliverance; none of them all that would open his mouth against this Friend for all this. What say you, O Paul and Silas, now your backs are raw, and your feet are in the stocks? Their singing speaks significantly enough for them that they were not over-sad; and they are so busy in crying Hallelujahs, that they can't attend to give an answer to so sorry a question. What say the martyrs out of the flames? Doth not their love burn as hot then as ever? Did ever any of them, from Abel to the least that suffered in Christ's cause, say that God was an uncomfortable Friend? Do not all the children of wisdom, from first to last, justify wisdom, and say, that "her ways are ways of pleasantness, and all her paths peace?" Of those that have God for their Friend, and know it, bring me any of them all that complains of God. How doth he come and cheer them up when all the world is against them! John xvi. 33. What made that holy man in Ps. xxiii. say, "Though I walk through the valley of the shadow of death, I will fear no evil?" What not fear then? Why, what friend is it that keeps up your spirits, that bears you company in that black and dismal region? He will soon tell you God was with him, and in those slippery ways he leaned upon his staff, and these were the cordials that kept his heart from fainting. I challenge all the gallants in the world, out of all their merry jovial clubs, to find such a company of merry cheerful creatures as the friends of God are. It is not the company of God, but the want of it, that makes sad. Alas, you know not what their comforts be, and strangers intermeddle not with their joy. You think they can't be merry when their countenance is so grave; but they are sure you can't be truly merry when you smile with a curse upon your souls. They know that he spoke that sentence who could not be mistaken, "Even in laughter the heart is sorrowful, and the end of that mirth is heaviness," Prov. xiv. 13. Then call your roaring, and your singing, and laughter, mirth: but the Spirit of God calls it madness, Eccl. ii. 2. When a carnal man's heart is ready to die within him, and, with Nabal, to become like a stone, how cheerfully then can those look that have God for their Friend! Which of the valiant ones of the world can outface death, look joyfully into eternity? Which of them can hug a faggot, embrace the flames? This the saint can do, and more too; for he can look infinite Justice in the face with a cheerful heart; he can hear of hell with joy and thankfulness; he can think of the day of judgment with great delight and comfort. I again challenge all the world to produce one out of all their merry companies, one that can do all this. Come, muster up all your jovial blades together; call for your harps and viols; add what you will to make the concert complete; bring in your richest wines: come, lay your heads together, and study what may still add to your comfort. Well, is it done? Now, come away, sinner, this night thy soul must appear before God. Well now, what say you, man? What, doth your courage fail you? Now call for your merry companions, and let them cheer thy heart. Now call for a cup, a whore; never be daunted, man. Shall one of thy courage quail, that could make a mock at the threatenings of the almighty God? What, so boon and jolly but now, and now down in the mouth! Here's a sudden change indeed! Where are thy merry companions, I say again? All fled? Where are thy darling pleasures? Have all forsaken thee? Why shouldst thou be dejected; there's a poor man in rags that's smiling? What, art thou quite bereft of all comfort? What's the matter, man? What's the matter? There's a question with all my heart, to ask a man that must appear before God to-morrow morning. Well then, it seems your heart misgives you. What then did you mean to talk of joys and pleasures? Are they all come to this? Why, there stands one that now hath his heart as full of comfort as ever it can hold; and the very thoughts of eternity, which do so daunt your soul, raise his. And would you know the reason? He knows he is going to his Friend; nay, his Friend bears him company through that dirty lane. Behold how good and how pleasant a thing it is for God and the soul to dwell together in unity! This 'tis to have God for a Friend. "Oh, blessed is the soul that is in such a case; yea, blessed is the soul whose God is the Lord," Ps. cxliv. 15. Nay, David when he seemed to be somewhat out of tune, leaves this upon record as undoubted truth: "Truly God is good to Israel, even to such as are of a clean heart," Ps. lxxiii. 1. Let the devil and his instruments say what they will to the contrary, I will never believe them; I have said it before, and I see no reason to reverse my sentence; "Truly God is good." Though sometimes he may hide his face for a while, yet he doth that in faithfulness and love; there is kindness in his very scourges, and love bound up in his rods; he is good to Israel: do but mark it first or last: "The true Israelite in whom there is no guile shall be refreshed by this Saviour." The Israelite that wrestles with tears with God, and values his love above the whole world, that will not be put off without his Father's blessing, shall have it with a witness: "He shall reap in joy, though he may at present sow in tears. Even to such as are of a clean heart." The false-hearted hypocrite, indeed, that gives God only his tongue and lip, cap and knee, but reserves his heart and love for sin and the world, that hath much of compliment, but nothing of affection and reality; why, let such a one never expect, while in such a state, to taste those reviving comforts that I have been treating of; while he drives such a trade, he must not expect much of God's company; but of that hereafter. What a charge doth God give to his ministers to keep up the spirits of his people: "Comfort ye, comfort ye, my people," saith their God; "speak ye comfortably to Jerusalem." It's a gross mistake to think that God loves to see his people drooping and hanging down their heads; no, no, he counts it his honour to have his servants cheerful. Oh why then should any of the precious sons and daughters of Zion walk up and down, as if their

Friend's company were not sufficient to solace them, even in the lowest state that a child of God can be conceived to be in! While you think God is honoured by you, you can't imagine what wrong you do him. The world stands by and looks upon you, the devil bids them look on still, and asks them how they like such a dumpish life and the service of such a Master, all whose servants and friends lead such a doleful life. Stay, hold there, Satan! that's a lie, and a loud one too; there are and have been thousands of God's children that have lived as it were in the suburbs of heaven, while they have been upon earth; many thousands there have been that have spent their days in true solid joy and peace; many that have gone from one heaven of comfort here, to another of glory and comfort in that other world. As I said before, so I say again, It is not the company of God, but the want of it, makes him sad whom you see so; besides, let me tell you, tears and joy are no way inconsistent. It may be, also, those tears, that sad countenance may be for thy sake, O sinner. When he sees what comfort thou despisest, and knows what a God, what a Friend thou refusest, he can't but weep; it's no rarity for the people of God, in the midst of their spiritual enjoyments, to pity poor foolish sinners, that slight those things which they know to be so refreshing. Thus David did when his heart was solaced with the love of God; when his soul was ready to be over-burdened, over-powered with the abundant in-comes of God's kindness; he can't but with grief and pity think of their state, who have nothing to live upon but husks, whilst he feeds thus high. Oh let my soul be but acquainted with God; let me but taste more of those true comforts, drink of that river of pleasures that is at his right hand, and then I could spare these lower sensual pleasures; then I could scarce envy the most merry ranting blades their comforts; I will not say but then I should with sorrow think of their wants. It was spoken by Galeacius Caraxiola, one that sometimes had none of the least shares of worldly enjoyments, and might have had more, could he have dispensed with the absence of this Friend, could he but have been willing to have wanted those spiritual comforts: "Let him perish that values not one hour's communion with God, and the comforts of a divine life, above all the pleasures and comforts that the earth can afford." Give me such comforts, such a Friend, whose smiles may refresh me upon a deathbed, whose presence may revive me when nothing else can. Naturalists tell us of a bird called Charadius, that, being brought into the room where any one lieth sick, if he look upon the sick person with a fixed eye, he recovereth; but if he turn away his eyes, the person dies. It is true, I am sure, of this Friend, in whose favour is life, and in whose frowns there is death. (Ar. Epic. l. xiii. c. 24.) " Can you help me to such a friend" (may all say with as good reason as he) "that can keep me from all fears?" Oh for such a friend! This is instead of all pleasures to me, to think that God is my Father, and to know that I have loved and obeyed him to the utmost of my power, not only in words, but in deeds; this, this is the pleasure; here is a Friend indeed. Now, what do you say to all this? Is God to be desired? Is his acquaintance to be sought after? Can such a Friend be too much valued? The truth of it is, I would not give a rush for any of your comforts which come not from a sense of our interest in Christ, and which have not a solid foundation, Scripture consolations. It is not he that smiles, but he that can look up to God as his, and look into his soul, and see things there in a good composure, and kept in a cheerful subjection to his Maker and Redeemer: this, this is the state, here dwell joys and comforts that deserve such a name. This lower region sometimes is stormy, but above there is a constant calm. (Sen.) And is God still to be slighted? Are his favours, is his acquaintance little worth? I know you can't be an enemy to comfort and joys. Why, let me tell you, here is the well of consolation, here is the fountain, and all other joys which are drawn out of the cisterns will erelong be dry. Come away, therefore, poor soul, and do not refuse such joys as all the carnal world cannot parallel for their hearts. And this is the next motive, taken from the consideration of the nature of this Friend, whom I would persuade you to get acquainted with.

First, He is a loving and kind Friend.

Secondly, He is the most cheering, comforting Friend.

Thirdly, He is the most able and powerful Friend. He hath all power in his hand; and as long as he is but thy Friend, whoever is thy foe, thou shalt never be overpowered, never be crushed. Thou mayst challenge all the devils in hell, and all his instruments upon earth to do their worst; God is on thy side; thou needst not fear. Thou art in thyself a poor, weak creature, easily conquered and broken by a thousand enemies; but if thou hast a God to fly to, thou mayst sing as well as those did, Isa. xxvi. 1, "We have a strong city; salvation will God appoint for walls and bulwarks." No wonder, then, if every wise man think it abundantly worth his while to secure this great privilege to himself, that God may be his Friend. This is his best hold, his one thing necessary. "One thing have I desired of the Lord, that will I seek after; that I may dwell in the house of God all the days of my life, to behold the beauty of the Lord, and to inquire in his temple," Ps. xxvii. 4.

Sin, the world, and the devil, may tempt a sinner, but they can never guard him from the power of this great and almighty God.

And now, you that are contented to live as without God in the world, let me request you to consider:

Canst thou spread out the heavens as a curtain, or cover the sun with darkness? Canst thou call to the lightnings? and will they answer thee, and say, Here we are? Shouldst thou speak to that hasty champion, and command him to stand still one quarter of an hour, would he obey thee? If these things be too much, why dost thou boast? thou art but a worm. Alas, poor sinner, when this great God appears in judgment, thou art not able to deal with a fly or a frog.

Oh, then, is it not good prudence for all the sons of men to come and agree quickly with this adversary, while he is in the way? for whoever goes on in an enmity and rebellion against this Lord of heaven and earth shall not prosper, and be sure his sin shall find him out.

And this is another qualification of this Friend, whom I would commend to your acquaintance: He is an able Friend,

1. He is the most kind and loving Friend.
2. He is the most comfortable Friend.
3. He is the most able and powerful Friend.
4. He is the most active Friend. He commands his to be diligent and industrious, always abounding in the work of the Lord. Surely he will not be slow.

If the inanimate creature, such as the sun, resolveth as a strong man to run his race; how active, then, must the Maker of that sun be! If he command you not to deal with a slack hand, surely he himself will not deal with a slack hand. Should you behold this Friend of yours riding upon the wings of the wind, and making the clouds his chariot, would you not say, Oh, how swift, oh, how active is this glorious Friend of mine! The feet of this beloved One are as hinds' feet, for the good of his friends. Yea, his very eyes run to and fro through the whole world; for their good he keeps constant watch and ward about them, and he that can injure any of his out of his sight shall go unpunished, Isa. xxvii. 3.

The Lord speaks this under the metaphor of a vineyard. And doth this great Husbandman neglect his vineyard? Doth he not dig, manure, and stone it, and keep out the wild boar and foxes? Doth he not prune it, and tend it charily? I the Lord do keep it night and day; none shall come into it to gather the fruit of it without my leave. I will water it every moment. So that you see what pains God takes for his. Do you believe this Friend sits in heaven, and looks down upon the earth for nothing? Be not deceived, O sinner, thou wilt not be persuaded to get reconciliation with this great and holy Majesty. "The Lord is not slack concerning his coming, as some account slackness." Let his stay be never so long, when he comes to judge the world, it will be before the sinner looks for him. Indeed there is nothing that a wicked man more pleaseth himself with, than the thoughts that it will be a long time before God and he meet; but he little considers that a thousand years are but as one day compared to the days of eternity. Now, by faith, these things are made real to the considerate Christian; and as for the supplying of his wants, he knows if he comes at midnight to borrow bread of him, he will not put you off with this excuse, that he is a-bed, and cannot rise from his children; but will presently help, making their necessity his own opportunity to give them what shall be convenient for them; as knowing, that, let the wind sit in what corner it will, it shall fit their sails, and bring them nearer the harbour.

The world's friends are infinitely below this Friend. One hath chosen silver and gold, and a great estate, and such a one in the world's calender may be written down for one of the wisest in his choice. Well, let us see now what this Friend can do for you. Your body is on the rack, your hands are weak, your legs tremble, your stomach fails, your sleep departs from you. Where is now your friend? Call for him speedily. Come, let us now see if he be a friend indeed. Let us see it. Can he give you one hour's sleep? Can he help you to one moment's rest? Can he give you no refreshment, no help? Take him; lay him by you on your bed. Oh, it is so heavy, I cannot endure it. Lay it in your bosom. Oh, I cannot breathe for it: take it away, take it away; it will not do. Why, sir, do you know what you say? It is your old friend, which you valued above God himself; it is a bag of gold. I know it, I know it; it presses me down; it is so heavy, I cannot bear it; away with it, away with it. And is this the friend you prized so very highly? Is this all the kindness that he hath for you now? Is this all the help he can give you at such a time, when a friend should stand one in some stead? Were you not told as much long ago, how you should be served at last?

5. He is the most humble and condescending Friend. He doth not scorn to be acquainted with the meanest: the beggar may be as welcome to him as the prince: the poor and rich are all one to him: he takes as much notice of Job on the dunghill as David on the throne: he knows any of his friends in rags as well as in silks; in sheep-skins and goat-skins as well as in scarlet and fine linen.

Look up, poor creature, and see what a privilege thou hast. God himself, the King of glory, is willing to be acquainted with thee. What sayest thou to this? Doth not thy heart leap within thee for joy, when you consider the infinite goodness of God, that reveals these things to babes, "which are hid from the wise and prudent: even so, Father, for it hath seemed good in thy eyes." That is a strong expression; yet He spoke it that cannot lie. Therefore, O you humble ones, that value the favour of this Friend, hear and read it, and make the best of it: it is yours; feed upon it: it is a sweet bit indeed: "Thus saith the Lord, Heaven is my throne, and earth is my footstool: where is the house that you will build me? and where is the place of my rest? For all those things hath mine hand made, and all those things have been, saith the Lord: but to this man will I look, even to him that is poor and of a contrite spirit, and trembleth at my word," Isa. lxvi. 1, 2. I shall have occasion hereafter a little to open these words under another head; wherefore I shall now but name it. Oh, what encouragement is here for the most despicable creature in the world, that may be as happy in the acquaintance with God, as the mightiest lord in the world. Here is One that will not be ashamed to own thee, when others will take little notice of thee. Thou thinkest these things strange, it may be, and so they be indeed; but yet not more strange than true. It doth not a little engage the affections of the meanest rank, if a person of quality do but give them a kind look; especially if they may have freedom of access to him. Oh what a privilege they count it, for such a one to undertake the whole management of a poor man's affairs; for him to come to his house, and to look into his cupboard, and to take care of supplying all his wants, and coming frequently to him, and supping with him, and being with him, and to make great provision for him, as if he were a prince; where is such a thing as this heard of? But if such a thing were, it were a light matter in comparison of what I am speaking of. Where do we read of a great king's sending ambassador after ambassador to a poor beggar? What history doth record such a story as this, that a great monarch should make earnest suit for many years together to a worthless slave, that he can hang when he will, that hath not a rag to her back, to make her his queen: this is rare indeed, this is beyond precedent among men; but yet it is that which the great God doth not disdain to do; nay, let me tell thee, whosoever thou art, remaining in a state of nature, that readest these lines, that at this very time God is doing no less than all this comes to for thee; and I, in the name of my great Master, do come to expostulate the case with thee. That God that gave thee thy breath, and can take it away as soon as he pleaseth; that God that made heaven and earth, to whom all the nations of the earth are but as the drop of a bucket to the vast ocean, who holdeth the sea in the hollow of his hands, who weigheth the mountains in scales, and the hills in a balance; that God that hath no less than a heaven to reward with, and a hell and everlasting flames to punish with; He it is that doth by me beseech thee to be reconciled unto him; He it is that would be your Friend, your Acquaintance. O unheard-of mercy! O infinite and unparalleled condescension! I have often thought there are two great astonishing wonders in the world. The one is God's infinite mercy and condescension to rebellious apostatized man; and the other is man's insensibility and ingratitude; that there needs such a stir and so many words to persuade him to close with this wonder of kindness, and that so very few should be prevailed with. See this set forth to the life in Ezek. xvi.; Isa. i. 2, 3. "The Lord is high above all nations, and his glory above the heavens. Who is like unto the Lord our God, who dwelleth on high, who humbleth himself to behold the things that are in heaven and in the earth! He raiseth up the poor out of the dust, and lifteth the needy out of the dunghill, that he may sit with princes," &c. Ps. cxiii. 4–8. The Psalmist, therefore, had no small reason to cry out with admiration, "What is man, that thou art mindful of him? and the son of man, that thou visitest him?" Ps. viii. 4. "What is man, that thou takest knowledge of him? or the son of man, that thou makest account of him?" Ps. cxliv. 3. "What is man, that thou shouldst magnify him? and that thou shouldst set thy heart upon him? and that thou shouldst visit him every morning, and try him every moment?" Job vii. 17, 18. Behold his majesty, and yet how he stoops! Nahum i.; Ps. xviii.; Job xxxvii. xxxviii. xxxix.; Isa. xl. "Though the Lord be high, yet hath he respect unto the lowly: but the proud he knoweth afar off," Ps. cxxxviii. 6. That which Seneca the moralist speaks of wisdom may be said of God: (Epist. lxi.) "It is lawful to come to him without rich attire and great attendance. Come naked, and you shall be as kindly entertained as if you did shine in cloth of gold, and were besparkled with diamonds. He will not give freer access to the rich than the poor, neither doth he value a strong healthful person before a sick and crazy one, a beautiful and well-trimmed gallant before a cankered, old, deformed creature." Thus far Seneca and the Scriptures speak the same language. Neither Job's boils nor Lazarus's sores made God keep ever the farther off from them. I knew one all of a cleave with the small-pox, whom this Friend came to visit, and in that condition, how many kisses had that sweet creature from God! Oh, it would do one's heart good to have such a Friend! And this is the next qualification of this Friend, which may commend him to thy acquaintance, be thou ever so vile and sinful in thy own eyes: Such as thyself he hath made welcome; and upon his word, wilt thou but come away speedily, thou shalt be welcome too.

6. He is the most faithful Friend. Where is the man that can tax him with the least unfaithfulness? Who is the man that can say that he ever forsook any of his in their greatest exigency? He hath been trusted more than once with more than the world is worth a thousand times over; and they who trusted him most never accused, never thought their choicest jewels, their whole estate, could be left in safer hands; his promise and his performance have kept true; he never failed his in the least punctilio or circumstance of time. Ask Abraham, who was one of God's friends. God tells him that his seed shall inherit Canaan, and that they shall be strangers in a land that was not theirs, four hundred years; and did he not, at the expiring of that time, though it was at midnight almost, bring them out of Egypt? God keeps his time with them to a minute. Ask Joshua

whether he did not live to see this promise made good? Inquire of David, and he will tell you again, that no Friend is so trusty. The unfaithfulness is on man's side; there, indeed, there, I say, is many an unhandsome thing done, and yet for all God doth not (as you shall hear hereafter) presently break with them. If they forget that they are children, he will not forget that he is their Father. If God should have done thus by them, many thousands of them that are now in glory had been somewhere else. He promiseth indeed great things unto his friend; but does he not as he saith, if not in the very thing, yet in that which is better? and who would account himself wronged, if one that promised him ten pounds in silver should in the stead of it give him ten thousand pounds in gold and jewels? I believe such a one would not be thought to be worse than his word, nor the person to whom he made this promise count himself injured. And this God doth frequently, did men but understand the worth of what God pays them with. It may be God doth not clothe them in silks and satins, (neither do I know that he ever promised to do so,) but yet he clothes them with the righteousness of Christ, and bestows those glorious robes upon them, in which they look more trim and neat than in cloths of gold; he hath made him such a suit that is the handsomer for the much wearing; he may eat and drink, sleep and work in it, and keep it on his back day and night, and it shall not be wrinkled; it is the better for use. He is a faithful Friend; and none that ever had to do with him can say anything to the contrary. He never forgot any business that any of his friends desired him to do for them; he never neglected it, or did it by halves. Where did any of them come to him to reveal some secret loathsome distemper to him, that he reproached them with it? To which of them did he promise a heaven, and put them off with this world? When this Pilot undertakes to steer their course, their vessel shall never split upon the rock, run upon the sands, or spring a leak, so as to sink in the seas. To be sure, He will see them safe in their harbour. (Ar. Epist. xxvii.) He was no Christian; yet I suppose none will deny but he spake good divinity, who said, "If a man will choose

God for his Friend, he shall travel securely through a wilderness that hath many beasts of prey in it; he shall pass safely through this world; for he only is safe that hath God for his Guide." Doth he not speak a little like David himself, Ps. xxxvii. 23, who never expected to come to glory, except he were guided by his counsel? Now, if a poor heathen could say thus, and see good reason to trust God, and admire his faithfulness as he doth frequently; (and so doth Seneca, justifying God's faithfulness in all his dealings with the best men in all their sufferings, and the prosperity of the wicked;) what then shall the heavenly Christian say, who hath experienced so much of God's faithfulness in answering his prayers, in fulfilling his promises, and supplying all his exigences! David will tell you as much, and justify God in his most severe dispensations towards him: "In very faithfulness hast thou afflicted me," Ps. cxix. 75. In our earthly and bodily affairs, we should never count that Physician faithful that will not rather open a vein, or put his patient to exquisite torture, to save his life, than let him die easily. We believe a father may whip his stubborn child with more love than let him alone. To prevent the axe or halter with a rod, is no cruelty. "Faithful are the wounds of a friend," Prov. xxvii. 6. It was not for nothing that the Psalmist stuck so close to God; he had a little experience of the unfaithfulness of other friends: "His lovers and his friends stood aloof from his sores, and his kinsmen stood afar off," Ps. xxxviii. 9, 11. May not a great many complain as well as Job, that their "brethren have dealt deceitfully as a brook, and as the stream of brooks they pass away?" Job vi. 15. A friend may forget one, a brother may disown one, father and mother may cast one off, but here's a Friend that sticks closer than all. Nay, he is a better Friend to his than they are to themselves. When they loved themselves so little as to undo themselves, he loved them so well as to save them; when they loved themselves so as to poison themselves, he loved them so as to give them a powerful antidote; when they, like children, would have the knife, he takes it out of their hands, lest they should cut their fingers; when they are so careless as to surfeit themselves, he is so faithful as to keep them short, and diet them; and all this I hope they that understand themselves will not call unkindness or infidelity. David had in his time some friends that made no bones of hazarding their lives for him; some of them were willing to quench his thirst, though with their blood; and yet, for all that, in all his life he never met with so faithful a friend as his God. "O Lord of hosts, who is a strong Lord like unto thee, or to thy faithfulness round about thee?" Ps. lxxxix. 8. He had rather trust his God than any of them all. God is a real true faithful Friend; he tells us things as they are; he doth not speak more of things than the nature of them doth require; he doth not tell the best, and hide the worst; he doth not speak all of heaven, and nothing of suffering; but saith plainly, all that will live godly in Christ Jesus must suffer persecution. And Christ saith, those that will be his disciples must take up their cross and follow him; and that through many tribulations they must enter into the kingdom of heaven. He speaks of sowing in tears as well as reaping in joy; of affliction as well as glory. And when he speaks of the glory of another world, he doth not too highly advance his excellency. When he speaks of his wrath, or hell, or sin, he doth not make them greater evils than they be. The Lord is faithful in all his dealings, and that they who love him know right well. Whatsoever doth happen to the world doth happen justly and faithfully; and so, if thou wilt but well observe, thou shalt find. And what sayest thou after all this? thou who hast tried many and many a friend, so called, and hast by sad experience first or last found them all unfaithful, and art almost ready to say of all men, that they are liars, and that truth and reality are rarities; thou thinkest there is scarce a man upon the earth to be trusted. And wilt thou never be afraid of such a friend? Wilt thou at last be wise, and be acquainted with a Friend that never proved unfaithful? Behold such a one that would be glad with all his heart to entertain you, would you but forsake your old treacherous acquaintance! Here, here is one that never fails, nor forsakes those that put their trust in him. The heavens shall depart, and the hills be removed out of their places, but his faithfulness, his love shall never depart from his; and wilt thou not think such a Friend, after all this, worth the having? Come, come, never stand fretting thy heart out with discontents; men will be men, that is, unfaithful, as long as the world lasts. Do you expect, as long as sin reigns in men's souls, as long as Satan doth so much act therein, that they should forget to be selfish, covetous, deceitful? But now God will always be like himself, a God faithful, true, holy, just; and if any one in heaven or in earth can condemn God justly of the least unfaithfulness, my mouth shall soon be stopped. In this thing I confess myself to be of Antoninus's mind, who said, "If there be a God, as there is most certainly, why, that God must necessarily be most faithful, most wise, most good; but if there be no God, it is not worth the while to live in a world in which there is nothing but sin, confusion, disorder, and no hopes of a redress; the excellence of our being, our reason, would make our misery more exquisite, and our lives less desirable." But, blessed be God, it is not come to that pass, that we should need question the being of a God; for as one saith wisely, "Thou hast far more reason to question thy own being than God's." Now I say again, methinks he that had been so oft perplexed with many unfaithful, unworthy carriages from them whom he called friends, should be at last persuaded to try what this one Friend would do for him. Oh, what abundance of sorrow would it prevent, if men would but trust God more, and men less! This, this is the Friend, sick and well, rich and poor, living and dying, always the same. Make sure of this Friend, and thou art safe; thy all is then in safe and faithful hands.

7. He is a rich Friend: "The earth is the Lord's, and the fulness thereof: the cattle upon a thousand hills is his." He it is that hath the absolute disposal of crowns and sceptres; he it is that can easily raise all his favourites to a high estate. If the world and all its glory can do his any good; if kingdoms and vast dominions can advantage them; he can, with better reason than Satan did to Christ, say, "All this is mine, and if thou wilt love me and worship me, I will give you as much of it as will do you good;" and who would ac-

count it a kindness to be given that which will do one hurt? But these are but toys and trifles in comparison of what God hath to bestow upon his friends. Lift up thine eyes, and behold those glittering stars; look upon that stately canopy that hangs over thy head. Why, all this is nothing almost to the glory which shall be revealed; there is far greater disproportion between it and what we see and enjoy at the best here below, than there is between the footstool and the crown. Oh, could you but by faith draw the curtain and see what is within! Oh, did you but know what is behind those hangings which you see wrought so curiously, the work of his fingers! Oh, that is the place, there is a house indeed, there is a palace, couldst thou but by faith and meditation take a view of it; could you but make a voyage into that far country, and see that city of God, and discourse with the inhabitants of the New Jerusalem, what discoveries should you then have of the riches, state, and grandeur of that Prince's court; shouldst thou but see those treasuries opened, and know the worth of God's jewels, thou wouldst wonder what men and women meant, that they should need so much persuading to be acquainted with Him that had such things to bestow; you would judge him worse than mad who should not joyfully embrace any overtures of this nature; in a word, they would reckon that person besotted that should not, with all possible gratitude, close with such kind of proposals. Come along, therefore, with me, poor soul, thou that art not worth a groat, and hast never a friend that can or will give you anything to speak of; come along with me, and take a short prospect of the territories of this mighty Monarch; let us get up to Mount Pisgah, and make a survey of that goodly land; let us take a turn or two in the courts of his palace; consider well the pleasantness of this seat, how rarely it is accommodated, the richness of the furniture, the nobleness of the inhabitants, the sweetness of that harmony that sounds night and day in that temple, the inconceivable costliness, riches, glory, and excellency of everything. Do but look a little about thee. Are not thine eyes even dazzled at the sight? Do you see what building that is, whose walls are jasper, and the city is all of pure gold, like unto clear glass, and the foundation of the walls of that city are garnished with all manner of precious stones? Rev. xxi., &c. And what think you now? Where is the prince upon earth that ever was master of such an estate? What are his attendants? The meanest of those that stand in his presence is no less than a king; the least of his servants is more rich and glorious than the mightiest potentate that ever trode upon earthly mould, that was a stranger to God. This God doth not grudge to give that which is more worth than a thousand kingdoms to his darlings. I might tell also at what a rate they live who are fed always at his table, and what dainty dishes they feed upon; I might speak of their clothing and robes: all which speak the riches of that Lord who maintains his servants so highly. But what am I doing? Can I grasp the heavens in my arms, or take up the sea in the hollow of my hands? Can I measure the heaven of heavens, or weigh the mountains in scales, or the hills in a balance? Could I do all and a thousand times more, yet I could not give you account of the estate of Him who would be your Friend, your Husband: at the best, I can but give you a superficial gross relation of it; and when I have said all that I can speak, and all the men in the world, with all their tongues, have spoken too; nay, let angels with their heavenly rhetoric do what they can to set out the glory of his kingdom; I say, when all this is done, you must remember all falls short of what it is, and that since the beginning of the world men have not heard, neither can it enter into the heart of man to conceive what God is worth, what a Friend you may have of him, if you will but speedily be acquainted with him. His kingdom hath no bounds, and his dominions reach farther than both the Indies. The small love-tokens that he sends now and then to his beloved into a far country are of infinitely more value than all the lockets of diamonds and richest pearls and jewels in the world, Prov. viii. Behold how merrily Rebecca looks upon a sorry jewel or two presented by Eliezer from his master! How soon is her heart conquered! And why should we not be more taken with things of far greater worth? What is all this? As much as nothing with you! Methinks your hearts should be all on a fire. Methinks you should quickly say, Oh that I could but see him! Who will bring me acquainted with him? he shall have my heart, my dearest love. Methinks, should I ask you the same question that they did Rebecca, Wilt thou go along with me to such a Friend? you should readily, without any further dispute, say, Yea, with all my heart, and think long to be up and going. Why then do you talk of a year, a month longer? Oh, what makes poor creatures stand waiting so long for an answer? Do you ever expect a better offer? Do you look to advance yourselves somewhere else? Can you look for a better, a richer match? Go then and search out among all thy lovers which make suit to thee, which of them can feed you with such costly viands, which of them can clothe you in such royal apparel! Which of them can make you such a jointure? Consider wisely and speedily, that I may turn to the right hand or the left. What sayest thou? Canst thou, amongst them all, better thyself? Is there any one like Him? Is there any of the sons of the mighty comparable to Him? Are any of the kings or great ones of the earth able to make you such an offer? or should they, can any of them make it good? What, have you yet resolved upon the point or not? What is it you stand for? I pray, do you question the truth of what I speak? Do you make account I speak of the highest, and make the best of all things? Why, then, let me tell you further, I have not, I cannot tell you the half of what you will find to be true, if you would come to be thoroughly resolved, or of what you will believe hereafter, to your sorrow, if you still refuse him. And I must further add to what I have said before, that whatever riches God possesses, he will jointure you in, as soon as you shall in good earnest be willing to accept him for your Friend; all that I can speak of, and more too, you may call your own. Ask, and it shall be given without prescribing how much more than you can ask or think shall be given you. Your Lord and Husband is not so niggardly as Ahasuerus, who said, "What is thy request, and what is thy petition, Queen Esther, and it shall be given thee, to the half of my kingdom?" But God saith, What is thy request, and what is thy petition, poor soul, and it shall be granted, to the whole of my kingdom? What is it thou wantest? what attendants dost thou lack to wait upon thee to my court? Are they prophets, apostles, ministers, angels, they shall be given! Eph. iv. 11. Do but try him; he bids you ask, and you shall have. Let me give you this one memento, Ask like one that hath to do with a rich king, who hates to do anything below himself. Remember it is he that delights to give like a God; widen, therefore, thy desires as large as heaven; be bold, and speak a great word, and I warrant thee thou shalt not be denied. Tell God, that seeing, in his infinite goodness and condescension, he has been pleased to give thee leave to ask without restraint, thou dost humbly request his Son for thy Lord and Husband, himself for thy Father, God, and Friend, his kingdom for thy dowry, the righteousness of his Son for thy ornament, clothing, and beauty, the comforts of his Spirit, and abundance of his grace to bear thy charges handsomely, till thou comest to his house. This is high indeed! but thy great and noble Lord loves dearly to hear such covetous petitioners, who will be put off with nothing but such great things. When do any of these go sad from his court? When do any of the seed of Jacob seek his face in vain? This, this is the generation of thriving ones, who seek for life, immortality, and glory; who seek thy face, O God of Jacob. And now what do you say? Will you believe all this? Dare you take my word? I am persuaded none of you all think I dare tell you a lie, and do you any wrong; but for all that, I do not desire you should take my word, nor the word of any man living in a thing that concerns eternity; but take His word who cannot lie. "Riches and honour are with me; yea, durable riches and righteousness. My fruit is better than gold, yea, than fine gold; and my revenue than choice silver," Prov. viii. 18, 19. The wise man tells us, that "wealth makes many friends," chap. xix. 4; and that "many will entreat the favour of the prince; and that every one is a friend to him that gives gifts," ver. 6. If this might be in spirituals, I should not fear but that I should prevail with all my hearers to seek the friendship of God; if their real interest did weigh with them, if true riches and wealth could win their affections, if the most substantial good things might signify anything, if solid reasons might bias them, I should not fear going away without them. But alas, alas, how little power have all these things with the sensual world! What are men and women turned to! What sots and brutes are they in the concerns of their souls and the affairs of that other world! Men run up and down hunting after good things, and have taken a false scent; they hope to catch that at last which they will feed upon, and satisfy themselves with. I tell thee, O man who askest, Who will show us any good? here, here it is. Riches thou meanest? Well then, let it be so; and if I do not prove that what I offer thee from my great Master is a thousand times more worth thy seeking than gold or silver, and better coin than that which bore Cæsar's stamp upon it, then say you were cheated. Thou tellest over thy monies very fast, methinks; but are you sure all that is gold which doth so glitter? Is all that current silver? Will it go in another country? Is it not possible but that you may be mistaken? Here, here is the gold that is tried; it will go anywhere. Here is One that will give you, will you but desire earnestly his acquaintance, such treasure that will not perish, such silver that hath not tin, such gold that hath no dross, such true riches that cannot be taken away from you. Ask that saint who looks so merrily, who lives so bravely, how he got his estate, and how he came to be so rich all of a sudden; he will soon tell you how, and where his treasure lies, and yet not fear being robbed. He hath of late been acquainted with a Friend that hath given him that which makes him esteem himself more worth than if he were possessed of ten times more than ever Alexander or Cæsar was. A friend of Cyrus, in Xenophon, being asked where his treasure was, which made him think so highly of himself, his answer was, Where Cyrus his friend was. A Christian may with much better reason and cheerfulness, if asked where his riches and estate lies, answer, Where God his Friend is. Ask the poorest of them that are acquainted with God, the weakest of all his children, what they will sell their portion for, and what you shall give them to resign up all their interest in God, to quit their claim to this inheritance. Would they not all be of Paul's mind, and even scorn the motion, and count the glory of a thousand worlds but as dung and dross in comparison of the excellency of the knowledge of Christ Jesus their Lord? Phil. iii. 8. Nay, hear what one says that was far less acquainted with God than any of them whom I have been speaking of, when he talks of such kind of bargain as this. (Epict.) "Offer me a kingdom, and you offer me to my loss." For, saith the same author, in another place, "A good man may look up to heaven as the seat of his Friend, and not fear want." Inquire of David what portion God gave him, and he will soon answer you: A goodly portion indeed; and that he gave him no less than himself, and that the lines are fallen to him in pleasant places, and that he hath a goodly heritage, Ps. xvi. 5, 6. And therefore he counts himself richer than if he had all his enemies in chains, and their royalties at his disposal; he takes himself to be a far happier man than if he were absolute monarch of the universe, and were to give laws to the inferior world; he reckons himself now as well to pass and better too than Adam, when he was sole landlord of the world. It was truly spoken of somebody, I do not well remember who: "He that hath rich friends must not look upon himself as poor." Oh then that you would be indeed friends to yourselves, and have respect to your own real interests! And what, will not this mighty and powerful argument, which weighs as much as a thousand others, prevail? And do you still say, What profit will there be in serving the Lord, and what advantage shall I get if I be acquainted with him? To what account will it return? I again answer, To a very good account every way. Try but this trade with the wise merchant, and you shall soon feel the benefit of it. "Conceive to thyself mountains of gold and rocks of diamonds, and to this a vast immeasurable tract of ground, land of inheritance, the most fertile soil in the world, bringing in such a burden every year that shall trouble the owner to reap it; imagine his pasture as great as his arable, and all clothed with thousands of cattle, small and great, and none of them barren neither; suppose his barns and storehouses could never be emptied, and his presses should burst out every year with new wine." Again, " Let the merchant store his cellars with the most pure oil, and furnish him with such rich spices as the Queen of Sheba brought to Solomon; suppose he were provided with all the exquisite rarities that the air, sea, or earth can afford, yet for all this he were a beggar, in comparison of one that hath God for his Friend: such a one possesseth him that possesseth all things." (Bolton.) Well then, be persuaded at last to be wise. I remember the moralist (Sen. Epist. vi.) brings in one acting like a wise man, and a good proficient in philosophy, who begins to be a friend to himself. And this is that that I am pleading with you for. If I came to rob you all of hopes of happiness, and to bid you give away all that you have or expect, and to turn mendicants; if I came to persuade you to espouse a beggarly interest, and to match yourself so as that you should be sure to be undone, I should not wonder if, after I had spoken much, I should prevail but little. But when it is such a cause that I am pleading, when it is for your own unspeakable advantage, when it is riches, true riches that I would have you look after, an estate that I would have you mind, which may be had for the looking after, have I not cause to admire what need a man should have to use so many words? Had you money to spare, and could I tell you of a brave purchase, that you might have an excellent pennyworth, I am persuaded I should not be very unwelcome. Could I tell you of a vast estate that you might have, upon the matter for accepting or looking after, I believe I need not spend ten years in earnest begging and entreating you to look after such a thing. Should I offer to bring you to the place and person of whom you might buy it, should I not soon have your company? Should not your necessaries be quickly made ready for such a journey? Would you not be up betimes in the morning? Nay, would you not travel all **night,** and think it no folly nor madness, both to lose some **rest,** and to take some pains, so you might come to possess what I speak of? Nay, were there but a possibility of obtaining it, at least a probability, I persuade myself you would not fail to look after it the very first thing you did. I am ready to think you would neither spare for pains nor costs, so that, after all, you might but make sure of enjoying it. Why, what then is the matter, that I can do no more in the business that I am about? I am sure I bring you tidings of a better bargain, a braver purchase, and surer inheritance, and what need I then spend so much time in arguing with you? Good Lord! what mean people? Are they out of their wits, and quite beside themselves? What, is a feather better than a crown, brass than gold? Is a glass to be preferred before a diamond, finite enjoyments before everlasting riches, darkness before light, the world before God? Oh, how is man sunk below himself! What hath sin made men and women? If this be not folly and madness, what is? Such may go for wise men in the world's account that make such choices; and it is possible a man in bedlam may say his neighbour that tore all his hair from off his head is well in his wits. Oh that this should be the condition of the far greater part of the world! And what meanest thou, O my soul, that thou art no more affected to see such vast multitudes of brain-sick frantic sinners, that make light of the tender of the gospel, that take them for their enemies who would do their utmost to make them happy for ever? I must profess I am even ashamed of my own heart, that I do not mingle my words with tears; that I should speak for God and souls with so indifferent a spirit. Well, now you have heard of a great match, by which you may be made for ever; are you, for all this, of the same mind you were? Well, then, complain not if you be a beggar. Remember how you were offered; remember you might have been worth more than a world. Oh that inconsiderate souls did but know, and indeed know, what an offer this is! Oh that they would not carelessly undervalue such a proposal! Oh, what shall I do? How shall I persuade you? What arguments will prevail? O thou great and mighty God, give men and women but a spiritual understanding of these things, make them deeply apprehensive of their excellency and reality, and then I should soon have them with thankfulness complying with these tenders which thou commandest me to make unto them. Oh when shall it once be! How long shall the devil and an unbelieving heart undo so many millions? How long shall Satan triumph over souls, and cheat them thus miserably of their all? Oh pity, pity, dear Lord, the besotted foolish world, and give me more compassion to souls, that I may, with incomparably greater earnestness and tenderness, plead thy cause with them, and resolve to give them no rest, till I have persuaded some of them in good earnest to look after the great and weighty affairs of eternity, and the making sure of their Friend.

8. He is a sympathizing Friend. It goes to his heart (with reverence be it spoken) when any injuries are done to any of his; when his friends are wronged, it touches him to the quick. He is tender of them, as of the apple of his eye. Again, "He that despiseth you despiseth me." Never was tender-hearted mother more pitiful over her only child, than God is to them who love him; never was any friend so much concerned for another as God for his. What else mean those high expressions of pity in Isa. lxiii. 9, "In all their affliction he was afflicted, and the angel of his presence saved them: in his love and in his pity he redeemed them; and he bare them, and carried them all the days of old?" It was not once or twice that God did so by them; but in all their afflictions he was afflicted; which was not expressed in some cold formal words, such as these; Alas, poor creatures, they are quite undone, their enemies are very barbarous: but he showed it in real demonstration, by saving them by the angel of his presence. A verbal kindness costs little and helps little. But suppose his friends are carried captive, are they not quite out of the reach of his help? No, his love, pity, and power will find them out in any place under heaven; and if they be slaves, he will redeem them, though he give kingdoms and nations for their ransom. In his love and in his pity he redeemed them; and when, by hard usage, they are grown so weak and feeble that they can scarce go or creep, why, he will

carry them in his arms, and bear them. And thus he did of old; and his affections are rather greater than lesser now than they were then. The mother can be weary of carrying a dirty screaming child; she thinks it less trouble to whip him, or to let him lie till he hath cried himself weary; she is loath to lug such a troublesome thing up and down all the day long. But yet, such is the tenderness of this Father, that he carries his all the day long, though they be so heavy, so unquiet, so dirty. But of that presently. How oft do you read of strange pity in the book of the Judges, when they had, by their own folly, more than once brought themselves into calamity; how do his bowels yearn over them; and when any of his are groaning under any trials or temptations, what sending and running is there! How many cordials are prepared for them! What calling to this servant and that servant to attend them with all the care that may be, and to comfort them in this state! And in case of abuse, how doth he show his love to them! If you should ask Pharaoh, he would tell you that God's friends are edgetools. Why else doth the Lord lay about him with so much indignation, when they are oppressed; nay, for their sakes he rebukes kings, saying, "Touch not mine anointed, and do my prophets no harm;" if they do, be it at their peril. How did he bear the afflictions of his people Israel in Egypt! Did he stand still as if he were unconcerned? Did he shut his eyes and not see? Or did he stop his ears to their cries? No, no, he sees the sufferings of his in Egypt, and that both enemies and friends too shall know, the one to their comfort, and the other to their cost, Exod. iii. 7. How doth he awaken for their help, and gird on his sword upon his thigh, and march out with fury! How doth he clothe himself with vengeance as with a robe, and brandish his glittering sword, and sheathe it in the hearts of his and their enemies! Wherefore is it that God hath so many controversies with Edom, Ammon, and Amalek? Why doth he muster up his forces with violence against Babylon? Whose quarrel doth he engage in? What was the ground of that war? If you read over all the indictments that are before this great Judge, you will find this a common one, their hatred of his people; and this, to be sure, he will not put up with. And that which puts an accent upon all this, is the unworthy carriage of most of them towards him all this while. But of that under the next head, which is this.

9. He is the most patient Friend. Never any one in the world could have digested such affronts, borne such indignities, as God hath many a time, and even from the best of those that he takes into this intimacy with himself. Had it not been for this covenant of friendship, Judah and Ephraim too had been soon unpeopled; as for them, they soon forgot their covenant, yet for all that, God remembers his: though Ephraim forgot to be a child, yet God cannot forget to be a Father. Read that text, and wonder, Hos. xi. 7, "And my people are bent to backsliding from me: though they called them to the most High, none at all would exalt him." Though they had many compassionate prophets that called after them day and night, when they saw them turning their backs upon God, yet they were not minded. Who now would conceive that God should ever think a thought of kindness towards them more? Yet hear what God saith, "How shall I give thee up, Ephraim? how shall I deliver thee, Israel? how shall I make thee as Admah? how shall I set thee as Zeboim? Mine heart is turned within me, my repentings are kindled together. I will not execute the fierceness of mine anger: I will not return to destroy Ephraim: for I am God, and not man; the Holy One in the midst of thee: and I will not enter into the city," ver. 8, 9. Well, now tell me if ever there was such a compassionate, meek, patient Friend. Ephraim was up in open arms against his Maker; he did rebel most unworthily against his good Lord and Friend, to whom he was bound by infinite engagements. Ephraim had quite cast off God, and he will have nothing to do with him; and Judah is not far inferior to his treacherous brother; and what will God do? One would think, as I said before, he should ease himself quickly of such false friends; one would think that, after such unfaithfulness, he should for ever banish them his court; one would soon conceive that he should think of disinheriting such rebellious

children; for this was not the first, second, nor third time that they had served God thus. Who then could imagine that he should ever trouble himself with them any more? Should one not look every day when he should quite cast them off? Why, God seems sometimes to threaten as much, and seems ever and anon to act towards them as if he would never look upon them more while the world stands. Go, saith God, to your idols, let them save you! What do you come to me for? You have refused to have me for your God. Go, cry to your gods, and let them deliver you. Thus he seems to turn away his face; yet, for all that, see how soon he forgets his displeasure. Ephraim is his child, his dear child, and he cannot but pity him; and "how shall I give thee up, O Ephraim," &c. How hardly is God brought so much as to chastise his children; he never corrects them but when there is an absolute need of it. Ask the church under the rod, and she cannot but say as much. "For though he cause grief, yet will he have compassion according to the multitude of his mercies. For he doth not afflict willingly, nor grieve the children of men," Lam. iii. 32, 33. He calls judgment his work, his strange work: and when he doth correct his stubborn children, how doth he many times give them a lash and a kiss, a frown and a smile! Oh, what would have become of the holiest men living, if God should upon every provocation have broken with them. If God should mark iniquities, oh, who should stand? Which of the fallen sons of Adam hath not abused his high kindness? and yet for all that, how is his patience and goodness exercised towards them! Well might the Psalmist make that the burden of one of his songs, "Oh that men would praise the Lord for his goodness, and for his wonderful works towards the children of men;" and that of another, "For his mercy endureth for ever." What created being could have borne the thousandth part of that from any hand that God doth every day from his dearest children? What peevishness and unfriendly quarrelling, what murmuring and repining, doth he bear even from them for whom he hath done such great things! How strangely do they carry themselves! How seldom and complimental in their visits of him! How cold and formal in their addresses to him! How frequently are they conversing with his basest enemies! How much treachery and underhand dealing doth he find in them! Yet for all this, how great are his kindnesses, and how open are his arms, upon their acknowledgment, to receive them again! Little do we think what unkindness the Lord overlooks; nor indeed, except we knew what it was to be infinite in holiness, could we in any way conceive how infinite his patience is. "Many times did he deliver them; but they provoked him with their counsel, and were brought low for their iniquity. Nevertheless he regarded their affliction, when he heard their cry: and he remembered for them his covenant," &c., Ps. cvi. 43-45. Here, here is patience, here is love and goodness with a witness! What prince under heaven would trust a rebel that hath been in arms a hundred times against him, and that at the best doth serve him with so little delight? What friend would continue his familiarity and kindness there, where he hath found abundance of falseness? And who but thou, O God, is so merciful and gracious, longsuffering, and abundant in goodness and truth? As for the trouble that any of his meet with, most commonly they may thank themselves for it; and it is always sent them in kindness: there is none of them all but may say, This is my iniquity, this is the fruit of my backsliding, this I have got by my estrangement from God.

10. He is an honourable Friend, and to be acquainted with him is the highest honour in the world. This word honour sounds great in the ear of this proud world. What a running and catching to get a little of it! How do many undervalue their lives, and make nothing to hazard their blood for a little of what men call honour! Some prize it above riches and wealth, and care not almost at what rate they purchase it; and yet in the meanwhile they are farthest from that which they so greedily desire, and they run away from that which they seem to pursue. Poor ignorant man is fearfully mistaken; he calls that his honour which degrades him, and takes that for his glory which is his shame. How is he pleased with that which, when he hath, he neither sees nor

feels, and scarce knows what it is! (Epict.) What is it, O man, that thou losest thy sleep for? What is it that thou art at so much charge to buy? that rather than you will want it, estate, blood, life, and soul, and all must go for it? Knight, lord, earl, &c., worshipful, right-worshipful, honourable, excellent, gracious, are big words, and make a great noise; but is this the true honour? will these words, without the thing, do a man so much good? a man, I said, and so doth God say too, and death will make the biggest of them all know as much ere it be long, for all those big words. What if his breath stink that speaks these words, and his that hears them be not much sweeter? (Antoninus.) Is it such an honour to have a company of fools to call him wise, that, may be, is like themselves? Is it worth a soul, to have it said when I am in hell, There lived a brave gentleman, that kept a noble house and brave table; his cellar was always open; one might come when one would, and drink as long as one could stand, and never hear, Why do you so? and be always welcome; that is, in plain English, where a man might be encouraged to damn his soul. There lived a noble gallant person who bid defiance to the Almighty, that had courage enough to go to hell merrily, that had a desire to carry as many along with him as might be; damning, swearing, cursing was their language; eating, drinking, sleeping, whoring, and persecuting the people of God, their business. And are these your honourable persons? Nay, go higher, to bustle up and down in cloth of gold, with a vast retinue, to have men on this side and that side, bowing and cringing; and is this such a business? Is it worth the while to keep up such a stir about that which a wise man may want, and a fool have? (Anton.) Will those names, that grandeur and state, those high titles, render you more acceptable to God? Will they procure for you a freer access into the presence of that great King? Will those great words scare death? Will he say, when he comes to your house, This is a person of quality, I must not be so bold as to come near him? Will your honour procure you a protection from the arrests of this sergeant? Where is the honourable personage, the gentleman, knight, lord, king, or monarch, that hath lived a thousand years? (Lucian.) Are the worms afraid to gnaw thy heart? Will thy flesh never putrefy? Will your servants, or your master either, honour you in hell? And is this all that you keep such a stir for, that can do you no good in the grave or in another world? Can that be better worth than heaven, than God? Oh that we might but know what it is, that great thing is, which is preferred before Christ and everlasting glory! Again, I ask what is it that the grandees of the world do so much idolize? Is it to be called wise, great, and noble? But what if the wise God call such a one a fool? (Epict.) What if he know neither himself, nor his God, nor his interest? Hath he much greater reason to boast than a feather, that somebody will say it is heavy? or dung, that the swine saith it is sweet? (Juven.) What profit is it for a man to be made great for betraying his country, and flattering a tyrant who yesterday was the son of a stage-player, and to-morrow shall be shorter by the head? What good will it do a beggar that is ready to be starved, to be told that he is a prince, a brave fellow, worth some thousands by the year? But would you know which is the ready way to true honour? I tell you it consists not in the favour of them that must die like yourselves, and, before that few years be over, must stand but upon even ground with the meanest; it consists not in the sorry acclamations of them who measure a man's worth by his estate and their dependence upon him; it consists not in the praise of them whose commendations some wise men have counted a discredit. But he hath showed thee, O man, what is truly honourable; to do justly, to love mercy, and to walk humbly with thy God, Micah vi. 8. To bear relation to God as a Father, and to carry themselves as his children, to be a servant and friend of God; this, this is honourable, truly honourable; this is the height, the top of the creature's preferment. To converse with, and delight in his Maker; to love, admire, and rejoice in God, and to love God, to take complacency in the soul; this is something indeed, this is honour; a wise man would not grudge to venture his estate, his blood, his all for this. And how few of the gallants of the world understand the nature of this honour? How do most of them account that which is the only true badge of nobility, a term of disgrace; and that which speaks a person highly honourable, and to have brave blood running in his veins, to be low, sordid, and much beneath them; as if it were below a creature to serve his Maker, and a pitiful preferment to be advanced to glory. Oh that men of parts and learning, that persons of quality, should be so much mistaken! Oh what's become of their reason? Is it an honour, a preferment, for a man to become a brute? We are ready to pity madmen, and to laugh at fools; but whether there be not more reason to bemoan the condition of most of the honourable persons in the world, I leave Christ and Christians to judge. Well then, will you be informed, after all this, by Him who hath all preferments and honours in his gift? I mean the great King; and he will tell you that glory and honour are in his presence, 1 Chron. xvi. 27. Man's only honour and true dignity lie in his nearness and acquaintance with God. A practical knowledge of his Maker is the creature's greatest preferment. David was of the mind, that it was none of the lowest honours to be God's servant, Ps. lxxxiv. It is upon the account of Israel's near relation to God, that Moses reckons them the happiest, the most honourable people in the world. Because God had avouched them to be his peculiar people, therefore they might well be said to be high above all the nations which God had made, in praise, in name, and in honour, Deut. xxvi. 18, 19. And upon this account might a wise man have his choice, whether he will wear a crown and be a stranger to God, or rags, and be one of his nearest servants. He will not stand long before he determine the case; he will soon answer with him, that he had rather be a doorkeeper in the house of God, than dwell in the tabernacles of wickedness. If men's actions may speak their judgments, most of the gallants of the world are of a far different opinion. But, oh let me dwell for ever in his house, and stand always in his presence; happy are they that see his face, happy are they that behold his beauty. This, this is man's crown, this is his highest honour and dignity; for God to be mindful of man, and for his Maker to visit him;

this sets him but little below the angels, this crowns him with glory and honour, Ps. viii. 4, 5. This is that which puts a true personal worth upon any one; and therefore the Psalmist thinks those the excellent persons, in whom is his delight. Upon this account the Scripture saith, "The righteous man, who is in covenant with God, is more excellent than his neighbour." The purblind world, they judge altogether by the outward garb; they see the face, the rich apparel; they see the estate, but they see not that inward excellency and beauty that may be under but a mean habit; they are ready to despise the noble worthies of the world, such as can look upon kingdoms as small things in comparison of what they have an interest in, who can call God Father, and Christ Brother. Have you never heard of a king in mean apparel, of a prince without his robes upon his back, or his crown upon his head? and will you say that therefore he was but a common person? But those heavenly creatures that have a more spiritual refined sense, that understand something of things and persons, are quite of another mind; they can look upon great ones in the midst of their gallantry, without a Friend in heaven, as mean persons that have no interest to speak of; and many of them, for all their greatness, to be in a far worse condition than dogs and toads. They can also look upon a poor despised saint, a contemned Christian, though, to carnal eyes, he should look as if he could scarce speak sense, to be a favourite of Heaven, a person of quality; such a one as this the heavenly-minded values as the son of a king, a citizen of Zion, one of the royal race, one of that glorious retinue that stand always in the presence of God to serve him, the least of whom are kings and priests to their great Lord: by faith he sees their crown, and looks upon that royal diadem which shall erelong be put upon their princely heads, Rev. i. 6. This was the great preferment they sought, this was the honour they most desired; as for the world and all its glory, they can well spare it for those that shall never be advanced to any higher dignity, to any better preferment. As for the saint, as contemptible as he looks, he hath higher designs, nobler things, greater honours in his eye; and if that which the world so admires were the highest glory that a rational creature were capable of, the top of man's preferment, why, then he could look upon brutes themselves as his equals, except in this, that their pleasures are more certain, and their miseries less understood.

It is storied of Constantine and Valentinian, two Roman emperors, that they subscribed themselves *Vassellos Christi*, the vassals of Christ; and that Numa Pompilius esteemed it a higher honour to be a friend of God than a lord of men. Consider, poor sinner, consider what honours you slight, what preferments you refuse, what dignity you undervalue, when you make light of acquaintance with God. Had that brave Stoic, Epictetus I mean, known God in Christ, he would much more have wondered at the inconsiderateness of them who make nothing of being related to God as a Father; he would much more have pitied them who cleave to their lower, meaner kindred beast, who had rather be like swine than God, and rather be companions to their servants than their Maker. Seems it to you but a light matter to be a King's son? Is it but a small matter, think you, to call God Father? Is it nothing to be born to a crown immortal that fadeth not away? This is honour, this is preferment worth the having, worth the looking after, worth the venturing one's life for. This is true nobility, to stand thus nearly related to Him before whom the angels veil their glorious faces, and at whose feet the four-and-twenty elders lay their crowns. The Queen of Sheba thought Solomon's servants happy, who stood always in his presence and heard his wisdom; but what would she have said, had she but known the honour and glory of this Prince! Oh, blessed are those that stand always in thy presence! O God, blessed are thy servants; blessed are those who see thy glory and hear thy wisdom; blessed are they that may have free access to thee. Oh let me have this preferment, though I live like Job at his lowest, and die like Lazarus. Let others sue for the favour of princes; let them make the best of what the world can give; let them desire that which hath been dangerous to more than Haman; I hope I should never envy them, might I but have more frequent and intimate converse with God, may I be but acquainted with him. Oh may I have but a heart more to admire, love, and delight in him, and serve him with the strength and intenseness of my soul while I am here, and stand for ever in his presence, and behold his glorious face with joy hereafter. O my soul, what meanest thou, that thou still speakest so faintly and coldly of such infinitely glorious things? Why doth not a new life animate thee at the very mention of these things? Hast thou not far more cause to raise up thy desponding spirits with cheerfulness, than old Jacob, when his son Joseph, who was lord of that land, sent for him into Egypt? Thy Father, O my soul, thy Brother is Lord, not of Egypt, not of Goshen, but of Eden, of Zion; he is the King of that glorious city, the new Jerusalem; heaven is his throne, and earth is his footstool, and yet behold the waggons that he hath sent for thee! Behold the provision that he hath sent to maintain thee comfortably in thy journey from Egypt to Canaan! Is not this enough? O my soul, awake, up and see him before thou diest. Behold, he is coming, the Bridegroom is coming, Joseph is coming, to meet thee with a gallant train, in a glorious equipage. It is but yet a little while, and thy Husband will come and fetch thee in royal state, attended with a numberless retinue of saints and angels. Oh, hadst thou but an eye to behold their chariots and horsemen coming upon the mountains. He is coming, he is coming; he will be here quickly; he will not tarry; he is at the door. Contemplate sometimes on these things, and a little antedate that glory by spiritual meditation. Do but think what a brave sight that will be to see the mountains covered with chariots of fire and horses of fire, when the heavens shall bow before thy Friend, and the earth shall melt at his presence, and yet thy heart not faint within thee; when the King shall come in the clouds to fetch his friends to his own house, where they shall dwell for ever. This honour have all the saints.

11. He is a suitable Friend. It is suitableness that sweetens society. I can easily believe a poor country peasant can take as much content in the company of a poor

man like himself, as in the society of a prince; an unlearned countryman is no way fit to converse with courtiers and statesmen; the vastness of the distance would so much swallow his mind, and the unsuitableness of his spirit to such company takes off that content which otherwise he might enjoy. But yet in spirituals, though the distance between God and man be beyond a possibility of our conception, and the disproportion infinite, yet the soul of man, being immediately from God, and spiritual, like God, and having a divine new nature infused into it by the spirit of regeneration, it finds an infinite suitableness, pleasure, and content in the enjoyment of God's presence; and it is not sunk, but raised, by a union, converse, and society with its Maker. The truth of it is, did man but understand his own original aright, he would think it infinitely below his noble parentage to converse with, and have intimate delightful society with any but God and those who bear the same relation to God with himself, or to bring poor strangers acquainted with him as well as themselves. There is not a match upon earth fit for the soul of man to be matched to. But in that other country there is a Match indeed every way suitable; a Spirit for a spirit; an everlasting God for an everlasting soul; a precious Jesus for a precious soul; a holy God for those whom he hath made holy like himself; and that is none of the least of man's happiness, that notwithstanding that infinite distance that is naturally between him and his God, yet that God should make in his creature such noble dispositions, and such divine qualifications, that there should be the greatest suitableness in the world between God and the soul, and the soul and God, and they both take wonderful content in the enjoyment of one another. This is in part here, but completed in glory. This we may find often in Scripture expressed in the nearest relations and dearest affections. Hence God is said to be a Father, and they his children; a Husband, and they his spouse. Now what greater suitableness can there be than between father and children, husband and wife? God is also said to delight in them, and they in him; to rejoice in their company, and they in his; and how could this be, except there were a suitableness in them one to another. Their wills are suited; what God wills, they will; and what God loves, they love; and so what they love, as his friends, God loves; one doth not thwart and contradict the other. Oh how sweet then must the company, the communion, of such friends be! Oh were our hearts as they should be! Were we more like God, we should quickly experience, to the unspeakable joy of our souls, how suitable a Friend he is to a soul: we should soon find, that as clay and stones are unsuitable food for the body, so the world is unsuitable food for the soul to feed on, and that it is God alone that can fill and satisfy the vast desires of it. Oh, I say again, were we but as we came out of our Maker's hands, or, rather, were we trimmed up in our eldest Brother's robes, and brought into the immediate presence of this great King; were we set before that glorious throne, where the infinite brightness of his majesty shines, so that the angels themselves veil their faces before him; yet for all that, we should not long stand silent, as if the place and company were unsuitable to us; it would not be long before we should carry it as those that were nearly related, and had intimate acquaintance with Him who sits upon the throne. Oh the unspeakable sweetness that will be in the enjoyment of His company! no tediousness, no irksomeness at all upon our spirits. We shall quickly understand our work, our privilege. Oh infinite goodness! Oh boundless love! Oh let me be always solacing my soul in the contemplation of these things! Oh let the very thoughts of them be a heaven upon earth to my soul! But here, oh here's the grief; while we are here in a strange country, there is something—(in all the poor fallen children of Adam, nay, in those of them that are recovered, and by grace brought into re-union with God)—there is, I say, something in God unsuitable to them, and in them unsuitable to God; and this, oh this makes our lives so uncomfortable: but converse with God will wear off a great deal of that. When thou comest to lay off thy rags, and to put off thy old suit, and to put on that new one that is making for thee, I mean after death; when thou comest to glory, thou wilt find the case strangely altered with thee. In heaven there will be a perfect harmony, suitableness, and agreement between God and thee for ever; and thou wilt take infinite complacency and delight in him, and he in thee. And thus shalt thou spend eternity in inconceivable joy, delight, and pleasures. This is heaven, a perfect suitableness to God, and enjoying him for ever. Oh when, when, when shall it once be? "Come, Lord Jesus, come quickly;" come, O blessed Father, by thy Spirit, and burn up what is unlike thee! Oh create a greater suitableness between my soul and thee. Oh come thou down to me, or take me up to thee! Oh, could we but talk with one of those happy creatures that hath been in the very presence of God in glory, and should we ask him, whether he were not weary of the same work, of the same company, the same place; what answer do you think he would make you? "No more weary than a man upon the rack but just before would be of perfect ease; no more than a healthful hungry man is of eating; no more weary than the sun is of running, than the fire of ascending, or a stone falling towards the centre. (Sen. Epist. x.) I know not where I had rather be than with Him. I was once upon earth as you are now, and now I am in heaven; and in neither of both these places can I find one that I can take more delight in than God. I must say as he, Ps. lxxiii. 25, 'Whom have I in heaven but thee? and there is none upon earth that I desire besides thee.' I cannot desire a better employment than a delightful constant attending upon my God. Can I have better company than such a Father? Can a greater happiness be conceived than eternal glory? a pleasanter place than heaven? That which I can speak, you cannot hear; and could you, though in this perfect glory, I cannot express what you will find and feel when you come hither. Oh had I but known as much as I do now, when I was in your condition upon earth, I should with incomparably greater earnestness have sought after acquaintance with God than I did. 'In his presence is fulness of joy, at his right hand are pleasures for evermore.' Now I feel, now I know it. I thought one smile sweet upon earth, but now I see and feel infinitely more. What you enjoy now is a shadow in comparison of what you will enjoy hereafter. Oh, what do you mean, that you prize his favour no more, that you get no more intimate acquaintance with him? What do you mean that you are so unwilling to come to this place of joy? Oh, were you but possessed of what I speak of, you would say what I say; you would never be weary of praising and serving him; you would never wish yourself out of his presence, and think it not possible to be in more suitable society." Is it so, O my soul? What then doest thou here? Make haste, O my soul, stay no longer here below, but know thy privilege, understand where thy comforts are.

12. He is a wise Friend. All the men and women in the world have great mighty affairs to manage, and they want skill, wisdom, and discretion for the right management of these things; they are wofully averse to their great business; they are wise to do evil; but in spirituals they are become stupid, sottish fools; and as to the carrying on of their great work, they do it with the greatest imprudence in the world; and they will most certainly for ever undo themselves, except One that is wiser than themselves undertake to help them. All things go backward with them, and they labour in the very fire whilst they act without God; and it is impossible it should be otherwise as long as there is such a disproportion between man's business and his spirit. Man is carnal, and his work is spiritual. Would an ignorant poor creature, that is but one remove above a beast, be fit to manage the great matters of government? How ridiculously would he behave himself in a chair of state! How strangely would an unlearned man bungle, should he go about to solve one of the profound demonstrations of mathematics! But a natural man is far more unskilful than any of these, as to the carrying on of that great employment that he hath to look after, while he is on this side eternity; his business is to serve his Maker, but what pitiful work doth he make of it! Man is made for an everlasting state; he is sent into this world to provide for another: a good, a happiness there is, which he is to look after; he once had a fair estate, but he hath spent and lost it all, and he is to see to the recovering of it again. He

hath been in arms against his lawful sovereign, and been guilty of the highest treason, and thereby hath forfeited his life, his soul; now he hath his pardon to sue out, and how doth he go to work in this one thing? To mention no more, why, he goes to beg a pardon armed cap-a-pie and with his sword drawn; he comes to ask pardon for one treason, and he is found acting another. Lord, have mercy upon me, and give me leave to break thy laws, is the sum of all his prayers. He talks of heaven, and yet makes all the haste he can to hell. He is told he is out of the way, but he laughs at him that tells him so; and that's his best. Sometimes he rages, and desires with all speed to remove him that would set him in the road to Zion. He calls for a hatchet to cut down the bough upon which he stands. And this is your man of wisdom! The man is under sail in the midst of rocks and sands; and if he would but look, he might see many doleful spectacles, to the tops of masts, shipwrecked souls I mean; and though the pilots tell him of the danger, yet he says he will never believe but that it is the best and safest road to the harbour, and so on he goes as if he were sure he would not miscarry; and all this while he will not be persuaded but that he acts very wisely; he judgeth it one of his greatest comforts, that he runs to misery without any hinderance; and how can it otherwise be, except men were spiritually wise? And who can teach man this wisdom? Who shall instruct him? Who shall help him, now his affairs are upon the matter almost desperate? Why, if thou wilt but hear, here is One that will yet undertake thy sole cause, if thou wilt be advised by him; for this is he who will set all to right. And oh, how doth he call after you! how willing to give you his advice! how desirous to assist you! "Wisdom crieth without; she uttereth her voice in the streets: she crieth in the chief place of concourse, in the openings of the gates; in the city she uttereth her words, saying, How long, ye simple ones, will ye love simplicity? and the scorners delight in their scorning, and fools hate knowledge? Turn you at my reproof: behold, I will pour out my Spirit upon you, I will make known my words unto you," Prov. i. 20-23. And will you set at naught all his counsels, and have none of his reproofs? Will you rather be ruined than be beholden to him for advice. Let me put in one word. If this wise Counsellor be not for you, he will be against you; and if you find any that can order your sad affairs more to your advantage, I pray make use of him; but if you will be ruled by him, you cannot miscarry, though you are in an ill condition; though you be quite broken, yet he will give you such a stock as that you may set up again, and such directions as that you cannot but thrive, if you will but follow them. It is he that teacheth his spiritual frugality, not to part with that for a trifle which will be a rich commodity erelong; it is he who persuades us to make the best use of everything; it is he that teacheth fools more true wisdom than the great politicians of the world; though the world judge them weak, yet they have wit enough to make a good bargain, to value heaven before hell, to fly from everlasting burnings. They are wise enough to know what is for their real advantage, and what not. This is he that I would bring thee acquainted with. It is he who giveth his so much understanding, as to know the true worth of things, and the difference between good and evil, finite and infinite, time and eternity. Who is it that David goes to for counsel, when his politic enemies combine against him? Where doth he advise? Who brings him out of all his intricacies? Is it not He that I am persuading you to go to, who was never outwitted, who can easily turn the counsel of Ahithophel into foolishness? It is he who can infatuate the great sages of the world, and make them weaker than children in their counsels. And this is he who will be a constant Counsellor to all those that are his friends, his acquaintance. Seneca, Epist. xli. lxxxi., gives excellent counsel indeed, which if we will precisely follow, our matters cannot but succeed. "Art thou never in any straits? Are all thy affairs carried on with so much prudence, both as to time and eternity, that thou standest in no need of advice? Art thou sure that this will always be thy condition? If not, why then wilt thou not be persuaded to strike in here?" Why, if you will believe them who to their comfort have tried Him again and again, it is your unspeakable interest and wisdom to get God for your Friend, and then whatsoever you do shall prosper by his advice; a poor Christian can outwit all the policy of hell, and show himself more wise than those who call him fool and count him mad. David durst trust none else to guide him; but with His conduct he doth not fear but that he shall come safe to his journey's end: "Thou shalt guide me by thy counsels, and bring me to thy glory," Ps. lxxiii. 24. And again, he saith, by the help of this Counsellor he was wiser than his teachers, Ps. cxix. 99. Hear, therefore, what you had best do, as matters stand with you. "I have taught thee in the way of wisdom; I have led thee in right paths. When thou goest, thy steps shall not be straitened; and when thou runnest, thou shalt not stumble," Prov. iv. 11, 12. "Because the foolishness of God is wiser than men," 1 Cor. i. 25. That which looks most contemptible, if thoroughly understood, will be found to have more depth in it than the wisest men of the world can reach. To choose such a Friend, this is wisdom, this is prudence. The godly man knows that he hath a great cause to be decided erelong, and that it will be no lost labour to make the Judge his Friend. Well, what say you, sinners? Is this considerable that I do now propound, or is it not? Can you plead your own cause, can you clear your title to glory without him? If not, be well advised before you slight such a motion as I now make to you.

13. He is an immortal Friend. Ay, that's a friend indeed. If one friend could be sure to live just as long as the other; and were friends sure never to want the advice, comfort, society, and help of one another, it would not a little advance the worth of a friend. But where is such a one to be found? What histories can give us an account of such amities? Let persons be united in ever so close a union, conjoined in the fastest knot that nature can tie, yet death will first or last dissolve it. So that sometimes I have been almost of this mind, as to all worldly friends, considering them abstract from God, (for grace in any friend doth unspeakably sweeten the relation, and such a relation will not die;) if we compare the shortness and uncertainty

of possessing, and the bitterness in losing, with the sweetness of enjoying, that it is somewhat difficult to resolve, whether such shortlived comforts are worth the looking after. Not but that I think a friend, a true friend, a great mercy, and much to be desired; but really, if our affections be not for God's sake, if our love be not regulated by religion, I can easily believe that the bitterness in losing doth overbalance the pleasure of enjoying. And who would much trouble himself to get that with care which must be possessed with fears, and will be parted with with tears? All worldly enjoyments will serve us thus. When we expect most from them, and please ourselves to think what content we enjoy in them, ten to one, if God love us, but that he either imbitters or takes away that comfort from us. One saith I had a dear husband, such a one as never woman had, but he is dead, I have lost him. Another saith, I had a precious child, a brother, but he is gone. And everybody will be in this note first or last. And if the case be thus, who would be so foolish as to let out the strength of his soul upon that which he may soon be deprived of? But here is a Friend, whom you need not fear over-loving, nor losing; a never-dying Friend, one that will be sure to outlive you. "Say of what you will, that it is mortal, and you have disgraced it enough. For how can that be of any great worth which can die, and, when I have most need of it, I may want; but this cannot be said of God; he only is immortal, and not subject to changes. As for the favour of princes and great ones, at the best, it is but an uncertainty: for, it may be, all thy hopes are bound up in his life, and that hour which puts an end to his days puts a period to thy comfort." (Ar. Ep. l. iii. c. 22.) But it is another kind of friend that I would have you acquainted with. Oh why do Christians dote upon that which is so shortlived? Make but choice of this Friend, and you shall never say of him, He is dead, I have lost him. Wherefore, "put not your trust in the son of man, in whom there is no help. His breath goeth forth, he returneth to his earth; in that very day his thoughts perish. Happy is he that hath the God of Jacob for his help, whose hope is in the Lord his God, which made heaven and earth," &c., Ps. cxlvi. 3-6, that God who is called the Living God.

14. He is a present Friend, a Friend that is always in all places. Man's condition may possibly be such as that he may be deprived of the company of his dearest worldly relations; he may be sequestered from the society of his most helpful and necessary friends. How oft have the dear children of God been clapt up in dungeons, not only from the sight, but from the knowledge of their more affectionate acquaintance! It is no unusual thing for them to be banished from their native country. Wives and children, among savage men and beasts, have no man to make their complaints to, but such as will increase their sorrows. How frequently may they be in such a condition, as that they may not see, hear, nor speak to any friend! What bolts and bars, what walls and guards, to keep them from them, who if they could not free them from, yet might in some measure alleviate their misery! But now God is such a Friend, who cannot, who will not, be kept out from his by walls of brass or bars of iron; he will find out his friends in the darkest holes, and bear them company there in spite of all the powers of hell. Oh! how reviving are his visits! What cordials doth he bring along with him! This is that which makes the people of God so very cheerful, when their enemies make account their condition is such as that it had no mixture of joy or comfort in it. Was that a prison or heaven where those martyrs were singing Hallelujah? Was that a time to be so merry, when all the world disowned them, when they were loaded with reproaches, and irons, and chains, counted the troublers of the nation, madmen, heretics? The case is clear: the sight of this Friend makes them forget their scorns, and think their chains gold, and their prison liberty. It was God that spake it, and he hath been found to be as good as his word. "Thus saith the Lord that created thee, O Jacob, and he that formed thee, O Israel, Fear not: for I have redeemed thee, I have called thee by thy name; thou art mine. When thou passest through the waters, I will be with thee; and through the rivers, they shall not overflow thee: when thou walkest through the fire, thou shalt not

be burnt; neither shall the flame kindle upon thee," Is. xliii. 1, 2. Who was he who bore the three children company in the fiery furnace? Who was he who went into the lions' den to visit Daniel? Who brought Paul alive to the shore when the ship in which he went was wrecked? Was it not this Friend that I am now speaking of? I might be large in reciting the miraculous preservations which God hath vouchsafed to his, which is a manifest token of his presence; when none can come near, he will not be far off. In the greatest extremities, when none durst own them, then God reckons it time for him to show himself. It was not for nothing that the Psalmist could speak so cheerfully when others were quaking, Ps. xlvi. 1, &c. What was it that bore up his spirits, when there were such dreadful commotions? What refuge hath he to shelter himself under in time of such calamity? In what doth his strength lie, that he is so confident? Whence doth he expect a supply, that he holds it out so bravely, when his enemies are so numerous, and his friends so scarce? Why, David hath his invisible Friends, as well as visible enemies. Ask him, and he will tell you, that God is his refuge and strength, and he is his confidence, and he will come in when he hath the greatest need; he will be a very present help in trouble. And that is the reason that David will not fear, though the storm were far greater than ever yet he was in; though the earth were removed, and the mountains were cast into the midst of the sea; though the foundations of the earth were shaken; though the sea should roar and threaten the earth with another deluge, he can sleep as securely as a person little concerned; and this he can speak, not only for himself, but for the whole city of God; God is in the midst of her, she shall not be moved. The saint hath a Friend that will bear him company in all places, in all dangers, and in his company he need not be afraid. Let the least child that God hath give but one cry, and he will soon awake. It cannot but be so from the spirituality of his nature, the immensity of his being, and the infiniteness of his love. It was orthodox divinity and doctrine that Ar. Epictetus, l. ii. c. 14, preached (though but a heathen,) when he said that "the first lesson that became a wise man to learn, was, that there was a God, and then, that nothing in the world could be concealed from him, and that he knew not only our outward actions, but our most secret workings, our closest curtain-business; and not only so, but even our thoughts, projects, and principles: which speaks him everywhere, and consequently ready at hand to help his friends at a dead lift." "Wherefore," saith the same author, idem. l. iii. c. 22, "think not that thou art alone when thou art in thy chamber, in thy bed, when thy curtains are drawn, when thou art locked up in a prison, ever so dark, under ground; if thou art good, thou shalt have two companions in spite of the malice of all thy enemies, a good conscience and thy God." This made that brave moralist dare his enemies to do their worst, to exclude his friends from him. "Can," said he, "any man be banished out of the world? Wheresoever you send me, there will be the sun, moon, and stars; but if not, God is there, I am sure, with whom I may talk, to whom I may pray; he will bear me company, though all the rest of my friends be kept from me. And as long as you cannot banish me from God, nor keep him from me, I shall reckon myself at liberty; and should I be sent out of this world into another, even there I should find my Friend; and he will scarce complain that he is removed from a place where almost all are his enemies, to a place where all are his friends." One would have thought these poor heathens had been reading Ps. cxxxix. Do you hear, O Christians, what language those fore-mentioned persons speak? And shall these that never had the thousandth part of that advantage for the knowledge of God, speak and act thus, and shall Christians have such low thoughts of God? Because we do not see God, shall we therefore not believe that he is present everywhere? He that denies God's own presence, had upon the matter as good deny his being; for were it not so, how could he judge the world with justice? how could all things be sustained by his power? God takes this as a very high indignity, that any should in the least question this glorious attribute. "Am I a God at hand, and not a God afar off? Can any hide himself in secret places that I shall not see him? saith the Lord: do not I fill heaven and earth? saith the Lord," Jer. xxiii. 23, 24. And is not this a Friend worth the having, who will be sure not to be absent when you have need of him? The wicked indeed say, How doth God know, and can he see through the thick clouds? and therefore they sin with confidence, and oppress the friends of God without any fear; they hope God doth not behold, they think Omniscience knows not. I wish there were not something too like this sometimes in the thoughts of God's people too; but let me only leave that one Scripture with the first sort: "He that planted the ear, shall he not hear? He that formed the eye, shall he not see? He that teacheth man knowledge, shall he not know? The Lord knoweth," &c., Ps. xciv. 9-11. As for the desponding Christian that begins to think God is out of the reach of his prayers, let me ask thee, O thou of little faith, when did God ever absent himself from his in a time of need? When was he quite out of the hearing of their cry? I know indeed he may hide himself; yet then he is near them also, to try their love and hear their voice; for God loves to hear his children cry: earthly parents may correct their children for crying, but God chastiseth his children usually for their silence. When he seems farthest off, he is but behind the curtain, he is there where he with pleasure sees how earnestly his children look up and down for him; and then when they are ready to sit down weeping, as if they had lost their Father; when they think they are quite forgot, and their enemies begin to triumph, and to ask, where now is your God? then he lets both friends and foes know that he is near. And what say you to all this, you that as yet are strangers to God? Have you gotten such a Friend as he is, that will always be at your elbow, that can and will come to help you when other friends are far enough off, whether man will or no? Have you got such a friend? If not, why then will you not now accept of his acquaintance who will be such a Friend to all that love him? No good man is without the company of God; he walks with God, he talks with God, he eats with

God, he drinks with God, and is entertained by him, and he sleeps in his arms. God is with him in his shop, in the road, at home and abroad; and who can miscarry that hath so helpful a Companion always with him? When thy burdens are too heavy, do but complain, and he will either take them off thy back, or put under his own shoulders, and help thee to go away lightly with them; he will assist thee in six troubles, and in seven he will give thee help.

15. He is a soul-Friend. Soul-friends are the best friends. As soul-affairs are the mightiest affairs, so those that give us the greatest help in those matters ought to be valued. God is the great soul-Friend. Expect not to find him a Friend to thy lust. This scares the wicked from him, who would be glad to be acquainted with God, if he would gratify their lusts, and please their wicked humours, and give them eternal happiness after a life of wickedness; that is, would un-God himself for their sakes. But hold there, man; you shall sooner see the sun black, and have fire cold, and find a heaven in hell, than have God a friend to your sin. God doth not promise to furnish all his acquaintance with provision for their sensuality; he will not put a knife into thy hands to stab himself, or to cut thy own throat. There are too many of such friends in the world; and men are generally so foolish as to count them friends who deserve another name; these are they who help men to hell, and show them the shortest cut to eternal misery, and this must go for a special kindness. Sure men and women will scarce be always of this mind. Must poison in a gilded cup go for a cordial, and a kiss, though with a dagger, be taken for true love? Seneca had more wit than to reckon such among benefactors. He that can teach me the way to true happiness, he that can help me to adorn, dress, and trim my soul; he by whose instructions I shall be more in love with virtue, and out of love with sin; he by whose directions I may be acquainted with myself, and made truly to value that which is really most excellent, this shall be my friend, this shall be my companion. And where are such friends to be found? How few of them in the world! Do not most that go under that

sweet name of friends do one another the greatest unkindness that can be imagined? How do they encourage one another in an evil way? Prov. i.; Ps. ii. How do men tug and pull to get one another apace into damnation! and if the world may be judges, none must go for a friend but he that would do me most mischief; none must be counted an enemy but he that desires to do me the most real kindnesses. This sounds strangely. Yet for all that, did it lie in my way, I could easily prove it. Yet I must confidently affirm, that every one's experience, first or last, will say as much. Something of this I have taken notice of in my conversing with dying men. I remember, once more particularly, being by a poor creature that was just going into another world; one of his old friends looked in to see him, at the sight of which person he gnashed his teeth, and could not endure him in the room, but cried out, This was he that brought me to this; I may thank him, or I had not been in so sad a condition upon a death-bed. But this by the by: open enemies are better than such friends. I say again, do not expect to have God such a friend. God loves his too well to let them undo themselves; he knows the worth of souls; and pities them that would part with their souls for a trifle; and therefore he tells men plainly that which may be really prejudicial to the health of their souls; he cannot but let them know what is food and what is poison. What else is the meaning of those vehement expostulations? Why doth he send so many messengers one after another? To what purpose else doth he tender such promises, such encouragements? Be it known, therefore, unto thee, O man, if thou understandest the worth of thy own soul, and wouldst have that soul of thine to do well for ever, and wouldst have a Friend for thy soul, that there is but one such Friend to be found in the whole world, and that is God. Oh, hast thou no regard at all for thy precious and immortal soul? Dost thou never think of that excellent thing within thee? Dost thou not care though thy soul starve, be naked, and miserable for ever? Is it nothing to thee, that thy soul hath not so much as a shelter to hide itself under, when a dreadful storm shall rise, and death shall turn it out of its old tenement? Dost thou not believe that it must have a being somewhere for ever, and that either in everlasting glory or eternal burnings? And are these small matters with you? What, will you for all this take no care in the world about these grand affairs? Had a special friend committed but a dog to thee to take care of, you would have thought yourself engaged, in gratitude and honour, to have suited your care of him to your respect for the person from whom you had him. (Epict.) "But dost thou not know, O man, that thy God hath committed a soul to thy care, and hath told thee what thou shalt do to preserve the life and health of this thy soul, that it may be in good plight when he shall call for it? He doth tell thee what is its most natural food, and what is not wholesome. He tells thee what thou shalt do to have that soul within thee everlastingly happy." And is all this of so little consequence, as to go in at one ear and out at the other? Are these things to be indifferent in? If man's soul were like the soul of a beast, the case were altered; if, when his breath went out of his body, there were an end of him, the matter were the less considerable. If he had ever a friend in another world, that could do as much for him as God can do, I should have little to say in this business. But since this is impossible, how can I bear to see thee neglect the making sure of such a Friend? How can a Christian with any patience think, that those that he lives with and dearly loves should miss such a Friend, without whom their souls must be everlastingly miserable. If it were only for your bodies or estates, I should scarce use so many words, neither, I believe, need I; but when it is for your souls and eternity, who can be silent? Once more, consider what a Friend thou mayst have; it is a Friend for thy soul. Alas, man, it is thy soul, thy precious soul, that lies at stake; that spirit within thee, which is more worth than a world; it is that which is in hazard, and here is a Friend that offers thee to make that soul of thine happy for ever. Thy soul hath abundance of enemies. Some would debase it; others would rob thee of it; others would clap up a hasty match between that noble creature and a servant, the world, I mean. And there are very few that have any true kindness for it; and thou knowest not the worth of that jewel, thy soul: but here, here's a Friend; if thou wilt but leave it with him, he will take care of it; it shall not be marted away for nothing. Here's one will do that for its security, honour, and happiness, that all the world besides cannot do. If, therefore, thou hast any love for thy poor soul; if thou settest any price upon that precious thing within thee; in a word, if thou wouldst have thy soul do well in another world, oh strike in here, close with these tenders, listen to the counsel of Him who offers you the best advice in the world. He, he it is that now offers thee that thou canst never value enough; he it is that will feed, clothe, and portion that soul of thine, and after that marry thee to his only Son; by which match you will be made for ever. Oh, did men and women but know what a soul is: did they imagine what a dreadful miscarriage that of a soul is; did they but in any measure understand the things of their peace; could they but conceive what God could and would do for their souls, I need spend but little time in persuading them to commit their souls to him, to be acquainted with him, who will be sure to take special care of their souls, that they may do well, whatever is neglected. Oh could you but see, did you but know what a sad taking they are in that go into the other world with a poor, naked soul, and know nobody in the world there, and have never a friend that doth take any notice of them, you would then think I spoke what I do with reason enough, and that my words were too short, and my expostulations too faint, in a matter of such concernment. O sinners, I tell you, nay, God tells you, soul-matters are the greatest matters in the world. I am sure Christ thought so, or else he would not have been at so much cost about them; those that are in their wits and understand themselves know as much too, and so will you, ere a few years, it may be hours, be past. Those that now speak contemptuously of all this, when they have been but one quarter of an hour in another world, will say as I do, that a soul-friend is the only friend, and that soul-concerns are the great concerns; things of weight and moment indeed; and that it would have quitted the cost to have taken some pains to have looked out for such a one that could have stood the soul in some stead in that other world; and that, above all, it would have been no folly nor madness to have accepted of the kindness of one that desired earnestly to be acquainted with them, and to do their soul a good turn. Oh that they had but been so considerate as to have embraced such a motion when it was offered! And this brings me to the next qualification of this Friend.

16. He is a necessary Friend. There is an absolute necessity of being acquainted with him. It is possible for a man that hath very few friends upon earth to live as happily as he that hath many. Multitude of acquaintance, such as they are, may contribute much to a man's care and sorrow. And as for most friends, such as are commonly so called, it is better to have their room than their company. A man may live without the acquaintance of nobles; he may be as free, cheerful, and rich, without the knowledge of such as them. One may live holily, and die joyfully, and may be happy for ever, though he never saw the face of a prince, though he was never at court, though he lived and died a stranger to all worldly friends. One may be disowned by his father, hated by his mother, slighted by all his relations, and have never a friend under the sun that will own him, and yet for all that be in a state of truer felicity than those that are daily attended with troops of visitors, whose gates are seldom shut, whose houses are never empty; but amongst all that comes, God never comes to them, as for his company they are strangers to it; this man I may write miserable for all his great and many friends. And him that hath the company of God in acquaintance with his Redeemer I'll call happy, though he have never a friend in the world besides. Multitudes of friends seldom add much to our comforts, but always to our cares. A man may go to hell for all his great acquaintance with men; but it's impossible, if we are greatly acquainted with God, to miss heaven. When men are unkind, if God be kind, it's well balanced; but if God frown, whose smiles can comfort? I may be

happy though I may be very little in man's favour; but it's impossible to be happy without God's favour. To be a stranger to God is to be a stranger to peace, joy, heaven. Oh it's sad being without God! If I should declare the judgment of most in the world, at least if their practice may speak for them, they see very little need of acquaintance with God. They do not write *must* upon the things of religion. They must eat, they must drink, they must sleep, and if they want any of these things, they count themselves in a sad condition. But further, they must riot, they must be drunk, they must whore, they must have what their lust calls for, let it be what it will, they must get into the favour of such and such a great person whose displeasure they have incurred: these are things that the world say must be; they are reckoned among the necessary things: but they do not say they must have a Christ, they must be reconciled to God, they must deny themselves, they must seek first the kingdom of heaven; no, these are indifferent things amongst them, these are things minded by the by, if not matter of scorn and jesting; these the world thinks unnecessary things. It's necessary their flesh should be pleased; it's necessary the devil should be obeyed; it's necessary they and theirs should be somebody in the world: these are matters of weight; for these they think it worth the while to toil and moil, to ride early and late, and to lose their sleep, and think they can never do too much; and all this while they see no need at all of getting a friend for their souls, no need at all of knowing, loving, and delighting in God. Well, seeing the case is thus, seeing it is no great matter whether you know God, or be known of him; be not then troubled at the day of judgment, if God look upon you as a stranger, then be not grieved (seeing the knowledge of God is nothing with you) if God say he knows you not; if God's presence be no such material thing, complain not then for the want of it; be content, if you can, to hear him say, "Depart, I know you not." Oh, but shall I thus leave you, poor ignorant sinner? Consider, for the Lord's sake, for thy soul's sake, whether it be a necessary thing to avoid everlasting burnings. Is it a necessary thing to be saved? Is eternal glory and heaven necessary? Dare you say these are unnecessary things? If these be necessary, then I am sure God and Christ are necessary: "For this is life eternal, to know God, and him whom he hath sent, Jesus Christ." Oh how will the case be altered erelong, with the God-hating and Christ-despising world? When they shall be quite despoiled of all that which they prized above the knowledge of God, when all their friends shall appear to be enemies, when all their hopes shall be swept down like a spider's web, oh, will they not then be of this mind, that it was no such slight matter that I was so earnest with them about; that acquaintance with God was no such unnecessary thing as they took it to be; and that there was more need of getting an interest in Christ than of running to a playhouse or a whore-house? How will they rend the skies with their fruitless wishes! How will the mountains echo with their doleful lamentations! Oh that God would but know them! Oh that they might not hear that word, Depart! But seeing all that to little purpose, how then will they exclaim against themselves! Oh that they should be such fools; that they should be so madly besotted as to neglect the looking after acquaintance with God! Time was that God would have had them to come to him; he called after them, and sent for them again and again, but they would none of his company; they desired not the knowledge of the Most High; they said to him, Depart from us: and now they have what they then desired; now they see that the ministers had cause enough to say what they did, and a thousand times more. As troublesome as it was to hear of hell, it's worse to feel it. They see now *must* is for the soul, and not the body. Oh that men and women would be now as serious in their judgments about these things as they will be shortly! Consider, O man, that as little as thou mindest these things, these are the only things that are necessary. Thou must have a God for thy Friend, a Christ for thy Saviour, to save thee from thy sins, or else thou must be damned, or else thou must be cursed for ever. Thou mayst lie racked upon thy bed of sickness, where none can help thee; thou mayst rot in a stinking dungeon, where no man can relieve thee; thou mayst be roasted in the flames, and yet for all this be a happy man. Worldly ease, pleasure, health, riches, are none of those absolutely necessary things. A man may go to hell, and have them all; and a man may go to heaven, and want them. Thou mayst have eternal rest in another life, though thou hast scarce a day of ease in this. One may be a favourite with God, though as miserable as Job. But what will you say of that man that hath not a God to go to? This, this is the miserable man, with a witness! Oh that, seeing men's lives are so short, they would wisely husband their precious time in minding nothing but necessary things! Oh that unnecessaries might be cut off! When I am about to undertake a business, let me ask my soul this question: O my soul, is this a business of absolute necessity? Hast thou not something of greater importance that is yet undone? We enter not into the lists for honour, where it is no great matter whether we conquer or no; we persuade not men to busy themselves about toys; we are not so importunate about a thing of nothing. No, sirs, as unnecessary as you think these things we speak of are, erelong you will say as much as we do, and more too; you'll shortly find that it was as much as your life and happiness was worth that lay at stake. These are things we must mind you of, or else we hazard our souls; and they are things that you must mind also, or else you hazard yours. I want significant words enough to express the weight and importance of these things. Oh that what is wanting of that nature might be supplied with tears, groans, and compassions! I am, through mercy, ashamed of my own heart, (oh that I were more so!) that I should speak of such serious matters so slightly. It is not now a time to jest, O my soul, when thou art to discourse with miserable men and women, who refuse their happiness, and dote upon their misery. Thou art now about a work that concerns souls and their eternal state. Tell me, dear friends, do you in sober sadness believe that you have immortal souls? Do you indeed know that your souls are naturally enemies to God? and that, if you be not reconciled to God, you must be dealt with as enemies? Do you really believe all this? Do you believe what a dreadful thing it is to look such an Enemy in the face, when he shall sit in judgment? Further, do you believe what it is to lie down in devouring flames, and to dwell with everlasting burnings? Do you not think it a fearful thing to fall into the hands of the living God? And if you do not, let me tell you, you are worse than mad. If you do believe all this, why, then, let me ask you again, whether you conceive it unnecessary to use the utmost care and diligence to get acquainted with Him who can deliver you from the wrath to come? O friends! I call you so, and I believe most of you love me dearly. Oh that you would do me one kindness; I should count it the greatest kindness that you can do me. Why, what is that you say? Why, it is but to pity your own souls, and to mind that one thing necessary, and to pity them that are mourning for your dry eyes and hard hearts. What say you to all this? If you have anything to say against the necessity of these things, I am ready to plead the case with you. Well, if it be not necessary to know God and Christ, and lay in provision for eternity, what then is necessary? If it be not necessary to serve, love, and delight in Him who can deliver from everlasting death, and reward with everlasting life, what then is? Once more, for your souls' sakes, consider what you do, when you vigorously pursue worldly things, and look upon the favour and displeasure of God as small things. Oh, write not these things down amongst the superfluous things which are to be minded by the by. Remember this, that it is very possible for a man to be exceeding holy, and yet to be altogether unknown to the world; but it is altogether impossible to be truly happy, and yet unacquainted with God.

17. He is a tried Friend. Thousands and millions can from their own experiences say all this which I have said of him, and much more; but I shall pass this over at present, having hinted it already; and because it may be I may touch upon something of the same nature hereafter.

18. He is an everlasting Friend. I shall be but brief in speaking to this head, because what has been spoken of this

fell under that of his immortality. Nevertheless, it is possible to conceive God immortal in himself, and yet, by reason of man's default, his kindness to him to be finite: so it was in respect of the angels that fell from him. But now, blessed be free grace, man stands upon surer ground than ever he did; the children of God have a firmer bottom by far than Adam had when he was in paradise; his state is more secure, being once united to God in Christ, than that of the angels of heaven in their first creation. For, that their state was mutable, is *de facto* proved. But now, blessed be rich goodness, if we can but make sure of reconciliation with God, again it is impossible for us to miscarry. God hath sworn, and he will perform it, that the heirs of glory might have the more strong consolation: "For this is as the waters of Noah unto me: for as I have sworn that the waters of Noah should no more go over the earth; so have I sworn that I would not be wroth with thee, nor rebuke thee. For the mountains shall depart, and the hills be removed; but my kindness shall not depart from thee, neither shall the covenant of my peace be removed, saith the Lord that hath mercy on thee," Isa. liv. 9, 10. God's children need not fear disinheriting. His gifts and callings are without repentance. If God loved us while we were enemies, how much more, being reconciled, will he continue his love to us! Once a child of God, and a child of God for ever; once in favour, and never out of it again. "Who shall separate us from the love of Christ? shall tribulation, or distress, or persecution, or famine, or nakedness, or peril, or sword? Nor height, nor depth, nor any other creature, shall be able to separate us from the love of God, which is in Christ Jesus our Lord," Rom. viii. 35, 39. Who can pluck us out of the arms of the Almighty? Who or what is that which can alienate our Father's affections from us? If the promise of God, which saith, I will never leave nor forsake you, be valid; if his oath bind him; if the blood of Christ continue always to be satisfactory; if his mediation can prevail; if the nature of God be unchangeable; we are well enough, we are safe, if this be but clear that we are really reconciled to God; if we be acquainted with him, we are kept by the mighty power of God through faith unto salvation. If they had been of us, saith the apostle, no doubt they would have continued with us. It is possible indeed, yea, common for men to pretend love to God, and to seem to have a true friendship for him, and yet not to be truly so. To have a name to live, and to live, are two things. It is not unusual to bear God company (as I may say) abroad, and yet at home to have somebody that they have a greater kindness for. It is common to go along with God (if I may so call it) in the external actions of religion, and yet to desert him at last, Isa. lviii. 1, 2, 3; Matt. vii. 21. There are many that seem to bid fair for heaven, and if cap and knee will do, God shall have that; they will give him the husk and shell, that they may keep the kernel for one that they love better. Thousands there are of such persons in the world; and these profess abundance of kindness for God; they come oft to his house, and sit down there, and make as if they were his friends and his acquaintance; and some of God's servants, by a mistake, may bid them welcome; but yet for all this they may be strangers; only they have heard of God, and can talk of him, and it may be, have given him many transient visits, but yet they want the real properties of friends: they never knew what it was to be brought nigh to the Father by the Son; to have a sense of their lost state and estrangement from God, and under a sense of this, to make earnest inquiry after him; they never knew what it was to converse with God, to have an intimate acquaintance with him; to be sending out the breathing of their souls after him, and to be unsatisfied without him; they took up a trade of lifeless duties, and that was all. As for the life and power of religion, they never understood it: communion with God they heard oft of, but never understood what it meant; they never savoured and relished the things of God, nor with any suitableness or complacency engaged in his service: and as for those more secret actings of religion;—to take up the interest of God, to design his glory, to be deeply concerned for his honour, observing their affections, and the workings of their hearts in duty, to take notice of answers of prayers, or to look after their petitions when they are out of their mouths; they know not what these things are. So that from hence it appears that God and they were never really acquainted. No wonder then that they do forsake God, and are forsaken of him. The building might look neat, and the house seem to be strong; but because it was built upon the sands, it need not seem strange if it fall when the winds rise and the waves beat against it: but I say it, and say it again, the house that is built upon a rock will not, cannot fall: if a man be really united to God in Christ, and the work of grace thoroughly wrought upon him, it is impossible that God should forsake such a one. God cannot but be true, though man be false; he cannot but value the satisfaction and intercession of his Son; he cannot forget his own nature: "Can a woman forget her sucking child, that she should not have compassion on the son of her womb? yea, they may forget, yet will I not forget thee. Behold, I have graven thee upon the palms of my hands; thy walls are continually before me," Isa. xlix. 15, 16. I do not say but that God may suspend the refreshing intimations of his love; nay, he may quite hide his face, and his dearest ones may look upon themselves as free among the dead; they may reckon themselves such as have no acquaintance with God, and yet for all this be exceeding dear to God: this is cleared by every day's experience. Nay, I may say, I believe that there are very few of them who know what God's presence, smiles, and love is, but know in some measure what it is to have his face hid, to walk in the dark, and to see no light. It is no unusual thing for a child of God to question his state, to fear whether all that he ever did were not in hypocrisy and formality. Have not the best been made sometimes to question (especially upon some notable fall) whether what they did formerly did not proceed from mere common grace or some less spiritual principle than the life of grace and a divine nature within them. Were there ever any of the sons of Adam whom rich mercy hath plucked as firebrands out of the fire, to whom the Lord hath showed his marvellous kindness and love in Christ, that have kept their watch so exactly, that have walked so closely with God, so as never to have the least frown from him? Were there ever any that lived all their days under a constant lively sense of their interest in divine everlasting love? If there be, they have fared better than Job did; they enjoyed more than ever Heman or David did. A child of God may oft be in a sad state, but yet he is always in a safe state: the purpose of God stands firm. Though for a small moment he seem to forsake them, yet with everlasting mercies will he gather them, Isa. liv. 7. Oh, everlasting! That's a sweet word indeed in the saint's ear; he would not that one word should have been out of the Bible, left out of the promise, for a world. If thou be once truly acquainted with God, thy state is as safe, thy condition as sure, as if thou wert already in heaven. God may and will chastise his with rods, but his loving-kindness he will never remove from them, his mercy endures for ever. All that God gives to his friends and acquaintance, that is spiritual, is, like himself, everlasting. God is not like short-spirited man, every moment changing, one day doting upon an object, and the next day hating it as much. An earthly prince may one moment set his favourite at his table, and the next command that he should be hanged. But far be it from the unchangeable God that he should do thus. As for the great ones of the world, it hath been counted by some, and those none of the weakest, no small piece of policy to keep out of their knowledge: their favours are so dearly bought, their kindness so uncertain, their displeasure so dangerous, and yet so easily procured. But here it is far otherwise. It is God, and God alone, that is an everlasting Friend, in whose presence there is fulness of joy, and pleasure for evermore. Oh these everlasting things are great things! An everlasting Friend, and everlasting inheritance, everlasting glory, everlasting joy, everlasting life, and everlasting death, they are matters of weight! Oh, why should not our very souls be overpowered with the very thoughts of such things! Oh this unbelief, this unbelief!

19. **He is One that is willing and desirous to be acquainted with you.** What I have said before had signified little to us, were it not for this. It is a misery, and no comfort, to

hear and know the great things which we must go without. But this is that which puts life into all those powerful motives which I handled before. God is the most loving, most strong, and rich Friend, and withal he hath in him a sweet inclination to be acquainted with us. The terms that he offers are the most reasonable in the world. This, this is the comfort of all the poor fallen sons and daughters of Adam; that though they have run away from God, though they have left their Father's house, and turned prodigals; yet their tender-hearted compassionate Father is ready to receive them again; his arms are open, he meets them while they are yet a great way off, he runs to them, and falls upon their neck, and kisses them, and expresses the greatest kindness to them, and joy for their return. O unparalleled love! O infinite goodness! God hath expressed this, his willingness to receive poor lost sinners, abundantly throughout all the Scripture. If God had not been willing to have been friends again with man, what needed he to have given himself the trouble of parting with his dearest Son, and sending him into the world to manage this great work of reconciling man to himself? Why else was that precious blood shed? And to what purpose should he send so many prophets, apostles, and ministers, for so many hundreds of years, rising up early, and sitting up late? Why are they commanded to cry aloud, to use so much earnestness, to compel poor wandering strangers to come to his house, but that he might be acquainted with them? Can any one conceive that he should do all this without the least design of kindness? If all that God hath done to the reconciling man to himself, doth not speak his willingness to be reconciled to them, what can? Isa. v. 4. Nay, so willing is he to receive them, notwithstanding all their backslidings, that he teacheth them how they may address themselves to him most acceptably; he puts words into their mouths which they may use with good success when they come before him, Hos. xiv. 1, 2, 4. Nay, that sinners may be more confirmed in their expectation of his favour, he hath most solemnly sworn that "he delights not in the death of sinners, but had rather that they should return and live." Wherefore else is it that we are so straitly commanded, as we will answer the neglect upon our peril before God at that terrible day, that we preach the word in season and out of season? To what purpose should Paul expose himself to so many hazards both by sea and land? Why should he teach this doctrine of reconciliation night and day with tears? Doth he not tell you that he did all this by divine dispensation, and that it was as much as his soul was worth to waive this work? And doth not all this speak God's willingness to be friends again with man? Could not he have sent legions of angels, with flaming swords in their hands, when he sent his Son, and thousands of prophets, apostles, ministers, and teachers? Might he not have proclaimed war against them for ever, when he followed them with the ambassadors of peace? If he had had no thoughts of agreement with them, could he not have spoken to them in thunder and lightning, with fire and brimstone, as well as in the still voice of the Gospel? He could, if he had pleased, have made them to have known the breach of his covenant, by giving them up to the will of their cruel enemies. God could as easily have cut off a whole world of us, as we can crush a moth, and easier too. But he is willing to show forth the richness of his patience and goodness, that thereby sinners might be brought to repentance. How doth God further express his willingness to receive returning sinners, by engaging them by many temporal favours! Who preserved that tender creature in the womb, and brought it out of those dark chambers into light? Who kept that helpless infant after it was in the world? Whose flax and wool do we wear upon our backs? To whom is it that we are beholden for every crumb we eat, and every drop we drink? Who spreads our table for us, and makes our cups to overflow? Who brought us from the brink of the grave, when we had received the sentence from our doctor and our disease? And what is the language of all these mercies, but, "Return, O backsliding sinner, for in me is thy help found?" Love, delight in, and be acquainted with Him from whom thou hast received so many kindnesses. If thou wouldst accept of Him for thy Lord, Husband, and Friend, who hath sent thee these tokens, thou shalt have other favours than these. Is not this the meaning of all the common mercies that we daily receive from him? Why was not thy breath stopt with an oath in thy mouth? Why is it that so many thousands that were born since thyself, are gone to their eternal state, when thou art still standing? What hast thou done to engage God more than others, that worms should not be feeding on thee, when thou art feeding upon the fat and sweet? What is the English of all this? What are all these droves of mercies which God sends to thee, but to cool thy enmity against him, and to make thee, who art marching out in thy warlike furniture, to meet him with tears of joy and friendly embraces? Is not Love the Giver written upon all his tokens? What means his frequent visiting of thee but desire of acquaintance with thee? Had he had no desire at all to know you, and to be known of you, do you think he would have called so often and so kindly at your door? Would he have stood knocking with so much patience, and have spoken to you so lovingly, if he desired still to be a stranger to you? Is this like one that desires your ruin? Did God never plead with thee by his ministers, and urge the same argument that I do now? Did you never hear of such kind of expostulations as these? Why wilt thou go on to despise thy God, and to refuse his love? What reason hast thou to harbour such hard thoughts of him? Doth he deserve such unkindness at your hands? How long, ye simple ones, will you love simplicity? Why will you make light of that you cannot possibly overvalue, the favour of God, and acquaintance with your Maker? How often have you grieved his Spirit by your unworthy contempts! How many times have you given him cause to complain of your unhandsome usage, when he in very pity and compassion came to visit you! He hath reason to say now, as of old, "Hear, O heavens; and give ear, O earth: for the Lord hath spoken, I have nourished and brought up children, and they have rebelled against me," Isa. i. 2. "Do ye thus requite the Lord, O foolish people and unwise? is not he thy Father that hath bought thee? hath he not made thee, and established thee?" Deut. xxxii. 6. "O that they were wise!" "Be thou instructed, O Jerusalem, lest my soul depart from thee," Jer. vi. 8. Is not this the voice of mercy? Have not these been expostulations of the mighty God with his rebellious creatures? and yet how do they stand it out all this while, as if God were like to get so much by their acquaintance! Return, O foolish sinner; if thou makest anything of salvation and damnation, if thou valuest everlasting glory, if thou thinkest the commands, threatenings, and promises of the Almighty to be minded, come away, and make no delay. Oh, why wilt thou go on thus madly to undo thyself? Come away, poor soul, for all this, it is not yet quite too late, thy glass is not yet quite run, thy soul is not yet fully fixed in its unchangeable state. Once more I make such an offer to thee, as I am sure none but a madman will refuse; such an offer as none of the kings and lords of the world can make. The great and mighty Monarch of heaven tenders thee an alliance with himself; he sees how far thou art spent, how poor and low thou hast brought thyself by a dangerous and long war against thy Maker; he foresees what a condition thou wilt be in after a few more merry hours, except thou repent and turn. Wherefore, in compassion to thy precious soul, he hath commanded us to follow thee, and not to let thee be at quiet till thou hast given us a promise that thou wilt return and humble thyself to thy God; and what, shall we still lose our labour? shall all this come to nothing? O prodigy of unkindness! O wonder of patience! Thou hast slighted the friendship of thy God; thou hast set light by Christ, and undervalued heaven and eternity for ten, twenty, thirty years already; and yet the Lord sends us once more in his name to ask you whether you are willing to have God for your Friend! God hath not yet said, "Cut him down, bind him hand and foot, and cast him into that lake that burns for ever. Bring those mine enemies, that would not that I should reign over them, and slay them before my face." God hath not yet spoken that dreadful word, Depart. Oh, what is it thou stayest for? What is it that makes this business to hang so long? What lover is it that doth so long hold back thy heart? What is the matter, that we can no more speedily and effectually manage this great affair? What is it that thou dost prefer before God? What is it that thou thinkest more worthy of thy warmest love than Christ? What is that great thing that thou stickest not to venture thy soul for? Act like a man that is rational and not beside himself. If the world be God, if earth be better than Christ, then choose that; if Christ be God, then choose him. How long will you stand halting between two? Love that which will last longest; be acquainted with him that is willing and able to do most for thee. Is the world worth more now than it was in David's time, when he preferred the favour of God before thousands of gold and silver? Is the price of it raised? Can it bribe death, and stop the mouth of divine justice, and procure thee a real respect in another world? Go, chaffer, and see what bargain thou canst make; tell God that thou wilt give him thousands for thy brother's life, and as much more for the lengthening the lease of thy own to eternity. What doth God say? Is the bargain made? Is it not enough? Why, add a world to it; will that do? If it will not do this, if this purchase be too great for thy purse, then go lower; can all thou hast keep thee from fears, get thee a stomach, procure thee ease, rectify thy constitution; will it do this, or will it not? If not, why shouldst thou value that which can do so little for thee, before that which can do all things for thee? Be persuaded at last to be wise. What is God like to get by your love, or lose by your hatred? What have you to boast of? What excellencies to set you out? What portion to advance you, that you stand thus upon your terms? Come, let's hear a little what it is thou thinkest so highly of thyself for. I am sure your over-great beauty cannot commend you; for a blackamoor may with better reason brag of comeliness, than such a deformed loathsome creature can of beauty. I am sure your helpfulness will not speak for you; for thou art a crazy, decrepit, sickly creature, that will cost God more to cure than thou art worth a thousand times. It cannot be for thy estate that thou art so much desired, for all thy gold is adulterated, thy jewels counterfeit, thy all forfeited; and what is it then that thou hast yet to boast of? Come and set it before us, that we may acknowledge our mistakes. Are the clothes upon thy back (as fine as thou art) thy own? Is the food that thou eatest paid for? And is this the creature that must be wooed with so much earnestness? Behold, all ye inhabitants of the world, and admire! Hear, O heavens! this is that —— (I want a name to call her by) who thinks it below her to be matched with Christ, and an undervaluing to be acquainted with her Maker, and a shame to have God for her Father! From the crown of the head to the sole of the foot, there is nothing but wounds, and bruises, and putrefied sores; and running plague-sores that are broken, are her greatest beauty: and here's a thing to be beloved with all my heart! Ezek. xvi. Whosoever thou art that readest these lines, this was once thy condition; in these ornaments he found thee; when God came to ask thy heart, this was thy dress, though thou art thus highly advanced. And such were some of you; but ye are washed, but ye are cleansed.

And after all this, O sinner, art thou still as stout and proud as ever? Is Christ so willing as bring thee to his Father? Is he willing to clothe thee from head to foot with glorious robes, such a dress as may become thee in the presence of a king? Doth he offer to lead thee in his hands to his own palace? Is God so willing and desirous to be your Father, and Christ to be your Husband? Are all the ministers of Christ so willing to do their utmost to bring this match to perfection? Shall they lie at you day and night, to give your consent, and to be willing; and are you still unwilling? Well, if all this signify little, and you miss Christ at last, and be not acquainted with God after all, remember it was your own doings, and that you thought it greater wisdom to marry the servant than the Master, to obey the rebel rather than your loving Prince. Remember you preferred darkness before light, hell before heaven. I call heaven and earth to record this day, that I have set life and death before you, and you stand as if it were so difficult a matter to resolve which was the best. This sounds strangely, and every one will be ready to write *fool* upon that man's forehead that acts thus. Hold, man, be not too ready to pass thy censure before thou lookest within thee! Dost thou see an absolute need of Christ? Dost thou adore his infinite love and kindness? Dost thou give up thyself to him for thy Lord, and receive him for better for worse, come on it what will? Or dost thou not rather spend thy thoughts, and let out thy affections upon the vanities and pleasures of this world? Dost thou not love father and mother, wife and children, brethren and sisters, house and lands, more than him? Why, if this be the case, I must say that thou art one of the fools that lovest death and hatest life; thou callest that folly in another which in thyself thou countest wisdom. I wonder who it is that you strive to please all this while! Is not the hand of Joab in all this? Hath not Satan been deep in retarding this match? Hath not he a design to marry thee to some painted lust, though he undo thee for ever? And must he be pleased rather than God? Is it more necessary to gratify him that never yet intended to do any of the sons of Adam any kindness, rather than their best friends? Come away for shame, and let us lose our breath no longer; and let that time we spend in pleading with you for God, be spent in singing with you and praising God for you, and congratulating your happy acquaintance with God, and your matching to his only Son.

20. But because man is so wedded to the world, and dotes upon his lust, that all the arguments that we can use are most commonly unsuccessful, I shall add one more upon this sort of motives drawn from the qualifications of Him whom I would fain have you acquainted with, and that shall take in all that can be said on this head, and that is this: Consider that he is altogether lovely; he is made up of love, goodness, and all excellencies; and whatsoever pleasure, delight, and content you find in the creature, it is trancendently in him. He is the Chiefest of ten thousands. Ask of them that by faith have seen him; inquire of the spouse in the Canticles, and ask her what is her Beloved more than another beloved, what there is in God and Christ more than in the world? and she will almost wonder that any one that is rational should ask so foolish a question.

She thinks you might with as much judgment and reason have asked what there is in heaven more desirable than in hell? what there is in ease more than in torments? in gold and jewels more than in dross? in a living, healthful, beautiful creature, more than in a stinking rotten carcass? Did you but see his face, you would soon think there were something in him more than in another. Could you but see his eye, your heart would be in a flame. Did you but understand what it is to be brought into his banqueting-house, you would say that they are neither fools nor madmen that can find in their hearts to scorn the beauties and glories of this world in comparison of one look or smile from God; and believe that his love was better than wine, to be preferred infinitely before the greatest worldly pleasures, and think that the virgins had reason enough to love him, Cant. i. 3. How high doth the church run in his commendations! How doth she endeavour to set him out to the life, that every one may admire his excellencies, and be taken with his beauties, as well as herself! Neither doth she fear to lose him by this, nor indeed is unwilling that others should fall in love with him as well as she, Cant. v. 9, &c. She begins first with his face; it is white and ruddy, the most exact beauty; so that she must be blind that is not taken with him; and so she goes on as well as she can to set him out; but he is so infinitely above her commendations, that she wants words to express herself, therefore she speaks one great one: "He is altogether lovely;" and if you will not believe, come and see. Do but look upon him by faith and meditation, contemplate his beauties, and then, if you have anything yet to object, if, after you have had a true sight of him, and have well weighed all, you do not find that there is in him infinitely more than I can tell you, why then let me bear the blame for ever.

Well, now let us gather up all these things together; and if a multitude of arguments, and if weight and reason, if vehemence and earnestness may prevail, I should have some good hopes that I should not want success in this work, nor you of the acquaintance with God and everlasting glory. Therefore I say again, if kindness and love be taking, who so sweet and obliging as he? If comfort, joy, and pleasure be desirable, who is there, when the soul is surrounded with a multitude of perplexities, that can so much delight, refresh, and raise it? If power, glory, and majesty, if ability to defend from injuries and revenge wrongs, might signify anything with poor shiftless creatures, who is there that ever yet prevailed against him? Who ever contended with God, and prospered? If vigour, activity, and care in all the affairs of his friends, can entice the dull helpless sinner to receive him, who will take more care for, and do more for them than he? If his humility may engage us; if freedom of access, notwithstanding that infinite distance that is between us and him, signify anything as to the commending of him to our acquaintance; where can a poor beggar be more welcome than at the house of this mighty Prince? Can faithfulness in the greatest strait raise the esteem of a friend? Who ever yet trusted him that was deceived? Are riches and wealth taking? Who is there that can give a kingdom for a portion, a love-token, and give everlasting glory and heaven for a jointure, but God? Doth pity in misery, sympathy in suffering, compassion in distress, endear and commend a friend? who is more tender-hearted than he? Are honours and preferments such great things? Who is he who will make all his favourites kings and priests, and set them upon thrones, and reward, and commend them before the whole world? Is suitableness a considerable qualification to make up this match? Who so suitable for the soul, a spirit, as God, a Spirit? Who can satisfy its vast and infinite desires but Infinity itself? Have poor simple creatures, that have quite undone themselves by their folly and indiscretion, need of a wise counsellor, to wind them out of their sad intricacies? Who is there among the profound politicians and grave sages of the world, to be compared unto him? Doth a dying man that hath a never-dying soul, that is to pass speedily into an eternal state. lack an ever-dying and immortal Friend, that may stand him in some stead, when all his relations are dead and rotten? Is not God immortal? Are not friends sometimes farthest off from one when one hath most need of them? Is not he then a Friend highly to be prized, who can, who will never be absent? Doth not God fill heaven and earth? What think you of a soul-Friend? Is not such a one worth the looking after, who takes care that your soul shall not miscarry? Who ever did more for souls than Christ? Will it not be true prudence to make sure of such a Friend as we must have for our Friend, or we are miserable for ever? And where is such a one to be found but He that hath the keys of heaven and hell? Which is most considerable, time, or eternity? And whom shall I most value? him who promiseth present pleasures, that are lost as soon as felt, or Him who will bestow everlasting favours? And are there not at God's right hand pleasures for evermore? If the trial and experience of so many millions may speak his commendation, will not all that ever knew God say, Truly, God is good to Israel. Will God's willingness, desire, and earnestness prevail with you to come to him? What is the substance of the whole Bible? Doth not almost every chapter speak the desire that God hath to be reconciled to man? If the perfection of all excellencies meeting in one can render him amiable, how can He be slighted who is altogether lovely? And what say you now? Are you resolved, or are you not? Shall the infinite Majesty of heaven condescend to offer himself to be loved and embraced by sinful dust? Shall God say, I will be thy Father! and shall not the sinner say, I would be thy child! Why should not the heart of every apostate rebellious traitor that hath forfeited estate, life, and soul, leap at such good news, and say, Will God for all this lay aside the controversy, and conclude a peace? Will he receive the rebel to mercy? Will he open his doors to his prodigal? And is there yet any hope? Is it possible that such sins as mine should be forgiven? Can it be conceived that such a creature as I should be embraced? What! look upon me! Will God indeed take me into favour? Yes, thee! Behold he calls thee, he offers thee his Son, a kingdom, a crown; behold the Father meets, he makes haste to meet his returning prodigal. Behold, the King hath sent to invite thee to the feast: nay, he will give thee his only Son in marriage, the wedding-garment is made ready, the Bridegroom is coming, the wheels of his chariot run apace, the friends of the Bridegroom are come to bid you make ready: up, deck yourself, put on your glorious apparel, make haste, make haste, ye virgins; your companions are ready; all stay for you; the Bridegroom is at the door. Behold, he is at the door; and will you still let him knock? What! Father, Husband, a kingdom! What words are these? Wilt thou, O mighty Jehovah, be my Father? Wilt thou, O blessed Jesus, be my Husband? Shall I have a kingdom? What! me a child, a spouse for the King of glory, an heir of glory! Grace! Grace! Amen! Hallelujah! Be it to thy servants according to thy word! But who are we, and what is our father's house, that thou hast brought us hitherto? And now, O Lord God, what shall thy servant say unto thee? For we are silenced with wonder, and must sit down with astonishment; for we cannot utter the least tittle of thy praises. What meaneth the height of this strange love? Oh! that the God of heaven and earth should condescend to enter into covenant with his dust, and to take into his bosom the viperous brood, that have often spit their venom in his face! We are not worthy to be as the handmaids, to wash the feet of the servants of our Lord; how much less to be thy sons and heirs, and to be made partakers of all those blessed liberties and privileges which thou hast settled upon us! But for thy goodness' sake, and according to thy own heart, hast thou done all these great things. "Even so, Father, because so it seemed good in thy sight. Wherefore thou art great, O God, for there is none like thee, neither is there any God besides thee; and what nation on earth is like thy people, whom God went to redeem for a people to himself, and to make him a name, and to do for them great things and terrible? For thou hast confirmed them to thyself, to be a people unto thee for ever, and thou, Lord, art become their God. Wonder, O heavens, and be moved, O earth, at this great thing! For, behold, the tabernacle of God is with men, and he will dwell with them, and they shall be his people; and God himself shall be with them, and be their God." Be astonished and ravished with wonder; for the infinite breach is made up, the offender is received, and God and man are reconciled, and a covenant of peace entered, and heaven and earth are agreed upon the terms, and have struck their hands, and sealed the indentures! O happy conclusion! O blessed conjunction! Shall the stars dwell with the dust? or the wide-distant poles be brought to mutual embraces and cohabitation? But here the distance of the terms is infinitely greater. Rejoice, O angels! shout, O seraphims! O all the friends of the Bridegroom and bride prepare an epithalamium: be ready with the marriage-song! Lo, here is the wonder of wonders! For Jehovah hath betrothed himself for ever to his hopeless captives, and owns the marriage before all the world; and is become one with us, and we with him. He hath bequeathed to us the precious things of the earth beneath, with the fulness thereof; and hath kept back nothing from us. And now, O Lord, thou art that God, and thy words be true, and thou hast promised this goodness unto thy servants, and hast left us nothing to ask at thy hands, but what thou hast already freely granted. Only the word which thou hast spoken concerning thy servants, establish it for ever, and do as thou hast said, and let thy name be magnified for ever, saying "The Lord of hosts, he is the God of Israel. Amen. Hallelujah." And how do you like this music, O ye the lost sons and daughters of Adam? How do you relish these dainties? What do you think of this match? Some, you see, have been so wise as, with the greatest gratitude they can for their souls, to close with those happy offers of grace. You hear how bravely such and such have bestowed themselves, and now they are made for ever. And what do you say to the same proposals? Have they so much reason to bless the day that ever such a motion was made? Have they cause to rejoice for ever for those blessed overtures? and are they all to be slighted by you? Will Christ be worse to you than them? Is heaven and happiness less necessary for you than them? Will the loss of a soul be more inconsiderable to you than it would have been to them? Will not heaven, Christ, and glory, be as well worth your acceptance as theirs? What, are you willing to be shut out when the Bridegroom comes to fetch his spouse home? Can you bear it, to see such as you thought your inferiors advanced, and yourself despised? What shall I say? What words shall I use? What shall I do to prevail? Oh that I could pity you a thousand times more than I do! Oh that my eyes might weep in secret for thy folly! Oh that you also might do as some have done before you! though, indeed, they be but few that be so wise. Oh that you would also bestow your heart upon Christ! Give him your heart-love, or he will have your heart-blood. Do not make yourself miserable to please any living. Do not slight Christ, because most do so; go not with them to hell for company. But that, if it be possible, I might persuade you, I shall add some more motives, to prevail with you to get acquainted with God; which, I am certain, will either work those blessed effects, or rise up against you to the aggravation of your confusion, in that great and terrible day.

II. HEAD OF MOTIVES.

The next head of motives which I shall insist upon, for the enforcing of this duty of acquainting yourselves with God, I shall take from the glorious effect of this acquaintance with God.

1. The first effect of this acquaintance with God is, that it makes the soul humble, and consequently fits the soul for greater communications from God still, and to do God the greater service; but of that particular afterwards. Acquaintance with God makes the soul humble. When God comes into the soul, he brings such a glorious light along with him, that he makes the soul to see, not only his beauty, but its own deformity. "The entrance of thy words giveth light: it giveth understanding to the simple," Ps. cxix. 130. Before the soul was acquainted with the word of God, and by that had some discoveries of God made to it out of the word, why, it was in the dark, and saw nothing at all of its own vileness; it took no notice of that sink, that hell that was within it, considered not its own treason against the Lord of heaven and earth, and the dangerous hazards that it run every moment upon that account; but the soul thought very well of its own state, it flattered itself in its own iniquity; the man thinks he is rich and increased in goods, and hath

need of nothing; but when he comes to look into his purse, to open his treasury, and to tell over all his gold and silver in the light, why then, he perceives a sad mistake: all his silver is dross, and the best riches that he hath is but dung. When the light comes in, he sees the darkness of his understanding, the perverseness of his will, the disorderliness of his affections, the distemper of the whole soul. He before took himself for a beautiful creature, but, by this light and this glass, he sees his beauty is great deformity; he beholds heaps of lusts crawling up and down, which before lay undiscerned, and then that man that reckoned himself so happy, cries out, "Oh wretched man that I am, who shall deliver me? What shall I do to be saved? I am undone, undone! How shall I live? Where shall I dwell for ever?" Time was that the man admired what the ministers ailed to keep such a stir about sin, but now he wonders that they are no more earnest in their preaching of it down. It was a little while ago that he thought himself whole, but now he feels himself sick to the very heart, wounded, fainting, and ready to die; he made full account that he was pure, but now he cries out, Unclean, unclean! It was not long since he said with indignation, Am I blind also? But now he cries out, and will not be silenced, Have mercy upon me, Jesus, thou Son of David, and grant that I may receive my sight! His language is much altered; he cannot say, Was ever such a sinner as I pardoned? Will such a prodigal ever be received? Shall such foul offences as mine be forgiven? If God should look upon me, and give me a Christ, and pity me, and cast his skirts over me, while I lie in my blood; if the Lord should look upon me, it would be such a wonder that all that ever heard of it may justly admire. Now the man who thought himself the best of saints, believes himself as bad as the worst of sinners! When a man begins to be acquainted with God, he begins also to know himself. He that saw no need of washing by Christ, would now have hands, feet, head, and heart, all washed. He that thought himself sometimes far enough from hell, now begins to wonder that he did not fall into it; and although there be a sweet alteration in him for the better, and saints begin to delight very much in him, yet he wonders that any one should see anything in him that should cause any affection in them towards him, much more to inflame their hearts in such vehement love to him; if he hear of any reproaches that are cast upon him, he is ready to say with that wise Stoic, Epictetus, "If he had known me better, he would have spoken much worse of me." If any praise him, he judgeth that it proceeds from their ignorance of his weakness, rather than from any knowledge of his worth; and if he hear any such language, he is ready to tremble for fear of his own heart, and cries out, "Not unto me, not unto me, but unto his name be the praise: yet not I, but Christ who dwelleth in me." Thus it is with one that begins to have some saving knowledge of God; and the nearer he comes to God, the farther he goes from himself; the more he sees of him and his righteousness, the less he sees of his own; the more he is exalted, the more he debaseth himself; like those four-and-twenty elders, he lays his crown at the feet of God. Thus it was with Job, when God, as I may say, stood at a great distance from him: he is ready to speak a little too highly; he stands much upon his own righteousness; he stiffly justifieth himself; but when the holy God comes a little nearer to him, when he throws off that dark cloud with which he has mantled himself, and when he caused that glorious brightness to break forth upon Job, and made him see a glance of his holiness, wisdom, and justice, then how is he even ashamed and confounded within himself, that he should ever stand so much upon his own justification! "I have heard of thee by the hearing of the ear; but now mine eye seeth thee: wherefore I abhor myself, and repent in dust and ashes," Job xlii. 5, 6. When he comes to be better acquainted with God, how strangely is his note changed; and I might say, when he was thus abased, how speedily doth God raise him to a wonder! A man may hear of God twenty years together, and yet never abhor himself with dust and ashes, never see any vileness that is in his nature, never be brought off from his own righteousness, never admire that he is kept out of hell! Oh, but when he comes to see God, and to be acquainted with him, how doth he cry out of himself as unworthy to breathe in the air, as deserving nothing but wrath! Then he had not a word to say for the goodness of his own heart; now he can say with astonishment, Oh infinite patience! Oh immeasurable goodness! Oh the depths of God's love! He must be merciful indeed that can pardon such sins! That must be goodness indeed that can be so good to me! That is love with a witness, that can embrace such a loathsome monster! What was it that made Abraham call himself dust and ashes? What made David say he was a worm and no man? What made Isaiah speak so debasingly of himself? Why, these were the friends of God; they had visions of that holy One. When is it that the people of God are most ingenuous in their confessions? When do they most freely pour out their souls before God? When is it that they most readily open their sores, and desire that they should be searched, but when this great Chirurgeon comes to their chambers? Those who before were whole, are now sick, full of plague-sores, head and heart sick, dangerously sick, and no whole part in them; they can say more against themselves now than ever the minister could; they can aggravate their sins, and lay loads upon themselves; and they see themselves vile, and even are ready to wonder that the earth did not open and swallow them up before this; they admire that God should endure them so long, and think it no small miracle that they were not crushed in the egg, that they were not cast from the darkness of the womb to the darkness of hell. Now they can cry out of original sin, and the indisposition of their souls to anything that is good, and inclination to that which is bad. They say, as well as David, that they were "born in sin, and in iniquity did their mother conceive them." They think everything too good for them, all mercy on this side everlasting misery. They count every bit they eat, and every drop they drink, more than they deserve. They think themselves unworthy of the least of God's mercies, Gen. xxxii. 10. Others *say* thanksgivings, but they *feel* them; others *say* confessions, but they *feel* them. It is one thing for a man to speak of his own unworthiness, and another thing to lie under the sense of it. The heart and tongue are two distinct members. The heart may speak that which the tongue cannot utter, and the tongue may utter that which the heart never felt. But a man that is brought into acquaintance with God speaks what he experiences, or rather his experience is greater than what he speaks; so that he doth not dissemble with God when he confesseth his sin before him. They lay themselves as low as hell; this is humility, and this is an effect of acquaintance with God. Hence it is that Paul saith of himself, "Unto me, who am less than the least of all saints, is this grace given, that I should preach among the Gentiles the unsearchable riches of Christ; and to make all men see what is the fellowship," &c., Eph. iii. 8, &c. He wants words to express God's greatness, and his own smallness. Now, what was it that made Paul speak and think thus of himself? There was a time when Paul would have spit in any one's face that should have spoken as much against him as he did against himself. What is it that hath wrought such a strange alteration in this great Rabbi, and made him so little? Why, this acquaintance with God, the sight of Christ, was the thing that laid this proud Pharisee in the dust, and made him blind also. Mark this; always the more heavenly any man is, the more humble, Exod. iii. 11; 2 Sam. vii. 18. If I should appeal to the experiences of saints, and ask them when they had the lowest thoughts of themselves, would they not say, when they were nearest God? Now, would you walk humbly, you must walk with your God; would you see more of your own deformity, why then, you must labour to see more of his holiness, more of his beauty. Contraries set near one another appear more visible.

2. Another excellent effect of acquaintance with God is, that it will make a man fall upon sin in good earnest. When the soul sees how infinitely good God is, it cannot but see an unspeakable evil in sin, which is so directly contrary to him. When the soul hath really entered into a league with God, it presently bids defiance to all his enemies; when he begins to be at peace with God, he presently commenceth a war against his adversaries. Friendship

with God makes enmity against Satan. That which formerly the man rolled under his tongue as a sweet morsel, is now like gall and wormwood to him. He that sometimes did commit iniquity with greediness can now say that it is the greatest folly and madness in the world; he knows that it is an evil and a bitter thing, as sweet as it tasted when his palate was distempered; he that gloried in his wickedness now accounts it the greatest shame in the world, and hates the garments which are bespotted with the flesh, which sometimes he took for beautiful raiments. The burned child dreads the fire. Sin hath cost his friend dear, and him dear too. The child cannot love that knife which stabbed his father. He knows how sweet God is, and how much he hates sin, and that if he would have God's company, he must bid an everlasting farewell to his dearest beloved sin; and therefore, rather than he will offend so dear a Friend, he will hew Agag in pieces before the Lord; he will as soon cut off one hand with the other, and be pulled limb from limb, as again draw his sword against his covenanted Friend, and again venture into the field in the cause that sometimes he did so deeply engage body and soul in. He that thought before that it was no great matter to damn, curse, and tear; but a trick of youth to whore, and no harm to do what one had a mind to; to eat and drink, and talk, and sleep as one lists, to give one's lusts whatsoever they called for; he that could once make a mock of sin, and sleep securely upon the top of a mast, and thought it a piece of gallantry to dare the Almighty, and was ready to laugh at them who durst not be so prodigal of their souls as himself; the case is now wonderfully altered with him: he now sees the harlot stript naked; he beholds how loathsome the whore is, now her paint is washed off; sin and hell are alike to him; tempt him to folly, and he will soon answer in Joseph's language, "How shall I do this great wickedness, and sin against God?" He that sometimes thought sin the only pleasure, and looked upon the devil and the world as the only friends, now sees his dangerous mistake, and blesseth God that his eyes are opened before he comes into another world; he knows now that holiness is the only pleasure, and

God is the only Friend, and sin and the world are as mortal enemies as the devil himself; he believes that if he venture upon sin, he must venture upon the displeasure of his Friend, whose favour he sets more store by than all the delights under heaven, and whose loving-kindness he judgeth to be better than life itself. When the soul is once acquainted with God, how strangely are its apprehensions of things altered! Now he calls things and persons by their right name; good he calls good, and evil evil; whereas before he called evil good, and good evil, and put light for darkness, and darkness for light. He now believes that the zealous compassionate ministers who spoke so much against sin, had reason enough to have said ten times as much as they did; he sees that it was not for nothing that they were so earnest with him; he hath tasted the gall, wormwood, and poison that is in sin; he plainly sees what is the great makebait between God and man; he hath now the wit to understand what it is that hath kept good things so long from him. Tell him now of a revel, a whore; he had as lief thou shouldst persuade him to part with his strength and liberty, and grind in a mill; he reckons you might as rationally desire him to leap into a bottomless pit, to take up his everlasting lodging in a bed of flames, and to make light of damnation. Let men and devils use what arguments they will to prevail with him now to close with temptations, he is sure he hath a stronger against them; he hath a sensible argument within, which will answer all. If they had ten thousand times as many more than they can produce, the love of Christ makes him abhor the motion; God is my Friend dashes all. Shall such a one as I take up arms against God? Shall I that have found him so infinitely good? shall I that have experienced the faithfulness of this Friend to me, be so infinitely ungrateful, as to be thus abominably unfaithful to him? Shall I that have forfeited my life and soul, and instead of hell have received heaven, instead of damnation, salvation; shall I, instead of thankfulness, again rebel? Because the grace of God abounds, shall sin abound? God forbid. To argue from mercy to sin is the devil's logic: to argue from mercy to duty is true Christianity. One that is acquainted with God can expostulate the case with his own soul, and say, What meanest thou, O my soul, to stand parleying with Satan? Hast thou known what that hath cost thee already? Look back to Eden. Who was it that dispossessed thy grandfather of that brave seat? What did Eve get by discoursing with such a cheater? Have you not lost enough already, but you must be venturing still? Was it nothing for God, of a Friend, to become a Stranger and Enemy? Was it so slight a matter to be divested of all that glory that once thou didst shine in, that now again, after thou art brought into some favour, thou must be tampering with that gamester who had liked to have robbed thee of all? Art thou talking of returning again into Egypt? What, hast thou so soon forgotten the iron and the clay? Is this all the thanks that you give the Lord for his unspeakable mercy? Doth he that hath done such things for you deserve no better at your hands? Is this your kindness to your Friend? What was it, O my soul, that that undone creature said unto thee? Did he say, It is a little one, and thy soul shall live? What, did he ask a few merry hours, that I should spare myself, that I should not be righteous overmuch? Did he so? A special friend! I thank you for nothing! And why didst thou not answer the tempter, as Solomon did Bathsheba, when she asked a small thing (as she thought) for Adonijah? "And why dost thou not ask the kingdom also?" And why did not Satan ask thee to part with heaven, and thy interest in Christ, and those favours? As the Lord liveth, as small a request as thou thinkest his was, that word was spoken against thy life, thy soul. A virtuous man, or as the Stoic Antoninus calls him, "one that hath God for his Friend, when temptations are presented, remembers who he is, and how he stands related to God, and how little grateful such an action would be to his Friend." And thus he doth resist the temptation with a great deal of gallantry, when he remembers himself. Nay, sometimes temptations to sin do make grace more to abound: the water which was intended to cool divine love, proves oil, and makes that noble flame to burn more vehemently, Cant. viii. 6, 7. He desires to exercise that grace which is contrary to the vice which he is tempted to with more than ordinary vigour. He stands like a rock in the midst of the sea unshaken; he is steadfast and immoveable, like a pillar in the temple of his God. He is much of the same mind, in that point, with that brave heathen, who spake thus to himself when temptation was strong: "Deliberate man; yield not rashly; 'tis a great work that lies upon thy hands, 'tis a divine work, 'tis for a kingdom, the kingdom of God." (Ar. Epict. l. ii. c. 18.) Now remember thy God, let's see what thy love to thy God is; remember his presence; he beholds how thou standest deliberating whether thou shouldst fight for him or against him. For shame! show not thyself so basely disingenuous. Remember what thy God, thy Friend, did for thee at such and such a time. Remember how kindly you were entertained by him the last time you were at his house. Whose sword is it that you wear by your side? Who gave you it? Did not God give it to you to fight against his enemies? And will you draw it against himself? Remember from whence you had all that you do enjoy; and can you find in your heart to take God's mercies, gold, silver, and food, and bestow them all upon that which he hates? Will you quarter and keep in pay, with God's coin, his greatest enemy? And if you feel your heart still staggering, and scarce able to keep its ground, then remember God stands by, Christ looks on, and sees how gallantly any champion of his will demean himself on his quarrel; and that there is not a more lovely sight upon the earth than to behold one of his friends rather venturing his life than he will bear that the least indignity or affront should be put upon his God! Oh happy are they that can always act as in the sight of God! And if the soul can have but a constant fresh sense of its relation to God and his eye, it is impossible but that it should hate sin, which is so directly opposite to him. Happy are those who by the thoughts of God are enraged against sin! Is it not enough, saith that heavenly soul that is acquainted with God, that I have done such and such things against God, when I knew him not, but that I should again engage against him after I have been obliged by a thousand mercies, after I have tasted and seen how good the Lord is? Is it a light matter that I did so long after fight against him then? And shall I now renew my rebellions, when I have had so much experience of the folly and madness of such a war, where I shall be as surely conquered as I draw my sword? And hath God kept me by a miracle of mercy out of hell, and after I had run out so wretchedly, and undone myself, set me up again, after I had played the prodigal, received me again into favour? And shall I after all deal thus basely by him? No, I'll die a thousand deaths before I will willingly yield to anything that may be in the least offensive to Him whom my soul hath such an infinite reason to love above the whole world. The knowledge of God's service, and Satan's too, makes a soul distinguish. He that knows what it is to be made free by Christ, abhors his old master; he remembers full well the great hardship that he then underwent, when he had nothing to live upon but husks; he calls to mind the clay and mortar, he cannot forget the cruel vassalage that he served under; garlic and onions were his dainties; and truly he cannot desire to leave his manna for such kind of food; he is not in love with the whip and scourge; he doth not dote upon the fetters, or the iron which went into his soul; but he is glad with all his heart to be free from those taskmasters who made him serve with rigour; he hath no mind to return to his old work. My meaning in all this is: he that was a servant and a drudge of Satan's, and a slave to his lust, when he once comes to taste the sweetness of spiritual liberty, to be made free by Christ, he hath no desire again to be enslaved, but doth, with the greatest detestation, reject all the proposals and promises that the devil makes, to bring this business about; he knows Satan too well to love his service; he remembers that all his pay was promises, and no more; he remembers that he fed him with poison, and made him do that which had like to break his bones, and undo him for ever; he sees what Satan's designs were; and what had become of him quickly, if he had gone on in his service; he believes chains to be chains, though they be of gold; believes that poison will kill him, though it may be sweet in the mouth; he hath now such a sense of the evil and baseness of sin, as being so infinitely loathsome to God, that he hates it with a perfect hatred; he hath a will in some measure conformed to the will of God; and what his Friend the Lord loves, he cannot hate, and where his God hates he cannot love. "Do not I hate them, O Lord, that hate thee? and am not I grieved with those that rise up against thee? I hate them with perfect hatred; I count them mine enemies," Ps. cxxxix. 21, 22. Now, what is it that stirs the Psalmist's choler so much? Why, he had been working upon his own heart, in the former part of the psalm, the doctrine of God's omniscience and goodness, and by meditation upon this subject, he was brought under a lively sense of the greatness of divine kindness; and while his heart did thus muse, the fire burnt, his soul was in a flame against sin: "How precious are thy thoughts unto me, O God!" ver. 17. Oh, when the soul, hath sweet thoughts of God, it will have sour thoughts of sin. When the soul loves God dearly, it cannot choose but hate sin entirely. None behold such deformity in sin as those who behold most beauty in God. Hence it is that some of the people of God have (nay all of them that are really acquainted with God are of the same mind) counted it more desirable to leap into the flames than to venture upon a known sin. It was no untruth in the absolute position, though falsely applied by Job's friend, that it is a great wickedness to choose the least sin before the greatest suffering, Job xxxvi. 21. What was it that made Paul so weary of himself? What burden was it that made his back to ache? What pains causeth those bitter groans? Rom. vii. Was it not sin? And why did not Paul groan before as well as then? Was it because he then had no sin at all, or less sin than when he made that bitter complaint? No such matter; but because he had then less acquaintance with God. But now he is become acquainted with God, the more he doth abhor himself for sin. He now knows better than he did; his eyes are opened, and he sees sin in its colours, and he looks upon it as so great an evil that he doth want words to express the odious nature of it; therefore, because he cannot find a worse word, he calls sin by its own name, sinful sin; which he thought a more significant epithet than if he had called it devilish sin. What makes the children of God to be so weary of this world, and so desirous to be upon the wing? Why, it is because of better acquaintance elsewhere. They know that then they shall put off that carrion that now they carry about with them, sin I mean, which, like a dead carcass bound to a living, doth now stink so abominably in their nostrils; they know that then they shall have a sweeter smell, and themselves also smell more savoury in the nostrils of God; they know that poverty shall be swallowed up with riches, want with fulness, sin with holiness, misery with happiness; they have an inheritance, a city wherein dwelleth righteousness, and nothing that is unclean shall enter into it; and when they come thither they know the case will be altered with them, and that though now they bear about with them a body of death and sin, yet then they shall have a body as pure, as bright, and glorious as the sun; they shall be presented by Christ to the Father without spot or wrinkle, or any such thing. Each knows that as long as he is thus sullied by his sin, his great Friend will not take so much pleasure in his company. Isaac and Ishmael, the ark and dagon, God and sin cannot dwell in the same heart; therefore he desires to have less of sin's company that he may have more of God's; none of sin's company, that he may have always God's company. Observe that constantly in your own experience and others', those who walk most close with God are most tender as to the matter of sin; and those who are less in converse with God are more bold in venturing upon sin, and after it is committed they have less regret. What is the reason that one can swallow anything almost, and another is afraid of the least appearance of evil? he hates the garment spotted with the flesh; he is as fearful of clothing himself with wickedness as of putting on the garments of one that hath had the leprosy or plague upon him; he hates vain thoughts, because he loves God and his laws, Ps. cxix. 104, 113.

3. Another glorious effect of acquaintance with God is, that it makes one to have very low and undervaluing

thoughts of the world. When the saint hath been, with Paul, raised up to the third heaven, when he hath had some intimate converse with God, he can look the world into almost nothing; nay, if it stand in competition with Christ, he counts it but as dung and dross in comparison of the excellency of the knowledge of Christ Jesus his Lord, Phil. iii. 8; he can then set a higher value upon the light of God's countenance than upon corn, and wine, and oil. It is because that poor creatures know no better, that they dote so much upon the world. Did they but know what it is to have one look of love from God, were they but acquainted with the glory of another world, they would soon disrelish everything else; nothing will down with them who have been feasted in God's house but those royal dainties. Taste the world who will, saith the saint, give me but more grace, more of Christ's company; let me but maintain an intimate familiarity with God; let me be but better acquainted with him, and be more frequently refreshed with his smiles; this is all that I desire upon earth; this is all that I expect to make my happiness complete in heaven. "Whom have I in heaven but thee? and there is none upon earth that I can desire besides thee." It was not without good reason that the Psalmist prizes the commands of God above gold and silver. It was no mistake in Solomon to count wisdom more excellent than the finest gold, and more precious than rubies. That spiritual merchant knew what he did when he sold all that he had for that pearl of great price; he was sure he should be no loser by such a bargain. Bring me a heavenly creature that hath had a view by faith of the glory of God's countenance, that hath been in his company, that hath been brought into his banqueting-house; such a one I am confident can easily spare that which most keep such a fearful stir about; he can spare the world for them who are like to have no better portion. Give him but more of those spiritual pleasures which he hath had in communion with God, and he desires no more. He can now speak it, and speak it in good earnest, that there is no comparison between this world and another; he can now call this world a shadow, and the glory of it grass, and write vanity, emptiness, and vexation upon its beautiful face, and contemn all its smiles and frowns, and look upon its greatest lovers as persons that deserve to be pitied rather than envied, whose portion is so small, whose happiness is so short, and whose misery and mistake are so great and dismal. It is a common thing for men to declaim against the world, and to say it is but a little muck; it is no unusual thing for its greatest lovers to speak against it, and say that it is that which passeth away; but yet for all that they pursue it more than heaven, and are more earnest for it than the salvation of their souls, and more troubled at the thought of parting with it than at the thought of their parting with God; and the loss of it troubles them more than if we tell them of the loss of their souls. Such as these will not say but that God is infinitely more to be loved than the whole world; but yet if the world and God stand in competition, they stand not long disputing which must give place; the world hath the uppermost room in the heart. But whence is this mistake? How comes the servant to ride, and the Master to go on foot? Why is the world preferred before God? Why, hence it is man knows not God, he is not acquainted with his excellency; the world is sensible, he sees it, he feels it, he tastes it. And so he doth not the things that are invisible. And no wonder, then, that sense bears the sway; the man wants faith to realize invisibles; he wants senses spiritually exercised. But now he that knows God, and is acquainted with spiritual things, hath quite another apprehension of the world; and that not only from faith, but sometimes from a spiritual sense, and he can say that divine pleasures, riches, and enjoyments do as sensibly refresh him, yea, abundantly more than ever the world did. And when he hath been newly taking a walk in that heavenly paradise, he looks back upon this world with grief and indignation, that he should ever love the world with his heart, when there was One that did infinitely more deserve his love, when there was a God, Christ, and holiness to be loved; that he should be such a child, such a fool as to run after butterflies, quarrel for a feather, hunt for a shadow, while God, Christ, and glory, those great substances, lay by unregarded. Now he grudges that anything should have his love but his God; his dearest relations, if they stand in God's way, must be run over, despised, hated. That which the men of the world fight, and kill, and spare not to damn their souls for, he sees now to be a pitiful worthless thing, which cannot defer death a moment, nor stand him in any stead in another world. He is all for that coin which will go current in another country; and if he be but rich in promises, rich in spiritual relations, rich in grace, he takes himself for no unhappy man; let the world speak or think what they will of him, he doth not much pass upon it; he believes that he is but a pilgrim and stranger here, and if he meet with no great kindness, it is but that which he expected. The truth of it is, he is almost afraid of the smiles of the world, not being ignorant of this, that whom it kisses, it intends to betray; he cannot be over-fond of that which in all probability will keep God and him at a greater distance, and make his passage to glory next to impossible. He reckons that it is better being rich in grace than rich in purse; and that he who lays up for his body, and provides not for his soul, is the greatest fool in the world. Tell such a one as Moses of riches, honours, and preferments; he thinks them but poor sorry things for a man of Israel to be taken with, and he will rather see them in the dirt, than part company with his suffering brethren, much less with God. It is storied of Anaxagoras, that he seemed to be very little concerned when his country was in a flame; upon which, being taxed by some, he made this reply, "There is none of you all care more for your country than I do for mine," pointing with his finger up to heaven. Thus it is with the people of God; let others talk of riches and honours; but there is none of them all do value true riches as they do. But here is the difference: one thinks he hath riches when he hath the command of a great deal of gold and silver; the other knows he hath riches when he hath Christ and grace, and can have good returns out of that other world. And which of these is the wisest will erelong be seen. One looks upon heaven and glory as a shadow, a fable, and the things of this world as the only realities; the other looks upon heaven, God, and eternity, as the greatest realities, and most worthy of his highest valuation, and the things of this world as flying shadows, which cannot fill the arms of him that doth embrace them. And under this apprehension and sense of things, no marvel that he doth prefer the substance before the shadow. He believes with that worthy, that he was born for other things than to eat and drink, and sleep, or to take his pleasure, or to get an estate; he knows that the business in this world is to provide for another, to get his peace made with God, to contemplate heaven, and to get thither; and therefore you must not count it strange that such a person as this is somewhat cold and remiss in his carrying on of lower designs; he knows that the disproportion between finite and infinite, time and eternity, is no such inconsiderable one as the most count upon. Again, he hath more than once experienced this, that the very joys and comforts that are to be had in the enjoying of communion with God, even in this world, are unspeakably more intense and refreshing than the highest sensual pleasures in the world. One that is acquainted with God will take the word of his Friend for true, which word tells him that whatsoever is presented to his sense, the world and all that is therein, must erelong be burnt up; whereupon he thinks it no imprudence at all to hazard present enjoyments for future hopes, no folly to look after something that will bear the flame. He thinks it scarce worth the while to be born to possess, if it were a whole world, except he were sure of having something after it that were better than what he met with here; he had rather have one smile from his Friend than thousands of gold and silver; he would not for a world have his portion here, though it be never so large a one: he had rather by far be with Lazarus upon a dunghill than sit with Dives in a chair of state, before the richest fare that the sea, or air, or earth could afford him; he would not change conditions with those who enjoy the most of the things of this world; he can thankfully want that which most commonly makes its possessors miserable. Oh, could you but talk with a man that lives in heaven while he is upon earth, and could you but see and hear how much he slights that which you adore! Give me neither poverty nor riches, but food convenient for me, is the highest that he dare pray for. He had rather live in a smoking cottage, and have God for his companion, than dwell in the greatest palace, and have the devil for his neighbour, counsellor, and master. When a man hath been in heaven by contemplation, though his body be upon the earth, yet the best part of him, his affection, his love, joy, and heart, is still there. "One that doth converse with God here is indeed that earthly lump, his body is below; but could you see his thoughts, could you look into his heart, and see the inward actings of his soul, you should see the man out of the world discoursing with God; he sticks close to the company of his Friend: he is like the sunbeams, which, though they reach the earth, yet still abide there from whence they are sent, and are most intensely hot nearest the fountain, the sun." (Sen. Ep. xli.) So the soul and thoughts of a child of God, they may, nay, they cannot but glance upon the world; but his most vigorous spiritual actings are towards God, and the heat of his affections are abundantly more remiss and cold when they beat upon earthly objects. He that knows what it is to have the company of God is almost ready to wonder how any one can be content with anything below God; and as for himself, he takes himself for little better than a prisoner, while his soul is pent up in a body which is so unwieldy as to all spiritual employments, till it be refined by the grave. He would not dwell here for ever, for a world, though he might enjoy more content than ever any since the fall did. A soul acquainted with God is a noble creature indeed; he scorns petty low things; he thinks no estate big enough for him, but that which is infinite; he looks upon himself as a citizen of no mean city, a denizen of Zion, a freeman of the New Jerusalem, one of the royal society, over which Christ, that King of glory, is the President; his inheritance is greater than that which the sun compasseth in its course. Oh when, saith such a one, shall I leave these cities of Cabul, and dwell with the King at Jerusalem? Oh when shall my soul be safely asked? Oh when shall I be upon the wing for heaven? Oh when shall I leave this body there whence it first came? When shall I go out of this cell, this cage? Oh that I were once safe in heaven! Oh that I were in the immediate presence of God, and might stand for ever before him, and have his blessed society for ever and ever! Neither am I quite without him; but how little, oh how little is it that I now enjoy! Oh when shall I enter into the possession of that better, longer life? I stay and long for that separating, or rather uniting hour, which will separate my soul from my body, from my dross, but perfectly unite me to God. Look then, O my soul, upon all that thou seest below but as so many inns and resting-places for a pilgrim to take some little refreshment in, and then to be gone. That day, O my fearful soul, which thou sometimes fearest as my last, is the birthday of eternity. Oh what mean we to love our prisons, fetters, burdens? Why are we so much pleased with our miseries, and afraid of our happiness? Oh this unbelief! Oh were Christians but more in the company of God by faith and meditation, they would look upon God as great, and the world as a very small thing. He that knows God to be great, sees everything below him little. It is an infallible argument of a divine and excellent soul, and one that hath acquaintance with God, when he can judge all beneath God as low, sordid, base, and utterly unworthy of the respect of his soul.

4. Another glorious effect of acquaintance with God is, that it will ease us of all sorrows, or cure all sorrows. As soon as any one hath but a saving knowledge of Christ, he is in such a condition as that he need not trouble his head with care, nor his heart with fear; no more than a rich heir that hath a tender-hearted, loving, wise father, need trouble himself what he shall do for bread and clothing: as long as the great cause of fear is taken away, so long he is well enough. As for those that are unacquainted with God, they either are always afraid, or have cause always to be afraid: but as for a child of God, that scripture buoys up his soul under the mightiest ways of fear: "There is no condemnation to them which are in Christ Jesus," Rom. viii. 1. He that is in covenant with God may in this world undergo

some petty injuries, some insurrection may be made against him; but this is his comfort, he is sure never to be quite overpowered, never to be finally conquered. Oh the disquietments and fears that strangers and enemies are compassed with, or will be! And oh the joys, the security, the true security that some have! at what a rate do they live, and how bravely do they die! "Mark the perfect, and behold the upright man; for the end of that man is peace." This was touched upon before, when I opened the nature and qualifications of this Friend, and therefore I need say the less here; yet it being the great inquiry of the wisest, how they may be sheltered from this storm, what they shall do to be cured of these heart-qualms, how they may be freed from fears, I shall not altogether pass it over in this place. I cannot but encourage poor strangers, as they value the truest comforts, as they would be free from fear and trembling when the foundations of the earth shall be shaken, when the mountains shall tremble, and melt at the presence of God, the mighty God of Jacob, when the heaven shall be rolled together as a scroll, and be all of a flame. Make sure of this Friend. It is impossible that one that hath such a One for his Friend should be much daunted. When he hears of wars, and rumours of wars, when the pestilence rages, when there are dreadful earthquakes in sundry places, and such distress of nations and perplexities, that the stoutest heart shall sink that hath not this to support, then a child of God may lift up his head with comfort, because his redemption draweth near. There is a vast difference between a godly man and a wicked, as to their affections, fears, joys, desires, hopes. The godly thinks long for that which the wicked wishes with all his heart might never be,—the day of judgment. The righteous man is even delighted with the forethoughts of that, the thoughts of which doth put a damp upon all the comforts of the ungodly; he rejoiceth in that which makes his neighbour tremble. As for death, a gracious heart that hath kept his watch, and maintained a sweet and constant correspondence with God, and hath had his heart in heaven, and can look upon the great Jehovah as his Friend, cannot be very much affrighted at his approach; he is not much appalled, when he looks out at the window, and sees this messenger making haste to his house; and when he knocks at his door, he dares let him in, and can heartily bid him welcome; he understands whence he comes, and what his errand is; and though he look somewhat grimly, yet as long as he comes to conduct him to his Friend's house, he can dispense with that: he hath more reason to speak so than he who said, "Let me make haste away to my country; there are my excellent ancestors, there dwell my noble relations, there is the constant residence of my dearest friends." (Plotinus.) "Oh happy will that day be when I shall come into that glorious assembly, when I shall have better company than Homer, Orpheus, Socrates, Cato, when I shall sit down with Abraham, Isaac, and Jacob, in the palace of their Friend and mine! O happy day, when I shall come to my Father's house, to that general assembly, the church of the first-born, to an innumerable company of angels, to Jesus, the Mediator of the new covenant, and to the spirits of just men made perfect!" (Tull.) A man's knowledge of other things may add to his fears, and make his miseries greater; but the more knowledge we have of God, the less our fears and sorrows must needs be: and when our knowledge of God is perfect, all our fears and sorrows shall be for ever blown over. I cannot omit a brave speech of that noble Stoic which comes to my mind: "If the acquaintance and favour of Cæsar can keep you (as you are made to believe) from some fears, how much rather to have God for your Father and Friend! How little cause have such to be afraid at any time of anything; death itself is not evil to a friend of God: he may say, Come, let us go quickly to our Father's house; our Father calls us." (Ar. Epict. l. i. c. 7.) And doth this seem a small matter to you? Believe it, when you come to die, you will be of another mind then: you will think that it is a cordial worth any money, that will raise your spirits at such a time, and make you, with a smiling countenance, pass into an everlasting state. It is but a folly to expect that anything in the world should do this for us but the knowledge of our interest in God. It is possible indeed to get some stupifying intoxicating stuff, that makes a man die like a beast, without any great horror; the devil's shop will furnish poor dying creatures with enough of that; nay, he is glad if he can keep men asleep till death awaken them; but miserable is that man who is beholden to the devil for his cordials; miserable is he who has nothing to keep him from a hell upon earth but his own ignorance and the devil's word. I promise you, 'tis none of the most joyful spectacles to an enlightened soul, to look upon one that lived wickedly and died peaceably. You would think that a poor man that is going to execution had little cause to smile, though he should ride to the gallows upon an easy-going horse, or in a coach. The swine is usually very still, when the butcher is making preparation to plunge the knife in his throat. It is no unusual thing for a vile unsanctified sinner to leap with a mad confidence into eternity; but he alone hath a solid peace who hath God for his Friend. This is the only man that hath just cause to sing for joy when his soul is going into another world. It was none of the worst counsel which he gave, whosoever he was, who said, that it doth highly concern us seriously to think of terrible things, which we must most certainly see erelong, and to lay in such provision as may make us fit to grapple with them when they come. Oh for that which will keep us from crying out hereafter, What shall I do? woe is me! I am undone! Were it so that there were such rare extraction to be made as would certainly prolong our lives as long as we would, and make us always cheerful, what striving would there be to get such a receipt! Oh, how would the great ones bring out their bags to purchase it at any rate! How willing would they mortgage all their lands, part with their richest jewels to buy it! and yet how little will they expend for that which, if they had, would prove far more effectual! Oh, would men and women but understand themselves, and mind their business, what sweet lives might they lead! what a calm might there be constantly upon their spirits! How cheerfully might they live, and how joyfully might they die! Tully saith that he and many others had been gathering the most powerful herbs that they could find to cure all fears; "but," saith he, "I know not what is the matter, the disease is still stronger than the remedy." And dost thou not know, O Tully, what's the matter? Why then, I will tell thee. One principal ingredient was left out, viz., faith in the blood of Christ, and union with God by virtue of that blood. He that is by Christ brought to be acquainted with God need not much fear griefs, sorrows, and such things as Christ was acquainted with for him; he hath unstinged death, and sweetened the grave: all his troubles are now but as physic, the poison of them is corrected; though the pill be bitter, yet it is of his Friend's composing, and therefore he may take it without any turning away of his head. "Show me a man," said old Epictetus, "that is happy truly in his life, and happy in his death, happy in his health and in his sickness; happy when poor, scorned, tormented, and banished; in a word, happy in all conditions." Oh that I could but talk with such a man! Oh that I could see such a spectacle! Such a one as my eyes never yet beheld! Why, I will tell thee the reason of it, O Epictetus, it is because thou never sawest a Christian, one that was acquainted with God; for let me tell the world, through grace I have seen such a sight, and do believe it to be the most lovely sight on this side heaven. I have seen one smiling when his jaws have been falling, and eye-strings breaking; rejoicing, when most about him were weeping, and accounting it a high act of patience to be willing to live. And how do you like such a condition? Is it better to lie quivering, shaking, and groaning, or rejoicing, and praising, and admiring free grace, and setting forth the riches of God's love and goodness? Which of these would you choose? I can easily believe that few are so bad but that they could be contented, as well as Balaam, to die the death of the righteous, and to have their latter end like his. But would you die joyfully? Why then, you must live holily; get acquainted with God, and then this may be your state. I remember Seneca speaks of one Pacuvius, who, when he was drunk, cried out, "Βεβίωκα—I have been alive," very merrily. But had he well understood himself, he would have thought he had had much better reason to have cried out, "I am dead, I am dead." But, however, what he said ungroundedly and wickedly, a child of God may easily and thankfully say; when he is going to his last sleep, he may with joy and cheerfulness say, I have lived, and, through grace, I have kept a fair correspondence with my God, my Friend, with whom I am now going to dwell for ever. Do not think, therefore, that I come to take away your comforts and joys, when I come to persuade you to get acquaintance with God; no such matter, I would have you learn to rejoice, but yet I would that that joy should be born from above, that the foundation of it should be the knowledge of your interest in God's love. Other joys may make you have a smiling countenance, but they do not raise and fill the soul; for I must tell you, I am far from thinking that every one that laughs is joyful and without fears. Give me a man that knows that God is his portion, and heaven his inheritance, that knows with what Friend, and in what a happy state he shall live after death; this, this is the cheerful man: such a one as this can overlook momentary sorrows; he understands full well that the case will be quickly altered with him; and the thoughts of eternal happiness do swallow up his temporal miseries. Tell one of God's acquaintance of poverty, he values it not, as long as he knows he hath a brave estate that cannot be confiscated, riches that none can take from him, a treasure that thieves cannot break through to, and steal. As for all worldly things, he knows that before a few years are over he must part with them for ever; he is of that man's mind, who, having a considerable sum of money and precious jewels hid in his saddle, and a little odd money in his pocket, was set upon by thieves; who readily went to his pocket, and took what was there, and looked no further. Now the man, escaping clear with his main treasure, is so joyful that he takes no notice of what was stolen from him. Thus a child of God, if he lose his estate, his liberty, and all his outward enjoyments, counts all these but inconsiderable, as long as his soul is safe, his great treasure is out of their reach. Tell him of torments, racks, flames, or what the policy of hell can invent, he is not ignorant of this, that the more he suffers for Christ's sake, the greater cause he hath to rejoice, to be exceeding glad, for great shall be his reward in heaven, and while they add to his sufferings, they add to his glory; and though against their will, while they would injure him, they do him the greatest kindness; this light affliction works for him a far more exceeding and eternal weight of glory. As long as his torments want that dreadful epithet, *eternal*, he doth not much pass; the thoughts of God's love makes man's hatred inconsiderable. Oh how sweet are the thoughts of his Friend, when his enemies are most bitter! Blessed be God, as for those intolerable torments, he knows it's beyond man's power, and far from God's will to inflict them upon him, and so long he cares not much. All other tortures are but a flea-bite to the pains of hell and an enraged conscience; he can almost dare the world and the devil to do their worst, as being confident of this, that as long as he is dear to God, his soul is out of their reach. Threaten him with banishment, he remembers that he hath a Friend that will find him out, and bear him company wheresoever he is. Tell him of the barbarous unkindness and treachery of former friends; he reads that his betters have been worse handled by their pretended friends; above all, this cheers him, to think that all his friends will not serve him so; he hath one Friend that will never forsake him, never be unfaithful to him. Now, bring a wicked man upon earth, that is without his sorrows; I know there is none, no, not one; there is none of them all, but if he were within the sight of those devouring flames, would tremble. Those that have wickedness enough to dare God, will not have courage enough to look him in the face when he shall appear in flaming fire to execute vengeance upon the ungodly; he that will not now be troubled at the doing of wickedness, will be troubled hereafter at the suffering for it. Let sinners say what they will, I am sure they cannot be long without fears, to behold Christ and his dear servants coming together in the clouds, with millions of mighty angels, to judge the world; I am confident it will be such an amazing sight as cannot choose but cool their courage, and make the stoutest heart of them all to ache; I am sure that as light as they make of damnation and God's displeasure, that the day is coming when they will believe it was no such cowardice to be afraid of an angry God, to fly from the wrath to come, and to run away from so formidable an enemy as sin; so that it is clear that a wicked man will first or last be a fearful man; a "*Magor missakib*—Fear on every side," shall be his name. But now he that doth exceedingly fear to offend God need not exceedingly fear anything else; and he that fears not God hath cause enough to fear everything. Oh sirs, it's a brave thing to be able to take death cheerfully by the hand, and to walk with him joyfully into another world; and this, I say again, a man acquainted with God may do; he hath this to comfort him, death doth more properly give him life than take it away from him, and as soon as he is dead his sin shall die too, and his grace live and act without control; then he shall live a life of joy, a life of perfect holiness, such a life as saints and angels live, such a life as Christ lives, the life of God, a life without death, an everlasting life; and why then should he be afraid of dying? As for his old companion the body, it is gone to rest, and will erelong be awakened, and rise from its bed more vigorous and fit for those noble employments in which it must be engaged for ever. And soul and body shall meet with more comfort than now they part with pain, when the body shall be in another kind of dress than now it wears, and that also shall in some respects be like the soul, agile, holy, and immortal. This is such a man that I can call happy, and so erelong will those that now scorn and persecute him call him too. Blessed is he that in his life is holy and cheerful, but most cheerful and perfect at his death. This is the happy portion of God's acquaintance, this is the heritage of the friends of the Bridegroom. I have read of a wise man that would commend and be thankful for everything, because he was sure a Friend of his had the management of everything, whose understanding was infinite, and whose wisdom was unsearchable, who could and would work his own honour and his friends' comforts out of everything, yea, though seemingly evil; for the greater the evil seems to be, the greater will be the real kindness which makes so much good out of it. Oh, but I have lately lost many of my most near and precious relations! If thou art one of God's friends, let me tell thee for thy comfort, you will meet them at your Friend's house, when you come thither. It was no unsuitable advice that *he* gave to his friend Lucilius, to cheer him up after the loss of a dear friend: "Let us consider, my dear Lucilius, that we ourselves should be glad to be in that place, and to enjoy that company, which you are so sad that your friend is gone to; and he that you say is lost, is not so, but happy before you." We do not judge rightly of things. Well then, would you know what a man is? Would you pass a true estimate of him, and understand his worth and value? Why then, consider the man without his riches, lay aside his honours, take away all his externals from him; nay, further, let us see the man naked out of his body, and how doth the soul look? Is it now rich, beautiful, joyful? Can it stand confidently before God? Doth it appear cheerfully in the presence of its Maker? Why, this is something; it matters not much whether his body were fed with pulse or dainties, clothed with rags or scarlet; it matters not whether his soul went out of his mouth or at a wound, whether he died in a bed of down or in flames. Methinks by this time you should be ready to think that religion is an excellent thing, that God's acquaintance is desirable, and that no life is like the life of a Christian, all whose sorrows end in joys, whose miseries make him more happy, whose shame for Christ will make for his glory; in a word, whose death brings him into life. "This is the generation of them that seek thee, that seek thy face, O Jacob."

5. Another effect of acquaintance with God is, that it will make us honour him more highly. Here familiarity is far from breeding contempt. Those that are strangers to God see not his worth and excellency, they honour him not, but they have the most vile, low, contemptible thoughts of the infinitely glorious majesty, and they think anything will serve his turn; they make more bold with him than they would do with a man like themselves; they put him off with the leavings of the world; when they have been feeding their lusts, and serving their pleasures, and gratifying the devil all the day long, then they come between sleep and

awake, and pretend a great deal of love to him, and anger with themselves for their sin, whereas God knows they do but play the hypocrites in all they do, and mean nothing that they say: lip-devotion, knee-religion God shall have, and but a little of that too, and that pitiful stuff that they present him with they think God is very much beholden to them for. As for the sanctifying the Lord God in their hearts; as for inward heart-love, as for high prizings and admirings of God; as for a real honouring of God, and worshipping of him in spirit and in truth, it is that which they understand not; and as for those who do, they laugh at them, as if they were guilty of the greatest folly in the world. But now he who converseth with God beholds such a beauty, excellency, majesty, and glory in him, that it is ready quite to swallow up his soul; he speaks much of God, but yet he thinks more; he wonders that a God of such infinite goodness should be no more loved, that a God of such infinite greatness, justice, and holiness, should be no more feared, that a God of such unspeakable power should be no more obeyed; and while he remembers his own contempt of God in former times, and the too mean thoughts that he hath at present of him, he doth even stand astonished to think that he should be on this side the state of the damned. He that before thought everything too much for God, now thinks nothing enough for him. The man is strangely changed by his new acquaintance, so that he may not improperly be called a new man, all things are new with him. In honour to this new guest, he hath got on new clothes, he is clad with righteousness as with a garment; new food, it is his meat and drink to do the will of his Father which is in heaven; new drink, wine on the lees, well refined; he draws all out of those wells of consolation, the promises: he hath new thoughts, words, and actions; God, invisibles, and all the things of faith are now substances with him. Now the threats or promises of a God are not counted small matters; heaven, hell, and eternity, go for the greatest realities, because God saith they are such. So, he that sometimes lived without God in the world, had no respect at all to his glory, but valued himself and his most base lust, and the devil himself, before God, doth now respect God's glory in all that he doth; he ventures upon nothing deliberately, but what may please him; religion runs through all he doth; he eats, he drinks, and sleeps, and clothes himself, he prays, he works, he recreates himself, with a design for God. The grand project he still is carrying on, is the honour of God. He will undertake nothing of importance before he consult with his Friend and hath his advice and direction. Whatsoever he hath that is worth anything, he sends it to this Friend, he presents him with his first fruits, he sacrificeth his male, the best of his flock; desires that his Friend may be always at his house, and that he may have the best entertainment that he can possibly give; and he is ashamed at the best, that he can make him no more welcome whom he so highly honours; he is grieved that his entertainment is no better; he would fain give God his first and last thoughts, his warmest affections; he would gladly have the strength and vigour of body and soul spent in his service; he studies how to improve all mercies and enjoyments for God, to take hold of all opportunities that he possibly can, and to make the best of them for the promoting that grand design which he hath on foot, his honour; he thinks not wife and children, houses and lands, body, soul, and all that he can make in the world, too good for him. Whatever temptations he conquers, whatsoever sin he slays, whatsoever piece of gallantry or prowess he hath done in his inroads upon Satan's kingdom, he gives the honour of all to the valour, conduct, and assistance of this his noble Ally and Friend. He sets the crown of the King of Ammon, like Joab, upon the head of this King David. He hath such a high esteem for God, that he thinks nothing well done but when it is done exactly as he would have it; he thinks everything then best, when it is done according to God's will; and he counts it no small weakness to be unwilling that infinite wisdom rather than folly should have the managing of all the affairs of the world. He desires to maintain a quick and lively sense of the divine majesty upon his soul, and that he may here and hereafter give him, as he hath infinite cause, all honour, glory, and praise,

6. Another effect of this acquaintance with God is this: it would put abundance of life and vigour into the soul; it would, as it were, oil the wheels, and set them a-running. There are none in the world that act at so high a rate as those do who are most acquainted with God. Oh, how indefatigable are they in their pains! With what earnestness and faith do they pray, as if they saw the glorious God before them, and were talking with him! With what reverence, seriousness, and delight do they read, meditate, and hear the word, and do all that they do! They know in some measure what it is to present their bodies and souls as a living sacrifice to God through Christ; they understand what it means to be fervent in spirit, serving the Lord. Such a man will not serve God with what cost him nothing; kneeling down, and saying a few formal words before God in the evening, repeating the Lord's prayer, and the creed, and the ten commandments, between sleeping and waking, doing nobody any wrong, and the like, is not enough to serve his turn; his conscience will not be thus put off; but he labours with all his might to stir up his soul to lay hold upon God; he is not content to go off from his knees without his Father's blessing. This is the friend and acquaintance of God; this is the brave Israelite, that spiritual prince, that will not let God go till he hath prevailed with him. He doth not go to his work as if he cared not whether he worked or no; he is not sick of the service of God, but he rejoices and works righteousness; his work is his pleasure, and he goes on merrily with his business. Those that are intimately acquainted with God are not so cold, faint, and dull in the service of God as others be. Such a one as knows God very well, and hath been oft made welcome by him, why, he comes with a great deal of confidence, and knocks at God's door, and, for his part, he will not go away, though the door be not presently opened; but he continues knocking, because he is sure that his Friend is within; he knows that he is never from home, and that he can never come unseasonably to him. He comes to prayer as if he were going to storm heaven, he gets spiritual things by violence; he comes to duty as to fight for a crown; he is

ashamed to offer the lame and the blind to God, but he chooseth for him the best in his flock; he desires to improve his interest in God to the height; this favourite of heaven comes frequently to the King to beg some great thing or other; and he is sure that his Friend will deny him nothing that it is not a greater kindness to deny than give; he knows that his King hath a large purse, and as large a heart, and he is not willing to lose such excellent things that are to be had for the asking for; he is not ignorant that spiritual things are worth the seeking for, and therefore he will seek, and seek earnestly; he hath tried more than once, and he remembers to his joy, that wonderful things are to be had, if we will but take pains for them, and prefer our petitions, or rather get them preferred by that great Master of requests the Lord Jesus Christ, and follow our business closely, that it cannot possibly miscarry, let it be what it will; the comfort in enjoying will abundantly pay all the charges we can be at in seeking; therefore he lays about him as one that is in good earnest; the confidence that he hath in the good will of God, puts life into all his petitions. A poor creature that very rarely enjoys any communion with God, that is very little or not at all acquainted with him, is ready to take up with a few formal complimental performances; he is weary of his work before he hath well begun it; he is quickly out of breath; but now, one that is very well acquainted with God is not so soon weary of his company; it may be, he may be somewhat cold when he sets out, but when he hath gone a few turns with his Friend, his blood grows warm; he is sometimes so taken up with God in duty, that he can scarce tell when to have done. Oh, he thinks it is good being there! Oh, it was a sweet season! These are the actings and experiences of some noble souls. I have heard some Christians say, that had not God made it their duty to follow their callings, they could be glad with all their hearts to do nothing else, day or night, but hear the mysteries of God's love in Christ opened, read, pray, meditate, and be immediately engaged in the service of God. Sure something is the matter with these persons more than ordinary, that their palate should be so spiritualized, as that it is their food, their wine, their dainties, to be actually employed in the great acts of religion. The more any one is acquainted with God, the more delight he takes in the ordinances of God; as one of God's children, he desires the sincere milk of the word. Before he was acquainted with God, he found it far otherwise; then nothing almost would down with him, the pure word could not be relished, except it was adulterated with flourishes of human wit. He had very little appetite to good wholesome food, his stomach was ready to turn at it, except it were so cooked, and sauced, and set out, that an understanding man could scarce tell what to make of it. What do you say to this, you that are so faint and cold in what you do in the service of God? Come a little nearer, get better acquainted with God, and you shall find such entertainment from him, that you will scarce be able to keep long from his house; get oft into his company, and you shall feel your soul strengthened with new spirits, animated with a strange life, heat, and warmth. You will not complain that the Sabbath is the longest day in the week; you will not say, "What a weariness is it! when will the new moons and sabbaths be at an end?" But you would think long till the Sabbath-day come, and when it is come, the pleasure that you take in the work of that day would make you think it the shortest day, and gone too soon: and when you have spent it in the most diligent attendance upon God, you would wish it were to begin again, or that you were to begin such a Sabbath as would never have an end. This is the condition of one that is very intimately acquainted with God; his nearness to his Master makes him follow his work, and he knows he shall lose nothing by it; something will be coming in ever and anon, which will more than quit his cost; so that when God calls, he is at hand, and readily answers, "Speak, Lord, for thy servant heareth." When God hath any message, any hot service to do, he accounts it his great honour to be employed in it, and saith, "Here I am, send me." I believe he that spoke it (Ar. Ep. l. c. 9) might be a little confident, when he said, "Lay what thou wilt upon me, O God, I have power to bear it; it shall not be my burden, but my ornament." Yet I am persuaded one that is acquainted with God can say it, and say it again in good earnest, "Lord, what wilt thou have me to do? Wilt thou have me to preach for thee, to run through fire and water for thee, to die for thee, to go or come? O Lord, do but bear me company, and give me strength, and it shall be done. I can do all things through Christ that strengtheneth me." This is one of God's champions; he watches, he keeps upon his guard, he fights stoutly, he stands his ground, in everything he demeans himself gallantly, he quits himself like a soldier of Christ; and that which makes him thus valiant, is because he is so near his Captain. Ask Epictetus what made Socrates do as he did, and he will tell you, "It was because he was a friend of God, his servant, and partaker of his kingdom." (L. iii. c. 22.) This is strange language from a heathen; but had he known what it was to live under the most lively sense of God's love, to have had such intimate converse with him as some Christians have had, what would he have said? As for the saint that keeps close to God, he keeps close to duty; his work is to serve, love, and praise God: this is his business, both by himself and with others.

7. Another excellent effect of this acquaintance with God is, it will make a man patient under all the dispensations of God's providence, in all conditions to be content, in quietness to possess his spirit. Acquaintance with God will make him be at peace, not to open his mouth against God, whatsoever he lays upon him. What was it that kept such a calm in Paul's heart, when there was such a constant storm without him? Was it not his sense of his interest in God's love? Though all the world were his enemies, yet as long as Christ was his Friend, he doth not care; though men and devils be against him, yet if God be for him, he passeth not much upon it: though men be never so unjust, yet God will never be so, that's his comfort. It's a small matter for him to be judged with man's judgment, as long as he is sure that God will acquit him; he knows that justice itself will do him no wrong, infinite goodness could not be unkind, and that wisdom itself could work glorious effects out of those things which the world call evil; if he do

receive evil at the hands of God, he is confident he deserves more; if it be good, and but a little, he is thankful, because he deserved none at all. Let the worst come to the worst, if all the devils in hell, and all Satan's instruments upon earth should combine against him, as long as he is sure of the love of God, and that none of them all can pluck him out of the arms of the Almighty, he is not very much concerned; heaven will make amends for all: whatsoever he suffers, it is nothing to the displeasure of a God, it is nothing to everlasting burnings. He believes that if his persecutors knew what he knows, they would as soon eat fire as do as they do; therefore he rather pities them than is angry with them, as seeing that their day is coming. How seldom have you either Paul or Silas complaining of their sufferings! how rarely bemoaning their condition! And what is it that makes them so patient? What have they to sweeten such bitter draughts? Why, God loves them; and so long, they do not much care though others hate them. Man's frowns cannot sink a soul to hell, nor his favour make one happy for ever. It is but a little while, and all tears shall be wiped away from their eyes. The kindness and faithfulness of God are enough to make a man hold up his head cheerfully when all the world is against him. When the most spiritual Christians do complain, it is more of themselves than of their persecutors. Oh my unbelieving heart! Oh that I should love God no more! Oh that my heart should be no more taken up with the great things of eternity! This is the condition in which those that are most spiritual are, in poverty, imprisonment, banishment, and all those things which most call dreadful. When they come to a man that is much in communion with God, they find him patient, meek, and calm; these are not the things which put him upon the rack; God is his Friend, and that answers all.

8. Another glorious effect of acquaintance with God is, that it will make all our enjoyments doubly sweet. He hath what he hath in love; he need not be afraid of poison in any of those dainties which come from his dearest Friend's table; he may eat his meat with a joyful heart, and not tremble for fear of the reckoning at last; what he enjoys is

freely given him; all his dishes have this brave sauce, they are seasoned with love, and come out of the hand of a Father. He that is the great Proprietor hath given him leave to use those things, and hath promised also to give him better things than these. He knows that this is not his portion, that this is nothing to what he shall possess; it is no small comfort to him to think that he shall never want anything that is needful for him; or that if he be brought into some exigencies, he hath a Friend that he can go to when he will, and be heartily welcome; he hath a portion, an estate, in another country that can never be spent, though he live at never so high a rate; and the more he spends upon it, the greater it is; he hath a key to that storehouse which can never be emptied, he hath an interest in Him in whom all fulness doth dwell: his Friend is noble, let him but "ask, and he shall have, seek, and he shall find, knock, and it shall be opened unto him." God is so free that he takes care of all his creatures; yea, so great is his royal bounty, that it doth largely provide for his enemies! And shall his friends, his children, starve? Hath he not fed them in ancient days? When his people were in the wilderness he sent them their diet from his own house, he fed them with angels' food. But if this should not be, if he kept them short, that may be done with as great kindness to them as the former: fasting may fatten the soul more than feasting doth the body; and this makes all welcome. If he have a great deal, he rejoiceth to think that he shall have more still one day; if he have but a little, he is satisfied; and so his condition is made more comfortable to him than the greatest enjoyments of the wicked are to them.

9. Another effect of this acquaintance with God is, that it will make a man wise. He that, before he was acquainted with God, had not the wit to know his friends from his foes, by his converse with God is made more wise than the great sages and grand politicians of the world. Upon his acquaintance with God, he is soon able to know right from wrong, to distinguish between good and evil. He hath now the wisdom to look after the salvation of his soul, to seek

the kingdom of heaven in the first place, and not to be laughed and jeered into hell. He is so wise, that he doth outwit the devil himself; he doth get so much wisdom by his acquaintance with God, that God will reveal many of his great secrets to him. I know one myself that was little different from those who are commonly called *naturals*, whom, when the Lord had wonderfully wrought upon, and brought near to himself, after his converse and acquaintance with God, his very natural understanding was exceedingly refined, and afterward he became more discreet, and fit to manage worldly affairs. But, however this be, I am sure the knowledge of God gives understanding to the simple. "A good understanding have they who love the Lord: and the fear of the Lord is the beginning of wisdom." Converse with men of wisdom doth not a little improve a man: but converse with the wise God makes a strange alteration indeed, they are made wise unto salvation. Of such as these David thought it best to make his privy council. These are the persons that are the fittest to advise with in businesses of the greatest importance in the world; they have learned the art of managing the affairs of greatest concernment with the greatest care and prudence. I know the wise world usually looks upon such persons as the veriest fools living. To converse with God, to take all possible care to make their calling and election sure, to do what they can to be happy for ever, passes with it for a ridiculous thing, and more than needs. But it is no great matter, they will not be beat from the work thus; they should be fools indeed, if such things as these should make them turn their backs upon God; they will not be jeered out of heaven, they pass not upon man's censures. He is wise that God calls so, and he will be found a fool whom God saith is so. As for the man that is acquainted with God, all his actions speak him a man of prudence, one that hath a deep reach with him; he is a man of an excellent foresight; he sees the clouds gathering a great way off, the storm before it riseth, and he hides himself; in him are hid the treasures of wisdom; he makes no foolish choice; he is a child of wisdom; he doth in some measure understand himself, and knows where his interest lies, and is faithful to it; he makes no foolish bargains, when he parts with dung for diamonds, brass for gold, earth for heaven, sin for holiness, present short-lived pleasures for sure and everlasting delights, the devil for God. How say you, ye mad gallants, that look upon the saint as a fool, and religion as a ridiculous thing? Are these such foolish actings? Is it so indiscreet a choice to prefer heaven before hell? If this be to be a fool, I wish I were more such a fool; if this be so contemptible a thing, oh that I may yet be more vile! Let me say further, as great a folly as it is, there are none of you all but erelong will wish you had been such fools. A few years will make you all of another mind, when you see what those that you counted fools have got, and what you with your wisdom have lost; then let's hear you calling them fools for choosing Christ for their portion, and yourself wise for despising him, and choosing this present world for your portion. Now, it is their being acquainted with God that hath made them thus wise; time was that they were as very fools as any in the world, till they fell into God's company, and ever since that, they have acted with a great deal more prudence: their being much in God's company hath much improved them. They may thank God for all that skill that they have attained to, for he it is that taught them; he is always at their elbow to direct them; when they are about to be cheated, he whispers them in the ear, lets them understand the fraud; and when God speaks, they listen to his counsel. It was no falsehood which Seneca spake (though he understood not the meaning of this doctrine of reconciliation) in the commendation of wisdom. "Wisdom," saith he, "is a great, spacious thing; it instructs us both in divine and human things, it teacheth a man how to demean himself in relation to things past, present, and to come: it informs him about things that are fading, and things that are lasting; and by it he knows how to put a true estimate and value on both: this learns one the difference between time and eternity." Thus far Seneca. But where is this wisdom to be found? Not in Aristotle or Plato's writings: the grand maxims of this wisdom were little understood in the Peripatetic or Stoic schools; flesh and blood, human wisdom improved to the height, reveal not these things to us. Where then is this wisdom to be found? and where is the place of understanding? Man knows not the price of it naturally. "The depth saith, It is not in me; it cannot be got for silver, &c. Destruction and death say, We have heard the fame thereof with our ears." There is talk of wisdom in hell; there they can say what reports were made to them of the excellencies of Christ, and how earnestly they were offered to be instructed in the ways of wisdom. But in hell there is no wisdom, though a world of them, which by their wisdom knew not God, be there. Where, then, is wisdom? God understands the way of it, and he teacheth man wisdom, and those that will come to him and submit to his instructions, may learn: the lesson is short, yet learnt but by few. He tells man, that to fear and love his Maker, and to be brought into union, friendship, and acquaintance with God, that is wisdom; and to depart from iniquity, that is understanding, Job xxviii. 12, &c.

10. Another effect of this acquaintance with God is, it will make a man rich. As soon as any one is acquainted with God, he is set in a thriving way. Man at the first had his estate in his own hands, and he kept up his trade for a little time, and but for a little time; for though his stock was great, yet meeting with the serpent, that great cheater, he was miserably overreached, and so sadly impaired in his spiritual estate, that he broke presently; and had not Jesus Christ stepped in and bailed him, and been his Surety, he would soon have had all his creditors upon his back, and have been laid up in that dismal prison, till he should have paid the utmost farthing; but through the kindness of Christ, the grand Creditor had patience, and offers to make up the business, and to compound upon better terms than the sinner could possibly expect. Christ undertakes to heal the infinite breach, to bring God and man acquainted, and to set him up again in case he will but accept of the gracious terms of agreement; and thus undone man, that was before in a beggarly condition, upon his return to God, is set in a better way than ever; God, his Friend, now takes such order

for him, that he shall be sure never to break again; he will be his Cash-keeper, he will have the oversight of all, he will teach him such an art, that he shall be sure to get by everything that he trades in; he shall gain by his losses, grow rich by his poverty, and drive the best trade, it may be, when he is forced to shut his shop-doors, I mean in a time of violent persecution. Whatsoever losses or crosses come, he is sure he shall never be undone as long as his Friend hath so great a bank; he hath a key, and he can go to an infinite treasury when he pleaseth, and fetch out supplies for any exigencies or occasions; and when all those that made such a great show in the world, and that were taken for merchants that were exceeding well to pass, shall be proclaimed bankrupts, and be found not worth a farthing, and be carried to prison for debt, then he hath money in his purse, coin that will go current in any country. In the meantime, though he be thought to be worth nothing, to drive but a pitiful poor trade, yet, when he comes to die, and when an exact inventory is taken of all that he is worth, he is found worth thousands: and no wonder, when he hath such a Partner, who will be sure to see that his business shall be managed to the best advantage, and that he shall never be out of purse: upon this account, the man cannot choose but thrive; he will have something to show for his gains, when others have nothing. When the rich ones of the world shall be begging a drop of water, he is at the fountain. If you would take a survey of that man's estate that is acquainted with God, you must lift up your eyes to those everlasting hills, you must look east, west, north, and south; all this is his, things present, and things to come; mount up to the top of Carmel; your sight is too short, you see not the hundredth part of his inheritance; all this is nothing: he hath a brave estate in another country; he is rich in bills and bonds; when he comes to age, he will have no man know what falls to him. And whence hath he all this wealth? Hath he not got every penny of it since he was acquainted with God? But I shall be but brief upon this head, because I have handled what might have fallen in here before; but the world laughs when I speak at this rate, and thinks that I am much mistaken. Godly men rich! That's strange! What, rich, with scarcely clothes to their back! rich, and fare so hardly! rich, and possess nothing! This is strange wealth. I grant it is; it is so, for their estate is in invisibles; it is not he that possesseth much, but he that wants little, that is rich. Will you call nothing riches but gold and silver, and houses and lands? Are virtue, grace, holiness, no riches? And will you call these little because he hath not so much trouble and vexation with his estate as some have? Are heaven, glory, the everlasting enjoyment of God nothing? Is the possessing that which is more worth than a thousand worlds, no riches? If to have all things that are good for them; if to have more than their hearts can conceive; if to be filled with all spiritual plenty be counted poverty; let me be thus poor, rather than enjoy the revenue of all the princes and great ones of the world. And what do you think of this, you that are worth never a penny? Are you desirous to have a great estate? You that go backward, and get nothing, would you be set in such a way as that you may be sure never to oreak? Why then, get acquainted with God, and you cannot but grow rich.

11. Another glorious effect of acquaintance with God is, that it makes a man like God, which is the top of the creature's honour. Company is of an assimilating nature. He that before was unholy, and like the devil, by conversion to God, and converse with him, is made holy like God. He that before was cruel, fiery, unmerciful, by his acquaintance with God is made kind, meek, and lovely. He that in his natural state was a nonconformist to the laws of his Maker, when he is well studied in this point, is the stiffest conformist; he sticks close to the righteous canons of the holy God, and will not by his good will turn to the right hand or to the left. He that was sometimes very unlike God, when he is brought nigh unto him, his countenance is changed, his features are altered, and the lineaments of God's image appear very lively in his face; and the more he is in God's company, and the older he grows, the more he grows like him. Oh how doth such a one shine! What a majesty, glory, and beauty is there in his face! The oftener

he comes to God, the more he is taken with his excellency, the more he labours to imitate him. He studies what God is; and as far as his nature is capable of it in this life, he desires to be like him. If God be true and faithful, he dare not be false, but he will hate the way of lying; if God be free and bountiful, he thinks it very ill becomes one of his children to hide his face from his own flesh, to shut up his bowels, to be void of natural affection. If purity be so eminent in God, he knows that impurity would not be commendable in himself. In a word, he desires in everything to carry himself as one whose highest ambition is to speak, act, and think as one that would be like God. It was bravely spoken of him, (Sen. Ep. xxxvii.,) especially if we consider what the man was, who told his friend that called him to heaven, *in compendium,* " To get as much happiness as this place, this soul, while in this body, is capable of; that is, to get God for his Friend, to be like him." This is a short cut to glory, a soul carried to heaven, or heaven brought down to the soul. A full and perfect conformity and likeness to God is the very glory of glory; and a partial conformity to him upon earth is an unspeakable honour in this life. Oh, were men and women better acquainted with God, they would sparkle and shine in their generation, so that their enemies should be forced to say that a saint is another kind of creature than a sensual sinner. Oh, why stand you then so far off from God? Come nearer him, and the rays of his glorious image will reflect from your lives. Be acquainted with him, and you shall be like him; keep much in his company by faith, secret prayer, and meditation, and you will be more holy, divine, and spiritual.

12. The last effect of this acquaintance with God which I shall name is this, it will make a man better, far more excellent in all states and relations; all his friends will have the better life with him, the whole family, it may be, where he dwells, will fare the better for him. If he be a child, he is more dutiful to his parents than he was while he was unacquainted with God. If he be a servant, he is more diligent and faithful than before; he serves not with eye-service, but doth what he doth with singleness of heart, as

unto the Lord. If he be a master, it makes him more exemplary, and makes him take care that his household should serve the Lord; he had rather his servants should make bold with him than God, he is concerned for the honour of God in his family, as much as his own. If he be a father, he is careful to bring up his children for God; he is more spiritual in his affections to them, and desirous to leave them God for their Father, Friend, Portion. As he is a neighbour, he follows peace with all men, and holiness, because he hath seen God. How sweet and amiable doth acquaintance with God make a man! how ready to heal divisions! how full of goodness and charity! how ready to do good unto all, but especially to those that be of the household of faith! how compassionate and tender-hearted! how ready to provoke others to love and good works: so that the whole parish lives the quieter, all the poor fare the better, all the neighbourhood, some way or other, is beholden to him. One that knows God himself doth what he can to get others acquainted with God too. How sweetly doth he commend the way of wisdom! With what earnestness and pity doth he plead with sinners, and labour to teach transgressors the paths of God, that sinners may be converted unto him! How doth he set before them the necessity of a change, the danger of their present state, and the excellent qualities of this Friend that he would bring them acquainted with; telling them that time was that he also was as they are, and thought his condition as safe as they do theirs; but that it pleased the Lord by his word to open his eyes, and to reveal to him the need that he had of Christ, and to enable him to accept of him, and to prize him above the whole world. In all conditions and relations, he commends religion, and shows that godliness, where it is in the power and life of it, is a brave thing, which makes so great an alteration in a man for the better. If he be sick, he rejoiceth, and thinks cheerfully of death, the grave, and eternity; and in this state demeans himself so, that standers-by cannot but be convinced of the reality of invisibles, and to think, surely there is something more than ordinary in acquaintance with God, which makes men so undaunted, and with so much gallantry to meet death; surely their condition is better than ours, or else they could never be so joyful at such a time as this is. Then he tells of the use of a Christ, the benefit of a Redeemer in a dying hour, and how infinitely it is for their interest in time to provide for eternity. If he be well, he desires to improve his health for God, and to serve his Maker with the strength of body and soul. If he be poor, he shows a pattern of patience, meekness, thankfulness, and lets the world understand that godliness with content is great gain; if he be rich, he desires to be rich in good works also, and to trade with such trifles as gold and silver, for rich commodities, as grace, peace, and glory, with the things of this world for the things of another; to lay up for himself treasure which neither moth can corrupt, nor thieves break through and steal, and to make to himself a friend of the unrighteous mammon; to be a faithful steward of those talents that his great Lord and Master hath committed to his trust: he shows how great a good it is to be great and good too. This is the man who doth adorn the Gospel; this is the Christian who doth credit his profession; this it is to be intimately acquainted with God! Oh how useful might men and women be in their generations, were they but more in God's company! Oh what a savour would there be of their graces in the place where they live! How would poor creatures, that receive good by their holy counsels and suitable lives, bless God for the day that ever they were born, and adore that goodness which brought them near such and such a one, by whose means God hath brought them out of the vassalage and captivity of Satan, and by whose help they have got acquainted with a Friend that is more worth to them than a world; for one that hath God for his Friend cannot but desire that others also should have an interest in him; he knows how ill it will go with them that know not God, and this makes him do what he can to bring God and man acquainted; he would make those that are good better, and those that are bad good? If those that he converses with, or stands related to, are enemies, he lets them know that a Christian can love them dearly whose sin he hates entirely, and that a child of God can pity them that have no pity at all for him. I might add, how oft are a great many wicked ones spared from temporal judgments, for the sake of the righteous that are amongst them.

III. HEAD OF MOTIVES.

The next head of motives to enforce this exhortation might be taken from the danger of not being acquainted with God. If you could live securely without God, and be in a safe condition though you still remained a stranger to him, the business then were not so very considerable; if you could find any in heaven that could do as much for you as God can, I should not be so earnest with you to get an interest in his favour; if you could by any means possible be everlastingly happy any other way; if without this Friend get to heaven, and without his alliance avoid utter ruin, I should have had the less reason to use so much importunity; I might then possibly have spared myself the trouble of speaking these things, and you the trouble of hearing them. But when I see and know that it is as much as your life and soul are worth, to slight and undervalue the motions that I am now making to you in Christ's stead, how can I with any faithfulness and love to your souls hold my peace? How can I stand looking upon men and women that are about to murder their own souls, and forbear crying out? How can I endure seeing poor creatures running with all the speed they can to that dismal place from whence there is no redemption, and not endeavour to stop them? Would you have me so cruel to your souls, as not to tell that which doth infinitely concern their well-being? for, let me tell you, God will not stand neuter; he will be either for you or against you; he is the Lord of hosts, and he will fight on one side or other. Now, see to your matters, as the nature of them doth require. What do you think of having a God against you? If God be against you, who will be for you? "There is no peace, saith my God, to the wicked." The safest condition you can be in, while God is your enemy, is sadly hazardous; such a one hangs by a twined thread over everlasting flames; he stands upon the brink of that bottomless pit, and one shove, one slip, sends him going for ever; he stands upon a pinnacle, which one little blast may blow him off, and then where is the man to all eternity? If he fall thence, there is no rising again; if he once go into that other world, there is no recovery of him, if one would give a world to bring him back again. I say it again, if God be not your Friend, he will be your enemy: and what do you think of such an enemy? It is but a word, a look, and they fall. Let me tell you, that except you speedily humble yourselves, you shall find that we do not make the danger greater than it is: "according to his fear, so is his wrath." You may know soon enough to your cost, what the displeasure of a God is, how dreadful his arrows, how sharp his sword. Not a man of them shall escape that will not accept of peace upon his terms, and that quickly too. Oh that will be a sad day, when God shall say, "Bring them out and slay them before my face." If God be your enemy, who do you think will be your friend? To which of the saints and angels will you fly? Where will you go for shelter against the storm of that terrible One? What armour will defend you against the dint of his weapons? What in the world can stand that man in any stead that hath such an adversary, especially when he comes to give his definitive sentence against him for high treason? Dives may say, Father; and Abraham, Son: but what comfort, for all that, had the miserable child from his holy father? Doth he not, instead of cooling his tongue with a drop of water, lay more burning coals upon it, and if it be possible, make the heat of it greater? "Son, remember that thou in thy lifetime hadst thy good things." Thus Abraham, by putting him in mind what his condition was, makes him with the greater sorrow to feel what it is. The memory of former joys under present sorrows makes them sting the more. Well then, if you would not hereafter reflect with an aching heart upon your lost enjoyments, think with a serious and thankful heart of the present offers, that you may in eternity reflect with joy upon your short sorrows in time. If you will not be acquainted with God, you shall be acquainted with the devil, and know whose company is best by woful experience. If you will not believe his word, you shall feel his sword. If his kindness and goodness will not melt you, his power and justice shall break you; for he that now is so patient will erelong roar like a lion, and tear in pieces, and there shall be none to deliver; he will break his stubborn enemies with a rod of iron, and dash them in pieces like a potter's vessel. Those that will not know his love shall know something else; I will not say what, for it is inexpressible. But only this remember: it is such a God that you will have to deal with, before whom the mountains quake, and the hills remove out of their places, before whom the great tyrants of the world have fallen; and shall you stand? Where are all those giants? Where are the inhabitants of the old world? What is become of Nimrod, that mighty hunter, and all his fellows? Where are all those daring sinners that scorned to accept of a pardon, mercy, and peace, and that had the courage to grapple with Omnipotency itself? Who got the day? Who had the worst of it at last? And art thou stronger than they? Is thy power greater, thy understanding deeper, thy allies more considerable than theirs? A fly may be too hard for Pharaoh; but Pharaoh can never be too hard for God. Because judgment is not speedily executed against thee, thou thinkest therefore, it may be, it is because God cannot deal with thee, and upon this account thy heart is fully set in thee to do wickedly; but know thou, for all this, that God will bring thee to judgment. Consider this, that as fair as it seems to be now, the winds may rise, the clouds may gather of a sudden, the heavens may be overcast in a moment; and what will you do then? When heaven and earth shall be in a flame, then you will be scraping acquaintance with God; then you will be glad to be owned by him; then you would willingly Christ should take notice of you, and say, "You blessed of my Father;" then you will stand at the door and knock, and cry, and pray, and plead, and say, "Lord, Lord, have I not been oft at thy house? have I not eat at thy table, and taught in thy name in our streets?" And yet thou shalt be dismissed with this short and sharp answer, "Depart, I know you not." How do you like such an answer as this is? How will you take it, when you stand begging at the door for one crumb of mercy, one drop of Christ's blood, to be sent away with a bitter scorn and denial, or else to be answered with silence? Whereas you were invited to the feast as well as those that went in, and you would not hear, though God sent messenger after messenger to fetch you; you thought your oxen better company than your God; you took more pleasure in your dogs than in the hunting after those nobler things. What do you think of such expostulations as these? What replies can you make to these accusations? Erelong you will find these things realities; erelong all your friends will be dead and gone; and if they would help you, they cannot; your estate will be consumed, your houses will all be burnt; all your attendants, except care and fear, will shortly forsake you; your gold and silver will not erelong be worth a rush; and what will you do then? nay, the greatest friends that you had will become your enemies. Little do you think, as kind as they seem to be, what your good fellows, the world and the devil, will do against you. Little do you think how false your friends will prove when it comes to that, that they see that all is going. Then they also will help forward your ruin. Those that you durst have trusted your life with, will accuse you and help to cast you. Those who encouraged to sin will witness against you for sin; your good fellows, your confederates in wickedness, your dear friends, that you loved more than God, that you did not spare to venture your life and soul for; oh! it will make your heart ache to see such come in against you, whom you thought loved you so dearly! Oh! to have a wife, a child, a husband, an old friend, to come before the Judge, and to make known such things as you hoped had been buried for ever! It will make your ears tingle, to hear one crying out, Lord, if it had not been for him, I had turned and repented; it's owing to him that I am in this woful condition; I was resolved many a time and oft to seek after another world, and to provide for my soul, but he would not let me alone; when I began to be serious, he laughed and jeered me, and would never be at quiet till he had made me as bad as himself;

he carried me from the alehouse to the tavern, from thence to a playhouse, from a playhouse to a whorehouse, from thence to the highway, from thence to the gaol, from the gaol to the gallows, and from thence I came hither; and I may thank him for all this. Oh how will men look when they see the best friends that they had come in thus against them! This 'tis to trust to faithless friends; this 'tis to make light of acquaintance with God. Your gold and silver will be a witness against you, and will eat your flesh as with a canker; your children, relations good and bad, will speak bitter things against you; your own family will curse you, and say, Lord, we never heard anything of God, except in an oath, from his mouth; we never heard anything of religion, except it were in derision of it, in his family; and those of us that were a little serious, and began to think of our souls, he would snub and browbeat, and never give us a kind look till we did as he did. Nay, the devil, who now doth so much flatter sinners, and make them believe that he is so much their friend, will then show himself; he will then be as cruel as he now seems kind; he that now tempts to sin so impetuously, will hereafter accuse for sin violently, and torment for sin unmercifully. The people of God, who weep over sinners, and pray for them, and wish them well with their souls, will then see justice executed upon their nearest relations without the least sorrow; nay, they also will come in against them too, and say, Lord, I told them of this woful day. O Lord, thou knowest I forewarned them of that which is now come to pass, I pleaded with them with all the compassion that I could, and they scorned my pity, they would not pity themselves, but made light of that glory which they are going from, and of that hell they are going to; and now, O Lord, thou art just and righteous, that thou hast thus judged them. This will be the language of those that are your best friends; the people of God will be your enemies one day, if you will not now mind the making of your peace with God; they must and will be on God's side against all the world; they must and will take part with their Friend, and clear him when he judges, and justify him when he condemns you. Oh that you who are now strangers to

God would but consider of these things! Oh that you would but think what this battle may be, where the combatants are so unequal! Stand still, O sun, in the valley of Ajalon, till the Lord have avenged him of his enemies! Muster yourselves, O ye stars, and fight in your courses against those miserable sinners that have waged a war against their Maker; plant your mighty cannons, shoot down huge hailstones, arrows of fire, and hot thunderbolts! Oh! how do the wounded fall! How many are the slain of the Lord, multitudes in the Valley of Decision, for the day of the Lord is terrible. Behold God's enemies falling by thousands, behold the garments rolling in blood, hear the prancing of his terrible ones, the mountains are covered with horses and chariots of fire. God's soldiers run from one place to another with their flaming swords in their hands, armed with the justice of God, jealousy, power, and indignation! Oh the dreadful slaughter that is made! Millions, millions fall; they are not able to stand; not one of them can lift up his hand; their hearts fail them; paleness and trembling hath seized upon the stoutest of them all. The bow of the Lord is strong: from the blood of the slain, from the fat of the mighty, the bow of the Lord turneth not back, the sword of the Almighty returns not empty. How do the mighty ones fall in the midst of this battle! A hot battle indeed, in which none escape! Who is he that cometh from Edom, with dyed garments from Bozrah? He that is glorious in his apparel, and travelling in the greatness of his strength, the Lord of hosts is his name. Wherefore art thou red in thy apparel, and thy garments like him that treadeth the wine-fat? I have trodden the winepress alone, and of the people there was none with me. For I will tread them in mine anger, and trample them in my fury, and their blood shall be sprinkled upon my garments, and I will stain all my raiment; for the day of vengeance is in my heart, and the year of my redemption is come. And I will tread down the people in mine anger, and make them drunk in my fury; and I will bring down their strength to the earth: the hand of the Lord shall be known, the power of the mighty Jehovah shall be felt, and his indignation towards his enemies. For behold he will come with fire and with chariots like a whirlwind, to render his anger with fury, and his rebuke with flames of fire: for by fire and by his sword will he plead with all flesh: and the slain of the Lord shall be many, and the saints shall go forth and look upon the carcasses of the men that have transgressed against me. For their worm shall not die, neither shall their fire be quenched, and they shall be an abhorring unto all flesh. Upon the wicked he shall rain snares, fire, and brimstone, and a horrible tempest. This shall be the portion of their cup! This it is to fight against God! This it is to defy the Lord of hosts! This it is to refuse a peace that would have been so unspeakably advantageous! To speak a little plainer, this is all that sinners are like to get by their standing it out against the tenders of grace and mercy. And are you still desirous to engage in this dreadful war? Will you still bid defiance to the Almighty, and make nothing of such things as you have heard of? Is the loss of your blood, the loss of your soul, your utter undoing for ever, no great matter with you? Well then, go on, bold sinner, arm thyself cap-a-pie, gird thy sword upon thy thigh, get thy shield and buckler ready, prepare to meet thy God. Go up, O thou valiant warrior, and let's see thy valour, behold thy enemy hath taken the field; go up and look thy God in the face if thou darest; come, show thyself a mark for God, and turn not thy back like a coward, venture upon the mouth of the cannon. Rush upon the thick bosses of God's buckler, if you long to perish everlastingly. You have heard what the war will cost you; and as you like it now, do. And what, do you laugh at all this? Well, then, go on, but be it upon your peril, your blood be upon your own soul. As for me I could not have said much more than I have to dissuade you from this desperate enterprise; I foresee what a case you will be in, when you are in the heat of the battle, and I desire to weep in secret for thee, as one that will most certainly be undone, if thou dost not speedily alter thy mind; wherefore my loins are filled with pain, pangs have taken hold upon me as the pangs of a woman that travailleth, I am bowed down at the thoughts of thy misery, I am dismayed at the seeing of thy destruction. The sinner ventures for all this! He is marched into the field! Set a watchman; let him declare what he seeth. Who meets that furious wretch? A lion, a lion roareth; he is torn in pieces, and none can save him; he is gone, he is gone! He is gone for ever! And who may the madman thank for all this? Who could help it? He would venture, though he was told as much. Well then, see what's like to befall the enemies of God. You hear what is like to be the condition of all them that will not be acquainted with God. First or last, you likewise may behold what a case you yourself shall be in ere it be long, except you do speedily repent of your folly, and meet your adversary in the way, and humble yourself before the mighty Jehovah. Speak quickly! What will you do? Turn, or burn; repent, or die! Yet you do but hear, you do not feel; but thousands and millions feel what the displeasure of God is, what the breach of his covenant is, and what the effects of a war with the Lord of hosts are. Oh, be wise by their falls; let their destruction be your instruction; take heed what you do, lest you be the next that God shall deal with as an enemy. As yet God offers to be friends with you; but whether God will do as much to-morrow as he doth to-day, I do not know. I tell you but so; it is hard putting it to the venture. Remember you had large proffers of grace and pardon made to you; God hath sent us to let you know his will and pleasure, and we demand of you from him to give us your answer speedily. And what, cannot you yet resolve? Is it so difficult a business to determine what to fix upon? O foolish people and unwise! O unspeakable madness! How just must their condemnation needs be, who are offered salvation so often, and refuse it! who are so oft told of damnation, and yet run into it! in a word, who might have God for their Friend, and had rather have him for their Enemy!

4. The next head of motives by which I might enforce this duty of acquaintance with God, may be taken from the examples of them who made all the friends they can get acquainted with God. Behold a cloud of witnesses, who do all with one consent speak high in the commendation of

this Friend whom I am persuading you all that I can to be acquainted with. Are you wiser than all your neighbours? is the ignorant objection of some that would take it very heinously if we should call them fools, when we put them upon a serious diligence in pursuit of the best things. Why, let me retort this objection upon themselves. Are you wiser than Enoch and Noah? Have you more understanding than Abraham, Isaac, and Jacob? Have you more wit than David? Are you wiser than Heman, Daniel, and many others of those brave worthies who were the wonders of the world, the nonsuches of their age, and a pattern to future generations? This was the greatest piece of their wisdom, to walk with God; this was the best of their policy, to get so potent an Ally; this spake them to be men of a deeper reach and a larger understanding than others, because they made it their business to get acquainted with God, and thus to make their interest as large as heaven, and their peace and prosperity as sure as the oath of a God could make it. Do you think that all these men were mistaken? Did their wisdom lie only in a prudent management of their worldly affairs to the best advantage? What, then, did they mean, some of them, by leaving all that they had so cheerfully upon the command of God? Dare you say that they prized the favour of God at too high a rate? As for their parts, they thought they could not value such a friend as God too much. What else was the meaning of their longing, panting, and breathing after him? Why else are they so glad of his company, his presence? How loath were they to do anything that might be in the least displeasing to him! What bitter moans did they make, if he did but withdraw a while, if he did but a little absent himself from them! How wonderfully desirous were they of enjoying communion with him! How earnest to live in his house for ever! Dare you say that they were all fools and madmen for refusing the embraces of this present world, for slighting its smiles, and undervaluing its greatest kindnesses, and choosing that favour of God, though with the scorns and reproaches of the world, rather than to hazard his anger, whose wrath burns to the bottom of hell? Behold, what a glorious company, as these stand upon Mount Zion with harps in their hands, with those hundred and forty and four thousand, and the Lamb, with an innumerable multitude of all nations, people, and languages! Why, all these were of the friends and acquaintances of God, or else they had never had those crowns, robes, and palms in their hands. Now, why should not our souls be as dear to us as theirs were to them? Will not heaven be as good for us as them? Is it not as needful for us to get a Friend of God, as them? Will not God do as much for us as them, if we will but do as they did, walk with him? The truth of it is, the number of them who are saved is but few, in comparison of the multitudes of them who know not God, and go the broad way; yet, for all that, take them absolutely, they are abundance; so many that the Scripture saith they are innumerable. Do but read over the history of some of their lives, turn over the holy records, look sometimes into those sacred chronicles, and behold how cheerfully they served God, how actively they followed the Lamb wheresoever he went, through thick and thin. Hear what their language is now they are got home safe, now Christ hath brought them to glory, and they are at their Friend's house. What do they talk of? What is their discourse about? Do they complain what a sad journey they had of it through a howling wilderness, after they had passed the Red Sea, through a thousand sorrows and trials? Do they say, now they are at their journey's end, that they are weary, and wish they had never taken so long and tedious a journey? Do they not rather speak the quite contrary, and that if it were to go again, they would do it with far more speed and cheerfulness than they did? Listen! hark! methinks I hear them from the walls of the new Jerusalem crying out, Come away, come away; fall on bravely; follow your business gallantly but a little while longer, and the city is your own; fetch your scaling-ladders, run up apace, mount the ramparts, fear nothing, though the devil play his artillery upon you; yet it is but powder; he shall never give you a mortal wound; resist him and he will fly, and the field is yours; the spoil, the crown, the honour will pay for your pains, blood, and danger. Fall on, brave souls, fall on; the more valiant you be, the more safe you are. Methinks I hear those noble saints encouraging you to get acquaintance with God, and saying to you that are yet afar off, Come near. Come away, poor souls, come away; what do you mean thus to delay? Oh, little do you think what a Friend we now find of God; it was but a little, a very little that was told us of the excellency of Christ and the glories of this place, to what we experience; it was no false report that we heard, when we were upon earth, of the happiness of heaven. Oh! here is a prize worth the running for; a kingdom, a crown worth the fighting for, an estate worth the looking after. We have not now our stint; we are not dieted with those spiritual dainties; we have not now and then a sip, a draught, a bit in a corner, but we are at the fountain, we are daily feasted with infinite pleasures, our hearts are full, brim-full, they run over, we swim in an ocean of spiritual enjoyments; these things are beyond your capacity now to understand. Were we to live upon earth again, and did we know what we do now know, we should ever pine with our earnest longing for God, the living God, to be in his immediate presence, and to be at that angelical work of praising, serving, and loving him for ever. Wherefore, brethren, let us encourage one another. " Come, let us go up to the house of the Lord; his dwelling is in Salem, his palace is upon Mount Zion." Why should not we go on as merrily in the paths of wisdom, as the wicked in the road of hell? How do the devil's champions encourage and hearten one another up! How do they laugh, sing, and roar, as if their life were the only life! For shame! let's tell them they lie in their teeth. Who have the best company, they or we? The patriarchs and prophets, the apostles and thousands of martyrs are gone singing before; some of our dear relations, fathers, brethren, and sisters, are newly welcomed by Christ to his Father's house; and they are blessing that rich mercy that hath conducted them to such a place, to such a Friend. We have many thousands of saints militant that are going along with us as fast as they can, and God himself will bear us company; and why do we yet linger? Oh that we were upon the wing! Oh that our souls were like the chariots of Aminadab! Oh that the Lord would strengthen poor short-winded creatures! Oh that we could run and not be weary, and walk and not faint! Oh that we might have now and then a hearty meal, and that in the strength of them we could travel to the mount of God! Oh that that acquaintance might now be happily begun, which may never have an end! Oh that God would visit us oft, and get into our hearts! Oh that He that gave those worthies in former times so much grace, would pour out of the same grace in abundance upon our souls! Oh that he would shed abroad his love in our hearts! Oh that we could maintain a constant intercourse with him here, till we came to a perfect enjoyment of him in glory hereafter! Oh that we may see thy face, thy blessed face, by faith! Oh that thou wouldst cause thy glory to pass before us! Oh that thy marvellous loving-kindness might be made known to a company of poor creatures of us, whose desire is to fear thee, who would fain love thee with the strength of our souls! Oh blessed are they that love thee, that are beloved by thee!

5. I might also insist upon another head of motives, which is named in the text, which is this: "Acquaint now thyself with him, and thou shalt be at peace." Though there be nothing but war on every side, you shall have peace. This peace of God, whatsoever you may think of it, is unspeakably advantageous; the benefits that would accrue to a soul upon this peace are infinite. It is a peace that passeth all understanding. When we have this peace concluded, we may drive a brave trade, without disturbance, for the richest commodities. If we are thus acquainted with God, we shall have such a peace as that we may laugh at the shaking of the spear, and not be much disturbed when we hear of dreadful things abroad in the world. He that is acquainted with God may safely venture up and down, he hath God's pass, a strong man-of-war for his convoy; he hath such powerful allies, that he need not fear; as long as he is at peace with God, he is sure not to be quite overcome by man. He is at peace with himself; when the air

echoes with drums and trumpets, and the roaring of guns, a music that pleaseth the devil's ear, he may still rejoice, because he hath a bird within, which sings sweetly; there is a harmony between his will and God's, a harmony between his heart and his mouth. This is no such contemptible thing; and if you knew what a wounded spirit, a fire in the bosom is, you would say so. This peace that such a one hath, is a well-grounded peace; not such a peace as is built upon ignorance and hardness of heart, but such a one as results from the sense of the pardon of sin, and reconciliation with God, through the blood of Christ: that blood of Christ hath washed his conscience from dead works. Sins he had, and hath, but some of them he sees lying dead, like the Egyptians upon the shore, others striving for life, with a death's wound upon them; and though he have enemies still living, yet they are such as shall never have the absolute dominion over him. As long as the great quarrel between him and God is at an end, all is well enough; the law hath nothing against him, all his accusers are silenced; Christ hath fulfilled and satisfied the law for him; the great Creator hath given a full and general acquittance; all debts are discharged for him; and therefore the man hath little reason to trouble his head much with cares and fears. Now he may go up and down anywhere, and not fear the sergeant; his noble Surety hath paid that vast debt, he hath laid down the ten thousand talents upon the nail, so that the man is at peace with God. He is also at peace with all the creatures in the world, from the glorious angels that are in heaven, to the meanest insect or plant; they are so far from doing him any real harm, that they all are servants to the friends of God, they all stand ready to oppose their enemies; and those of them that are mortal are ready to lay down their lives for one that stands thus related to God. For when any enter into covenant with God, God also makes a covenant for them with the beasts of the field. Great peace have they that love God's law, and nothing shall offend them; such are at peace with death and the grave. We read of some profane monsters that made a covenant with death, and were at an agreement with hell;

but this covenant will soon be broken, because he that hath the keys of death and hell, the power of life and death, never subscribed to the articles of their agreement. But now the godly man hath a Friend that hath made a covenant for him, a firm covenant with death and hell, so that none of them shall ever do him the least wrong. As for death, Christ hath taken out its sting; as for the grave, Christ hath spiced and seasoned it, its power is mastered, its terribleness is taken away. It's now no prison; Christ hath opened the doors of it; and now it is but a chamber of repose, a bed to rest in; and he that hath already opened this door, when it was bolted, barred, and double-locked, can and will erelong open it again, and awaken his from their sleep; and is this inconsiderable? Is not such a peace as this is desirable? Who that is well in his wits would not be glad to be in so secure a condition as this peace will put him in? And who are like to have the benefit of this peace but the friends of God? Oh, therefore, if you value your own peace, if you would be undisturbed from storms without and heartquakes within, if you would have all the creatures in heaven and earth at peace with you, if you would have death unstung, and the grave a chamber and not a prison, why then, get acquainted with God, and you shall be at peace.

6. The next head of motives I might take from these words, "Thereby good shall come unto you." "Acquaint yourself with him, and be at peace; and thereby good shall come unto you." But I shall here be but brief. Think of what you will that is good for you, and if you are acquainted with God, you shall have it for asking for, or that which is far better than that which you desire: for the Lord God is a sun and a shield; he will give grace and glory, and no good thing will he withhold from them who walk uprightly; that is, from those that are acquainted with him. All his ways are mercy and truth to such as be in covenant with him, and all shall work together for good to them that love him. Enlarge thy desires as wide as the heavens, request what you will, ask never so much, and you shall have it; and what would you have more? If it be the good of profit

that you desire, what greater gain than godliness? Who can give such rewards to his servants as God? Who will give greater portions to his children than this Father? Who is like to thrive better than he who hath such a vast stock, such a great trade, such quick and great returns, and, above all, such a Partner? Oh that those that are all for profit and gain, that cry out, What advantage shall it be to me if I serve God? and what profit to me, if I am acquainted with him?—oh that such would but do that which will be most for their profit! I would desire no more of them than this. Oh that they would but try what a gainful trade religion in its power is! The greatest merchants that ever walked the exchange, if they be not acquainted with God, and have not Christ for their Factor, are but pedlers to the saints. One that is acquainted with God gets more in one hour, in one prayer, at one sermon, in one meditation, than all the rich men of the world are worth, put all their estates together. One receives his peace, the other his pounds; the one hath, by way of return, a great deal of troublesome lumber, the other his box of precious pearls, and a jewel of an infinite value. Oh! little doth the laborious worldling think what poor and small gains his are, when he gets most, to what this spiritual merchant gets; he would not sell what he gets sometimes in one morning for all the riches of both the Indies. He trades in such commodities that will not suffer damage upon the sea. His vessel is light and strong; the master of it never made a losing voyage. All his wares are invaluable; and though his ship be in many a dreadful storm, though sometimes she be becalmed, though it be long before she returns; yet as long as she hath such provisions within, such a Pilot, such anchors, she cannot miscarry; she will come into the harbour richly laden. The world will not believe this; but I am sure there is never a man breathing, but will sooner say, that no gain is like the gain of Christ and glory. One return from Heaven, one answer of prayer, one smile from God, one look of love, the head of one Goliah, the death of one sin, one soul brought home to Christ, one drooping soul comforted, is a greater mercy (for all the ignorant world make nothing of such things as these) than to be invested with the greatest honours, than to be possessed of all the riches, than to enjoy all the pleasures that the whole world can afford. But oh, were men's eyes opened, were men within sight of those devouring flames, then they would believe that a Christ was worth the having, grace a pearl that cannot be overvalued, and that no trade was comparable to a spiritual merchant, no art like that by which one may turn everything into gold. But if it be the good of pleasure you look more after, can there be greater pleasures than those which are in the presence of God? Can there be any greater pleasures than to rejoice in God, and to be made welcome by him, than to drink flagons of that excellent liquor which is better than wine? Can there be better music than to hear so many millions of sweet voices singing hallelujahs? Oh, there's a concert! There's melody indeed! If you desire that other good, the good of honesty, a rare accomplishment, perfection of grace, purity of soul; wherewithal shall a young man choose his ways, but by taking heed thereto, according to His word? Well then, lay all these motives together, and let us see whether they will any whit prevail. If the nature of the Person with whom I would fain have you acquainted, if all these admirable qualities that are in him (if I may so call them) may signify anything; if all those glorious effects of acquaintance with God weigh anything with you, one would think by this time you should be well resolved. If the danger of not being acquainted with God may make you afraid of standing it out; if good or evil, if peace or war, if life or death, if all this be as much as nothing, what then is something? If the frequent pleading of mercy, if the blood of Christ have any voice, if the expostulations of his ambassadors may be heard, why should you not then be persuaded? If all this will not move you, what can we say more? If we could show you heaven, and the glories of another world, could we let you see the face of Christ, could we any way in the world reach your hearts, and persuade you by any means to mind the things of eternal peace, we would do it with all our hearts. If we were sure to get you with us, and to bring you acquainted with God, we could willingly come begging on our bare knees to you, and beseech you to be reconciled to God. We see that dismal day coming, and are grieved to think what a sad taking you will be in then; we know the case will then be altered with them who will not be persuaded to be reconciled to God. Oh what a woful condition will they be in, who have heard or read these sermons, and yet for all that would not mind the looking after acquaintance with God! How will such wish that they had never been born, or that they had their being in some of the dark savage corners of the world, where they might never have heard of the doctrine of reconciliation, being acquainted with God, and union with Christ, peace with their offended Maker, rather than, having heard of these things, to make light of them! Oh, to hear of such a Friend, and to have him for an Enemy; to hear of peace, and to choose war; to hear of heaven, and go to hell; this is sad indeed. It would have been far better for such that they had never known the ways of God, than, after they had known them, to go in the ways of folly. Oh that men and women had but such serious thoughts of these things as they will have erelong! Oh that they would but believe heaven, and hell, and eternity to be such realities, as shortly they will! Oh that men's hearts were but affected with things, as they will be when their souls are just a-going, or a little after they are in another world! But, oh the miserable condition of the world! Oh the lamentable state of professors, that make no more of the favour or displeasure of God! Nay, may I not say, oh the folly of the children of God themselves, that are no more in God's company, when they know they may be so welcome, when they have tasted so oft of his kindness, when they were made so much of the last time that they gave him a visit! Are not men in a deep sleep, that they do not hear? Are they not blind, that they do not see? Are they not ignorant, foolish, and mad, that they do not understand their interest any better? It is not without good reason that the Spirit of God doth so oft cry out upon sinners for their folly; the Scripture saith not in vain, that "there is none that hath understanding, no, not one." No wonder that they who have but half a cure see men like trees; that those who never had a thorough work do not prize Christ. Oh that those who have been brought nigh by grace, who were sometimes afar off, that such should be so much strangers; for those that have met with such kind entertainment at his house, for these to keep off so, to come so seldom; for them who have fed so high at the King's table, to fall to their trash, their husks; this is a shame indeed, as if the devil kept a better house than God. Christians, doth God deserve this at your hands? How unkindly do you think he takes this from you! What will the world say? Look how his own acquaintance despise him! How will the devil insult! Oh how do the hearts of your fellow-Christians ache, to see how strange your carriage is! How do they tremble to think, what if that fine house be built upon the sands! Christians, you who seldom or complimentally visit God, bethink yourselves well what you do, when you begin to be cold in your affections to this Friend; remember from whence you are fallen, and repent, and do your first works; remember what entertainment you have sometimes had at God's house; forget not all his kindnesses; of all the creatures in the world, you have no cause to carry yourselves so towards God. I tell you again, the world stands by and looks on, to see what there is in you more than in others; they mark your lives more than you are aware of, it may be. Wherefore, look to yourselves, take heed how you carry yourselves before them. Oh, why should they see your faces pale, when you may feed so highly? Oh, show them by your countenance that you feed upon wholesome food! Oh let your breath smell sweet, let your discourse be more savoury of the things of God! Labour to maintain a sweet, constant, uninterrupted intercourse with God, to walk with him. Oh, little do you think what you lose by your coming so seldom to this Friend. I appeal to your own experience. Was not that dish you eat last at his table sweet? And what, do you think that God doth not still keep as good a house as he did? Do you believe that he hath spent all his best wines? Can that fountain ever be emptied? Is there not bread and good cheer enough in your Father's house? Believe it, God hath other kind of entertainments, richer cheer, better fare still to make you welcome with, if you would not be so strange, if you would but come oftener to him. As for Christians, methinks I need not use so many words to persuade you, methinks you that know how sweet his company is should desire to be never out of it. Christians, I tell you plainly, if you ever expect true peace in your life, and true joy and comfort at death, it's your only way to keep close to God; visit him oft by secret prayer and other kind of duties, and then you shall ever and anon meet with that which will sweeten your greatest diligence, and abundantly make amends for your pains. Knock at his door, ask for him, and resolve to stay till he comes; though he come not at the first, second, or third knocking, yet I am sure he is within, and will come at last, if you will but wait; and when you have once again met with him, oh let him not go, but tell him seriously that you cannot bear his absence; he shall be your God and Friend, living and dying; death itself shall not part you. Go also and tell your friends you have found Him whom your soul loves, that you have met with Jesus, and see if you can get them too to come out and see him; bid them taste and see how good the Lord is; commend him all you can to your poor Christless friends. But you are not the persons that I intended to speak to, only thus a little by the by, that I may a little warm my own heart and yours in this great duty of maintaining an intimate close converse and acquaintance with God. But my business is to go out into the highways and hedges, and to invite poor wandering strangers that have nothing to live upon themselves, and that do not know what a noble open house God keeps, that never tasted of his kindness in Christ, to come to this royal feast, and to eat their fill of such food as they can never eat too much of, never be surfeited with. "Unto you, O men, I call; and my voice is to the sons of men. O ye simple, understand wisdom; and, ye fools, be ye of an understanding heart," Prov. viii. 4, 5. "Hear, O ye deaf, and see, O blind: let the dead hear the voice of God, and live." Then hear what I have been speaking of. I have almost done my message. Consider well of these things, as you tender the displeasure of God, as you value your souls; be serious; remember what it is that I have been discoursing to you about; read it over again, and study it; read and pray, pray and read, and turn this exhortation into prayer; take with you words, and say, Oh that this might be the sermon that might bring me acquainted with God! Oh that this might be the man that might bring me to some knowledge of Christ! Oh that this might be the happy day wherein a match may be concluded between my soul and the precious Jesus! But alas, alas, where are the hearts that are thus smitten? Where are the souls that are any whit taken with this infinite beauty? How few have any real love or good will for Christ! Oh, who hath believed our report, and to whom is the arm of the Lord revealed? Though I and many hundreds more have been pleading thus with sinners; though some of the ambassadors of peace weep bitterly, that their message is no more kindly entertained; though their public preaching be followed with private prayers and secret groans; though they expostulate the case with poor refractory creatures, with all the earnestness that they can for their lives; though we use the most powerful arguments that we can, and deliver them with all the vehemency, seriousness, and compassion that we can for our souls; yet how are the greatest part of our hearers unconcerned! Is not a great part of our auditory as stupid and senseless as the very stones they tread on? The more is our sorrow. We fear, as to the most of them that hear us, what we speak is lost. It may be they may be a little affected just at the hearing, or for an hour or two; but, oh that these truths might have a lively and abiding impression on men's hearts! I fear— oh that they were causeless fears!—I fear that most of you that have heard of these things will go away, and quickly forget what weighty things you have heard; perhaps some of you may say, The man was very earnest, and some of his expressions were piercing. O friends, I hope it is not your commendation that I desire! Oh that I may, with a single heart, respect God's glory! I say again, I would not be pleased with your praise, nor would I fear your dispraise; it's your souls I want; and may I but manage my great work in this successfully, and see you acquainted with God, before I leave you for ever, I hope I should be contented to be trod in the dirt. Oh that my heart may not deceive me! Oh that my compassion to your souls were greater, a thousand times greater! Oh that I could never speak to you of such things as these without tears! I must again and again profess I am ashamed of my heart, that it is no more sensible of these weighty affairs! But, O mighty and glorious God, if thou pleasest, thou canst out of the mouth of a babe and suckling ordain strength! Oh that thou wouldst make the worm Jacob to thrash mountains! Oh that thou wouldst make use of the most unworthy and weakest instrument, in that honourable service of bringing home some souls to thyself! Oh, if but any one soul, if but one soul that was estranged from God, might by these lines be brought acquainted with him, if I might prevail with any other stubborn enemy to lay down his weapons, and be friends with him, I should think my pains well bestowed; though (if that will make you to regard it ever the more) this work hath cost me many an hour's study, and it hath been interrupted with many bodily distempers, groans and sorrows, fears and sighs. Yet if, after all my travail, I may hear of any children born of God; if I may meet but one soul the better for it, by it brought to glory, I shall have abundant cause to bless my God, and to rejoice that my labour hath not been in vain in the Lord. But if I might have more, I should have still more cause to adore infinite goodness and rich grace! O my dear friends! O precious and immortal souls! What shall I say to you? What shall I do for you? Oh did you but know how hardly I fetch my breath at this time; did you but see what a crazy creature he is that writes to you; did you but know how faint he hath been sometimes in speaking to you, you would go nigh to pity him. Oh pity yourselves! Oh pity your own souls, that erelong must be turned naked out of your bodies, and hear the expostulations of a dying man, who would gladly live with you in everlasting glory, and meet you all among the friends of the Bridegroom; who longs to see you among the sons of God, in that great meeting, when the Father shall send his servants the angels to fetch all his children home to his own house! Oh pity your souls, and let not all my pains be lost, trample not under your feet the blood of the covenant, neither count it a common thing: remember that the slighting of Christ is a dangerous thing; the loss of his favour, and the loss of your soul, must go together! Oh, how shall I leave you! How shall I part with you! Shall I go before my work is done? What shall I say more? What arguments shall I further make use of? Oh that I knew what to say, that I might prevail! And are you still resolved to put me off with frivolous excuses? Can you put off your consciences thus? Are you still contented to be aliens and strangers? If you are, know this, that I must leave these lines to bear witness against you; remember this, that you were told of these things again and again. Those that can forget sermons here shall remember them hereafter? If you be not the better for this discourse, you will curse the day that ever you heard it; it will be a cutting reflection, when, another day, you shall say to your own soul, At such a time, such a one did beseech me in Christ's stead to be reconciled to God, and I would not: wretched man that I was! I made nothing of all the offers of grace and mercy, I made little account of these intolerable torments which now make me gnash my teeth! Hear, O unhappy creature, that art yet alive; be not thou past hope! Oh that thou mayest see thy sad state before it be quite past remedy! Oh let me take up a lamentation for thee, as one whose condition is beyond expression deplorable! Oh that I could speak as affectionately to you as one did lately, who spent his strength and life amongst you all, viz., that I can neither eat nor drink, nor sleep quietly, whilst I think of the danger that precious souls run every moment, while they are unacquainted with God! Oh that mine eyes were waters, and my head a fountain of tears, that I might weep day and night for poor Christless creatures, that laugh and are as cheerful as if no danger were near them; whereas that dismal day approaches apace, wherein they must bid an everlasting farewell to all their pleasures, and lie down for ever under the scalding wrath of an angry God! Oh stand astonished, O heavens, and wonder, O earth! Here's a man that had rather be a beast than a man, a devil than a saint, that prefers hell before heaven, that loves death and hates life; here's a man that makes nothing of going to hell; damnation is a thing that he jests with; 'tis but damning, he saith. But damning! Is that so light a thing—a thing to be laughed at? Well, if that damning be nothing, never complain of it, when you feel it. If it be nothing, never groan and bite your tongue, nor gnash your teeth for it. If heaven, and your soul, the favour of God, eternal happiness, be such small matters, never complain for the loss of them. Well then, belike you are pleased very well with your choice, and you do choose rather to enjoy the pleasures of sin for a moment, than the pleasures of holiness, which last for ever. There stands a sinner that hears all this, and frets and foameth at the hearing of it; it's a torture to his soul to be within the sound of such truths! Why, act like one in his wits. If the hearing of hell and damnation be so troublesome, what will the feeling of it be, thinkest thou? But that I may, if possible, prevail, I shall leave a few serious questions with you, which I charge you, in the presence of God, seriously to consider, and to give a wise answer to them.

Quest. 1. Are those things which you have heard, true, or are they not? Doth not the Scriptures speak the same things which I do? Dare you say that the Word of Truth is false? Do but open the Bible, dip where you will; what is that you read there? Is it not something that hath a tendency to what I have been teaching? Oh that you would but give yourselves the trouble of searching the Scriptures, to see whether these things are so! To what purpose, do you think, should we spend our breath? To what purpose should we follow you with such exhortations, if we had not some grounds for what we say? If there be no such thing in the word of God, why then do you not say so? Why do you not show us it, if there be such a place that saith there is no need of repentance, that man's condition is safe enough already, and that he may do well enough, though he be never reconciled to God? Do you think that we take delight in vexing men and women? Do you conceive that it pleaseth us to displease you, and to get your hatred? Do you not believe that a great many of us, if it might consist with God's honour and your welfare, had not far rather be excused? Can any man imagine that so many thousands of prophets, apostles, and ministers, in such distant ages, and in such distant places, should all agree in this, to impose a falsity upon the world? Would any man be so mad as to invent such things as these, which are so contrary to men's dispositions, if he had not abundant warrant from God himself? Is it possible that men should make such complaints, and shed so many tears, and be in such agonies about these things, if there were nothing at all in them? Are all the experiences of so many thousands of saints but mere fancies? Speak, Christian, speak. What do you say to this? Are all thy joys, thy answers of prayers, those sweet dishes that thou hast sometimes fed upon, but dreams? Doth not thy very blood stir in thee, at the very putting such a question to thee? Canst thou not say that thou hast seen, that thou hast felt, and that thou hast known undoubtedly, that spiritual things are realities, the greatest realities in the world, and that thou hast been as much affected with them as ever thou wert with the things of sense? Let me, the meanest of ten thousand, tell the stiffest atheist in the world, that I have seen these things so realized, that I shall sooner believe that I am turned to a stone, or am dead, than believe that spirituals are nullities and fancies. I am confident, if there be any credit to be given to both eyes and ears, then these things are true; and had you seen but what I have seen in dying saints, and heard what I have heard, you would easily have been convinced that there is something in communion with God, something in spiritual joys. I am sure, if there be any truth in the Scriptures, if the word of God be true, if Christ and the apostles were not all mistaken, then these things are true. If I should tell you a business that did concern your house, or your children, or body, or any worldly thing whatever, upon my own personal knowledge, would you not readily assent to what I say? I am persuaded you would be far from suspecting the truth of what I affirmed. I am ready to think that there is none of you all that think that I dare tell you that which is false. Oh then, why will you not believe me in a business of far greater consequence? And if you ask me, to what purpose I spend so much time for nothing?——What need I speak at this rate? What, will I make infidels of you all? What, do I think that you are such atheists, as not to believe that the word of God is true? Well then, you yourselves are witnesses that the word of God is true, and that you do believe all that is contained in it; and by rational inferences deduced from it. I shall therefore take it for granted that you give your assent to these things, if you be Christians in profession; your very name speaks as much. Now, my next question shall be this:—

Quest. 2. Are these things of weight and importance, or are they not? You hear that they are matters that concern your eternal life or death, soul affairs; and are not these matters of the greatest consequence? If acquaintance with God, the happiness or misery of a soul, your making or undoing for ever, be inconsiderable things, what then are great things? Is it a matter of greater importance to lose the sight of a lascivious play? Is it an affair of greater weight to have the frowns of a wanton mistress, or the frown of a God? You said even now, that the word of God was true; if you will stand to that, I desire no more. How is it written? Read a verse or two; turn to Matthew v. 20, "Except your righteousness exceed the righteousness of the scribes and Pharisees, you shall in no case enter into the kingdom of heaven;" and John iii. 3, "Except a man be born again, he cannot see the kingdom of God." And God will pour out his wrath upon the heathen, and upon the families that call not upon his name. Doth not the Scripture say that is the one thing necessary? Are not these things called by the Lord Christ the weightier things? Matt. xxiii. 23. I hope you will not say that God is mistaken, and that the Scripture speaks more of these matters than needs. What, are you gone from your word so soon? Did not you say that the word of God was true, and are you now of another mind, because you find that it requires more strictness than you are willing to submit to? But are you ashamed of that, and are you convinced of this also, that the doctrines of reconciliation, acquaintance, and peace with God, are affairs of the highest importance in the world? And do you indeed believe this? and will you stand to it? Well then, my next question shall be this:—

Quest. 3. What do you mean then, to mind such things as you acknowledge to be most unquestionably true, and of the greatest consequence, with so much indifference and coldness? What reason have you then for your strange neglect in your prosecution of them? What say they are the greatest things in the world? and will you say they are least to be looked after? Is it any prudence and wisdom to be very serious about trifles, and to trifle about the most serious things? Are heaven, the love of God, and the like, by your own confession, the most weighty, and will you make light of them? Oh, folly and hypocrisy! Out of thy own mouth thou shalt be condemned. Dost thou know that heaven and hell are before thee? Dost thou know that the one is unspeakably glorious, and the other unspeakably dreadful? and yet, for all this, dost thou stand demurring which of these thou shouldst choose? And darest thou for all this venture on in a way which leads to the region of eternal darkness? And though those that know the way better than you, and see you ride on so hastily and merrily, call after you with earnestness, yet do you still turn your back upon them? Consider whether you act in these affairs like one that is well in his wits. Is God the best Friend in the world, and yet his kindness least to be regarded? Man, what hast thou to say for thyself? Oh what brutes, and how irrational are men in their spiritual matters! How do they contradict themselves! How do they say one thing, and do the quite contrary! Oh let me, in a word or two, renew my expostulation with them who are loath to be accounted fools! What reason have you to undervalue the favour of God as you do? What reason have you thus foolishly to cast away yourselves, and to slight acquaintance with your

Maker? Let me plead with you in the language of a reverend divine (Richard Baxter) of our own. Look up your best and strongest reasons; and if you see a man put his hand into the fire till it burn off, you'll marvel at it. But this is a thing that a man may have reason for, as Bishop Cranmer had, when he burnt off his hand for subscribing to popery. If you see a man cut off a leg or an arm, it's a sad sight; but this is a thing that a man may have good reason for, as many a man doth it to save his life. If you see a man give his body to be burnt to ashes, and to be tormented with strappadoes and racks, and refuse deliverance when it is offered: this is a hard case to flesh and blood; but this a man may have good reason for, as you see in Heb. xi. 33–38, and as many a hundred martyrs have done. But for a man to forsake the Lord that made him, for a man to run into the fire of hell when he is told of it and entreated to turn that he might be saved, this is a thing that can have no reason in it, that is reason indeed, to justify or excuse it. For heaven will pay for the loss of anything that we can lose to get it, or for any labour that we bestow for it; but nothing can pay for the loss of heaven. Read on in Mr. Baxter's "Call to the Unconverted," page 169. Do you still believe the word of God to be true, and the things contained in it to be the most weighty, and yet will you still pass them over, as if there were nothing at all in them?

Quest. 4. My next question that I shall propound to you, and desire your serious and speedy answer to, is this: Do you believe than you can find a better friend than God? Can you mend yourself anywhere else? Is there in heaven or earth any that can do as much for you as God can? Is there any one that can take you off when you come to be accused of high treason against the King of heaven, and to be arraigned before that just Judge? Have you got that which will quit your cost in getting it, and countervail the loss of a soul? What is it that still hath an interest in your heart, that is thought to be an equal competitor with God for your dearest love? If it be indeed that which will shield you from the arrests of death and the wrath of the

Almighty; if it be that which can shelter you from the storm of his displeasure; if it be that which will do you as much good as heaven, and make you as happy as God can; why then, I have little to say; make your best of it. But consider well what you do first; be sure that you be not mistaken; have not many thought as you think, and found their mistake when it was too late?

Quest. 5. Do you think that this world will last always with you? Do you not believe that erelong you must die, and your soul appear before God, and by him be sentenced to its everlasting state? Where is all the glory of those great monarchs who despised God and oppressed his people? What is become of all their pomp? Which of them that flourished three thousand years ago stand alive now in glory? And are you better than they? Shall the worms which have made a prey of them, spare you? Is Death more favourable now-a-days than he was before? Is not the world still, as it was, but vanity? Is not all flesh still but grass, and the beauty of it as a flower that is cut down and withereth suddenly? Well then, this being granted, that nothing is more certain than death, and that it is appointed for all men once to die, would you not then be glad of something that will stand you in stead after death, a Friend in another world? Why, then, do you not speedily get acquainted with Him who alone can befriend you in that dreadful hour?

Quest. 6. What do you think will become of you, if, after all this, you go on in your old ways? What will become of you, do you think, if you should die without the knowledge of God? What hopes have you of life in peace, if you bid defiance to the Lord of life, and contemn the Prince of peace? How shall you escape if you neglect so great salvation? What do you think that those who once, as you do now, slighted Christ, and never looked after reconciliation with are now doing in another world? What would you do in this case?—should one come to you either out of heaven or out of hell, how wonderfully do you think you should be affected with the narration which he would give you of the affairs of the invisible world! Why then will you not now be affected with what we say? for assure yourselves, whatever you may think, our testimony is as true, and hath a better foundation of credit, than if one should tell you he came from the dead, and speak to you of these things.

Quest. 7. Another question I would propound to you is this: Are you willing to bear the displeasure of God? Can you undergo the weight of that wrath which made His back to ache who was mighty to do and suffer? Can you with any patience hear that dreadful word pronounced by the mouth of that Judge who will see to the execution of his sentence, "Depart from me, ye cursed, into everlasting torment; depart from me, ye workers of iniquity; for I know you not?" Can you endure without any trouble that scalding hot wrath which is abundantly more painful than fire and brimstone, more intolerable than to be shut up in a burning fiery furnace, or to be boiled in a caldron of melted lead, or whatsoever torments the wit of men or devils can invent? Can you with any patience bear the stone, gout, toothach, colic, or some such distempers of body which last but for a while? Oh, how long do you think the time when you are in that condition! How do you toss and tumble! What lamentable moans do you make! Do not you think you cannot be too much pitied in that condition? How then will you be able to lie down in those torments, the least drop of which is abundantly more painful than the greatest torment that ever you felt in your life? If these seem dreadful to you, why do you not go the way to avoid them? which is by getting an interest in Him who hath the keys of hell at his girdle; for there is no condemnation to them that are in Christ Jesus, to them that are brought into a state of reconciliation and acquaintance with God by his Son, our Mediator.

Quest. 8. Are you contented to lose everlasting happiness? Can you willingly see Abraham, and Isaac, and Jacob, and a great many from all the quarters of the world, sit down in the kingdom of heaven, and yourself cast out? How do you like to have those whom you scorned to look upon, set at the table at the feast, and yourself shut out with the dogs? Would you not be glad to have a word of comfort spoken to you, when your soul is just taking its leave of your body? Would you not be glad, then, to be conveyed by the blessed angels into the presence of God, and to be crowned with an immortal and glorious crown? Would it do you any harm to be perfect in holiness and happiness when you die? Would you not be glad to be saved when others shall be damned? In a word, do you not desire to be rejoicing and praising God in endless pleasures, when others shall be weeping and cursing God in endless torments? Why then do not you live the lives of the righteous, if you would die their deaths, and have your latter end like theirs? If you would be glorious and happy for ever, why do you not endeavour to be holy and spiritual in time? if you would have God your Friend in another world, what do you mean that you labour no more to be acquainted with him in this world?

Quest. 9. How would you take it at any man's hands, to be served as you serve God? Suppose you should take up a poor child that came to your door to beg, that had scarce a rag to cover his nakedness, or a morsel of bread to put into his mouth, and nowhere to hide his head; suppose you should strip this poor beggar of his rags, and clothe him in very good apparel, and take him into your own house, and take as much care of him as if he were your own child; suppose, after this, you should bid him do you some small piece of service, and he instead of it should say, Command your man, and do your work yourself; and instead of answering your kindness, should offer you the greatest abuse in the world, and afterwards conspire with a company of rogues to rob and murder you—how would you like this? Should you think that such a fellow as this did not deserve a halter rather than your favour? But now, if after this you should send after this ungrateful wretch, and tell him that you are willing to forget all that is past, and to receive him into the greatest favour, and never to cast his former wickedness in his teeth; how would you take it at his hands, if he should stand, I know not how long, disputing whether he should accept of your kindness or no, whether he should choose the gaol and gallows, or your house? But if, after all this, you should send messenger after messenger, and offer to give him all that you have in the world, and to bestow your only daughter upon him, and to settle presently a great estate upon him with her, how would you take it if this vile ungrateful beggar should put you off a great while together with some poor excuse or other? How would you like it if he should make light of your offers, and tell you he thanks you for nothing, and should undervalue your kindness? Would you not soon resolve not to trouble yourself any longer with such an unthankful monster? Would you not let him take his course, and not much pity him, if he afterwards see the difference between a father's house and a gaol, between liberty and a prison, between riches, glory, and pleasure, and poverty, dishonour, and sorrows? Would you not bid him never expect kindness more at your hands; but, seeing he would not be ruled, to take what follows? What do you say? Would you not do thus? I am persuaded you would. But should I unriddle this parable, who do you think would be condemned? Your own mouth would accuse you, and you would be your own judge. Thou art that man that hast dealt thus disingenuously with God; thou art that beggar to whom the Lord hath shown much kindness, and offered more; he hath sent messenger after messenger, and at last he hath sent his Son to invite thee to his own house, and he offers to make thee as happy as heaven, glory, and happiness itself can do; and thou standest still demurring, adding one delay to another, and art far from that grateful and speedy compliance which the nature of the thing doth require; and, instead of coming at God's call, and thankfully owning his marvellous kindness, how basely dost thou prefer thy company, thy lust, before him, and offer the most intolerable affronts to his majesty, and make nothing of his unparalleled goodness, and continuest in open rebellion against him! What, then, hast thou to say for thyself, why God should not, with a just abhorrence, cast thee off for ever? But now, that God should still offer thee as high as ever, and (instead of doing as I have said, and as thou thyself would have done in case of a less contempt) still follow thee with such a gracious proposal as this is, that I now make unto thee; is it not a miracle of mercy, a prodigy of kindness?

Quest. 10. And now, what will you do? Will you still, for all this, go on in your contempt of God? Will you still refuse to know him, and never mind acquaintance with him? Will you still be indifferent whether you have God for your Friend or your Enemy? Now you have been tendered such a match, will you make another choice? will you bestow your heart somewhere else? And when you have done that, dare you stand to your choice? and say that you have done very wisely in refusing God, and in embracing this present world? Will you maintain it at the day of judgment, that you have done well to refuse acquaintance with himself, and to run the hazard of his displeasure? But you will not, you say, trouble your head with such melancholy fancies as these are; they are enough to put a man beside his wits; you hope to do as well as others, and, so long, you care not. Well then, it seems you are resolved; though, let me tell you, if you are contented to fare as most shall fare at last, you must be contented to be damned; for the Scripture is exceeding clear in this, that the number of those that go to heaven is a very small number; and if you will not take my word for it, (for indeed I would not that you should take my word, nor any man's breathing, without warrant from God's word, in things of so high a nature,) look into the Scripture, and, at your leisure, ponder a while upon these following texts: Luke xiii. 23, 24, "Then said one unto him, Lord, are there few that be saved? And he said unto them, Strive to enter in at the strait gate: for many, I say unto you, will seek to enter in, and shall not be able;" Matt. xx. 16, "Many are called, but few are chosen;" and Luke xii. 32. Christ saith his flock is a little flock. And the church complains of the fewness of her number in this language: "Woe is me! for I am as when they have gathered the summer fruits," Micah vii. 1. I might heap up abundance of Scriptures of the same nature, all which speak this to us, that it is not so common a thing to go to heaven as most people reckon upon. But yet if you be resolved, come what will come, not to change your mind; if, after so many warnings and pleadings, you still continue of this judgment, I must speak a dreadful word. Your blood be upon your own soul. I have blown the trumpet; I have done what in me lies to convince thee of thy dangerous state, while thou art a stranger to God, and to bring thee to a speedy acquaintance with him; but thou hast, after many and many a tender, given in this answer, that as for God, thou dost not desire to be acquainted with him; as for your matching with his Son, it's that which thou carest not for hearing of, except thou mightst have his estate without his sovereignty; thou wilt not have him for thy Husband, except he will let thee do as thou list, and run a-whoring from him when thou pleasest; thou wilt not have heaven, except thou mayst have it without holiness; and as for the invitations of God, thou still makest light of them; neither promises nor threatenings signify much with thee. Well then, when you find by woful experience what you have done, know whom you must lay all the blame on. I call heaven and earth to record, and you yourselves are witnesses, that I have, with all the pity and earnestness that I could for my soul, told you of these great things: but you think the flattering offers that the devil makes more advantageous than those which God makes, and his service to be preferred before the service of Christ, and the friendship of the world to be esteemed before the friendship of God; and the pleasures of sin, which are but for a season, you value before those rivers of pleasures which are at the right hand of God for evermore. Now, if you continue in this mind, blame not me if you miscarry for ever; you must, whether you will or no, stand to your choice. Do not say that you were not told of these things; this is not the first time by many, but it may be the last that you may ever hear, for ought that I know. Remember you were once well offered. Do you think that God will always bear with such unworthy abuses? Shall God's justice never be righted? Yes, yes; be not deceived; slighted kindnesses will cost dear at last. What have you yet to say for yourself? Do you think that I mean you any hurt by all this, except you count salvation a wrong, and kindness itself an injury? But if all this will not do, go then and make the best thou canst of all thy friends; let us see how well and how long they will entertain thee. Ere a few days, it may be, shall be at an end, we shall hear how you like your choice; when they shall turn you out of doors, and tell you plainly, they can do nothing for you, you must shift as well as you can; as for them, they cannot provide for themselves, much less for you. And then let's see who hath made the best choice, he that is acquainted with God, and hath chosen him for his Friend, or he that hath taken the world for his friend. Let's see which will do most for their friends when a time of trial comes. When heaven and earth are all in a flame, when the trumpet is sounding, when the Judge and his attendants, Christ and all his holy angels, are coming, when the prisons, the graves, are opened, and the prisoners are brought forth, then let's see who will have the most cheerful countenance, —he that holdeth up his hand at the bar, or they that sit upon the bench with the Judge: for know ye not that the saints, the friends of the Judge, shall sit with him when he judgeth the world? We shall know, when the storm riseth, whose house was best,—that which was built upon the sand, or that which was built upon the rock. Oh that people were now of the same mind that they will be of at the day of judgment! Oh that they would consider, that if they will not now be at leisure to think of these things, they shall be at leisure to repent of them hereafter! Do not talk of scorns, and reproaches, and suffering; what, do you think that heaven will not make amends for all that? Which is most to be feared, the scorns of God, or the scorns of men? Which will do you most hurt, man's contempt, or God's? Where is the man that will be laughed out of a great estate? Because a fool saith that a jewel is not worth the taking up, will you therefore never stoop to take it up? The truth of it is, if you intend to make anything of your profession, you must be willing to be counted a fool and a madman; but you must remember it is by those that are so themselves. Oh, be not affrighted from your duty by the talk of the rabble! If the thing be evil, let the voice of it scare you; but if it be good, let not the fear of them who are very incompetent judges in such a case divert you from it. Do you think that such poor excuses will be taken at the day of judgment? What, do you intend to say to God then: "Lord, I would have laboured to have known thee, I would have taken some care of my soul, and I would have taken some pains about the things of eternity, but that I saw that almost every one that did with any seriousness look after such matters were scorned and laughed at. When I had got into the company of those that were godly, and I had half a mind to go with them to heaven, then my friends fell a-jeering me, and asked me whether I meant to be made to undo myself, to turn Puritan and fanatic?" Do you, I say, believe that such a plea will stop the mouth of the Judge, and keep him from pronouncing the sentence against you? Will this hold the hands of justice? Will the thoughts of this quench or cool the dreadful flames? Be better advised. Oh be better advised, for your soul's sake, and consider how such creatures will befool themselves, who would upon such a trifle part with heaven! that would be laughed out of glory, and jeered into hell! Is your mind yet altered? Have you any thoughts or resolutions to look after your soul and acquaintance with God? Are there none of you all that ask by this time, What shall I do to be acquainted with God? Are there none of you that begin to think that it is high time to look out for a Friend in a time of need? Have I all this time been beating the air, and labouring in vain? Shall I leave you all as I found you? God forbid. Methinks I hear some poor souls crying out by this time, Oh that I had but such a Friend that would bring me acquainted with God! Oh that I had but a saving knowledge of Jesus Christ! Oh that I did but understand what it means to have communion with the Father and the Son, through the Spirit! I see myself undone and lost for ever, except I have an interest in this Friend. Oh, who will bring me to him? How shall I get acquainted with him? Oh that's sweet language! That's a very good question, "What shall I do to be saved?" But do you speak in sober sadness? Do you speak in jest or in earnest? If any one would give you advice and direction, would you follow it in spite of all the opposition of hell? What do you say? Will you labour to keep exactly to those directions that shall be given? If you will, I do not question but that you and God will be acquainted before you die. But, oh let me not take a great deal of pains, and all to little purpose, as to you; do not now serve me as the Jews did Jeremiah—come and ask counsel of God, and take the devil's. But in hopes that some poor souls may in good earnest desire directions with an intent to follow them, I shall give them as follows.

DIRECTION I.

If you would be acquainted with God, labour to get a thorough sense of your great estrangement from him, and of the danger of such an estrangement. This is what makes people so well contented with their condition, because they see no great evil or danger in it. Men are ready to think very well of their condition, although they be enemies to God, and no friends to Christ. Enemies to God! They scorn your words, though all this while they express the greatest contempt of him conceivable; though they regard neither his commands, threatenings, nor promises; though they value the company of a drunkard, a whore, before the company of God; though they do all that they can against God, love nothing that he loves; though they side with God's greatest enemies, yet they abhor to be thought to be any other than well-wishers to Christ, and the friends and servants of God; though they never come near God, yet they take it very ill if they be not reckoned amongst his acquaintance and special friends. Where are the professors living almost that do not count it a high piece of uncharitableness, if one do not canonize them among the saints, though they live more like brutes? How heinously do they take it, if any one do but question their state! They ignorant of God! they enemies to the cross of Christ! they blind! they unconverted! Who is that man who dare question their condition? They hope to fare as well as any precise Puritan of them all; they will hope to be saved. Say what you will then, you shall never beat them out of their trust in God. And though, in faithfulness to their souls, we beg of them to make a more diligent inquiry into the state of their souls, because we know that the heart is so deceitful, and we have very great cause to suspect that they know not God; yet they will go on very cheerfully with this confidence, until Christ himself show them their mistake, and tell them plainly that he knows them not, and that he never accounted them any of his Friends. But now, did men but thoroughly understand their natural estrangement from God; were they but indeed sensible of the vileness of their hearts; did they but take notice of the rebellions and treasons that are within, the case would be far otherwise with them than it is. Oh, this, this is the reason why so many millions of professors miscarry everlastingly, and never come to desire the friendship of God, because they never believed that they were any otherwise than friends; they do not suspect themselves at all, but think that they are rich and increased in goods, and have need of nothing, whereas the Lord knows, and Christians know too, that they are poor, and blind, and naked. But now, when men begin to be thoroughly sensible of this enmity that is in their natures against God; when they see what mutinies and rebellions there are in them against their most gracious Lord and King; and when they are made to understand the consequences of this war, then how sensibly do they cry out, What shall they do? Was there ever any poor wretched creatures in worse condition than themselves? Was ever any one's heart worse than theirs? Are there any out of hell that are such monsters of sin as they are? Oh, what shall they do? They see the fire kindled, and themselves hanging over everlasting burnings: now all the world for Christ; they believe now that God and man are not equals; that there is no contending with the Almighty: Who can stand before his indignation? And when they see God's sword drawn, and the point of it set against their heart; when they behold the terrors of the Lord setting themselves in array against them, and themselves like to lose all, then how welcome would the news of a parley be! How glad would they be then to hear of a pardon? Then down go their weapons; they will sooner come before God with a halter about their necks than a sword by their sides; they will fight now with no other weapons but tears and prayers: as for their armour, they break it in pieces, and lay it at the feet of their offended Prince; and, oh! if they might but have any hopes of pardon, it would revive their hearts; if they might have but a look of kindness from God, it would be a greater comfort to them than all the world besides could afford them. To whom can a skilful physician be more welcome than to the sick? Christ came to seek the lost, and such as these we are sent to encourage: but till the soul comes to this pass, Christ is not valued at all by it. If sinners be not made thus to understand themselves, why, though we should plead with ever so much earnestness with them, we do but beat the air; all that we can say signifies very little. The man thinks his great work is done, though his hands have been all this while in his bosom; he is far onwards in his journey to heaven, though he never set one step out of his own doors; he hath an interest in God, and is very well acquainted with him, and hath an assured confidence of his condition, that he shall be happy, though he have not one drachm of grace. He is a good churchman, he hath sat at the Lord's table, and the like. But, oh how many are there who shall see and know that it is more than possible to come oft before God, and to compliment him much, and to sit oft at his table, and yet not to be any of his peculiar friends and special acquaintance! Now, if ever you would make anything of religion, and be made highly to prize God's favour, and to be really acquainted with him, you must labour to understand your distance from him, and the inconceivable hazard that you run while you are in a state of separation from God; that there is but one step between you and the state of the damned; for what would become of you, if God should say to you, This night thy soul shall be required of you? How easily can God in a moment stop your breath, and send your soul and body into that lake that burns for ever and ever! And is it not then time for you to look about you? Oh this ignorance of ourselves, how doth it expose us! He was not a whit mistaken who said that "the not knowing of ourselves was one of the chiefest causes of our sin and misery, and that the consideration of the state of the soul, and the thorough understanding its depravements, was the beginning of wisdom; for its weakness being well known, a man will not afterwards trust it in the determination of the greatest things; but man will be desirous to consult that great oracle, the will of his Maker; and finding his old guide is blind, and hath often missed him, thereupon he is the readier to be acquainted with such a one who may direct him in the way to true happiness." (Ar. Epict. l. i. c. 26.) If you would, therefore, be acquainted with God, you must get well acquainted with yourselves: you will, upon the knowledge of yourself, be afraid of yourself. He was none of the weakest men who said that "a true sense of folly is no small sign of some proficiency in wisdom." Look unto thyself, O man, search every corner, behold what abundance of armour there is in such and such a dark cellar; but is this armour strong enough to encounter a God withal? Canst thou with these fig-leaves defend thyself against the arrows of the Almighty? Behold what a condition thou art in, if thou stirrest a step farther! Yield speedily, and throw down thine arms, or thou art a dead man. Do you know this? Do you really believe this? Is it possible? What, believe that your treason is found out, and that you are within a little of execution; and yet not tremble, and yet not seek nor desire a pardon! When a man thoroughly understands how things stand between him and God, and how unable he is to carry on a war against him, he will speedily cast about how he may conclude a peace upon any terms. As soon as Benhadad knew what a condition his army was in, when he saw the crowns of his thirty kings shaken, and his warlike captains cut in pieces, or to tremble, and be like women; when, instead of a mighty army of gallant warriors in martial order, behaving themselves bravely in the field, he saw their carcasses upon heaps, their garments rolled in blood, the shields of his mighty ones cast away, and himself wofully deserted, how speedily doth he send away his servants, with ropes about their necks, to beg peace upon any terms! When the Gibeonites heard what dangerous fighting it was against Joshua, they were not long before they made means to make a covenant with him. So the soul, when it doth seriously consider what a sad condition it is in while it continues in rebellion against God—its impossibility to stand it out long, and utter inability to conquer him; when it perceives the designs of Satan, who first caused this difference between the soul and God, and hath still instigated and stirred it up to persecute with all the violence that might be; I say, when the soul sees this before it is quite too late, oh how doth it bewail its condition, how doth it cry out, O wretched man that I am, who shall deliver me! Oh what will become of me if I still make war against God! And as for flying, whither shall I fly from his presence, and where shall I hide myself out of his sight? And how shall I look Him in the face whom I have thus desperately and ungratefully opposed? Can such a traitor as I possibly expect any mercy; if the Lord should look upon me, and not immediately cast me into hell, it would be a miracle of patience. And thus the man that begins a little to understand himself, speaks to himself; and after that, he, with Ephraim, smites upon his thigh, and bemoans his condition exceedingly. Oh that he should ever take up arms against his gracious Prince! Oh what shall become of him? Well, I have heard that the God of heaven is a merciful King, I will go and cast myself at his feet; if I perish, I perish. If I continue in this rebellion, there is no hope; if I fly, there is no escaping; and if I yield, I can but perish! Oh sad, sad is my condition! Woe and alas, what shall I do in these dreadful perplexities? But why do I stay here? The avenger of blood follows after me apace. Well, I will go to my God, through Christ, and I have heard that this is the only way, and that there is not the least hope in the world, any other way, to get a pardon, to escape the wrath to come. Oh that the precious and merciful Jesus would pity me and stand my Friend now, if ever! Oh that he would speak a good word for me! "Have mercy upon me, Jesus, thou Son of David, have mercy upon me!" Oh make peace for me by thy blood; if thou wilt, thou canst do more with a word speaking than all the saints and angels in the world; if ever any poor creature in the world had need of mercy, then have I. Oh! mercy, mercy, mercy, for thy blood's sake! But because I shall speak to this under another direction, I shall be the briefer. Now, when a man is at this pass, he is in a fair way for peace; but as long as a man is ignorant of all this, he is quite in another. Note, He will never buckle, and therefore he shall be broken. Therefore, consider well your condition, observe the acting of your own soul; if you be one of the friends and acquaintances of God, what means your breaking and hating of his spiritual laws? What's the reason, if you love God, that you can take no delight at all in his company, no pleasure in his sabbaths? If you are a friend of God, how is it you come no oftener to his house, when he dwells so near you? Why do you knock no oftener at his door? Why are you so rare in your visits? Is this your kindness? Is this like a friend? How comes it to pass that there are so many arms found hid in your house? What are they all for? What is the meaning of all those meetings that you give to God's enemies? What do all those whisperings, plots, and projects signify? Is this friendship? Can you mean any good by all this? What do you say of your condition? Do you ever complain, and that feelingly, of your enmity against God? Did you ever observe what a desperate wicked spirit you have against your Maker; and were you ever made sensible of the danger of such a state, and ashamed and grieved to the very soul that you should ever engage against so good a God? Why then, I am confident you cannot but cry out with all the strength and earnestness of your soul for a peace, you cannot but desire to meet with your Adversary quickly, while he is in the way. But if you see nothing at all of the treachery and baseness that is in your heart, search, and search again; it's your ignorance and blindness, and not the goodness of your state, that makes you know nothing by yourself. What, are you better than David? He was so jealous of his own heart, that he dared not trust to his own examination of it, but he desires the great Heart-searcher to help him in this work. Are you more excellent than Paul after his conversion? Had he more reason to complain of himself than you have? Oh, be at leisure to look within and get David's candle and lantern to go into those dark corners of your soul with it, and, it may be, you may see that within which may make your heart ache, and your joints quiver, and your spirits faint within you. Paul was sometimes as confident as you: he took no notice of the enmity that was within against God, though he was as full of it as an asp is of poison; yet before he became acquainted with God, the case was altered with him; he was of another mind when that light shone about him, and he cried out, "Lord, what wilt thou have me to do?" He now thinks it is "hard kicking against the pricks," dangerous opposing God, and persecuting Christ in any part of his members; and he desires nothing in the world so much as to be reconciled to God, and to have him for his Friend whom before he fought against as an Enemy.

DIRECTION II.

My next direction to those who would be acquainted with God, shall be this: Get an humble heart, which is the consequent of the former. God will exalt none to this high honour of being his friends, but such as have low thoughts of themselves. The humble are the persons that he will raise; these are they that he will converse most with; these are the great favourites of heaven whom God doth delight to honour: "The Lord is nigh unto them that are of a broken heart; and saveth such as be of a contrite spirit," Ps. xxxiv. 18. God is nigh unto them, (with reverence be it spoken,) God takes so much complacency in the company of such, that he cannot endure to have them far from him; he must have them always nigh to him, always under his eyes: as for these broken ones, he will be sure not to leave them long, not to go far from them, but will be ready at hand to set their bones, to bind up their wounds to keep them from festering. It may be he may put them to much pain before he brings the cure to perfection, but it is to prevent future aches. He is a foolish cruel chirurgeon, who, for fear of putting his patient to some pain, never searcheth the wound, but skins it over presently: and a wise man will not think him unmerciful that puts him to exquisite pain, so he make a thorough cure of it. Thus God doth by his patients sometimes, when the nature of their distemper calls for it. But, however, he will be sure not to be out of the way when they want him most. It's possible they may look upon themselves as forgotten by God, they may not know their Physician when he is by them, and they may take their Friend for an enemy; they may think God far off when he is near; but when their eyes are opened, and their distemper is pretty well worn off, they will, with shame and thankfulness, acknowledge their error; nay, they do from their souls confess that they do not deserve the least look of kindness from God, but to be counted strangers and enemies; but God will let them know that he loves to act like himself, that is, like a God of love, mercy, and goodness; and that they are the persons that he hath set his heart upon; he will have them in his bosom, never leave them nor forsake them; and though these contrite ones many times look upon themselves as lost, yet God will save them, and they shall sing a song of thankfulness amongst his delivered ones. Again, The sacrifices of God are a broken spirit: " a broken and a contrite heart, O God, thou wilt not despise, Ps. li. 17. The proud sinner may bring his stalled oxen, multitudes of rams and sheep, and his rivers of oil, and yet all this while not be accepted. There is another kind of sacrifice that would be ten thousand times more acceptable to God. We read that sacrifices have been despised, prayers, long prayers, have been rejected; sabbaths, new moons, and solemn assemblies the Lord hath sometimes abhorred; but we never read that he despised the sacrifice of an humble heart, the prayers of such always have an answer one way or other; their poor performances, their chatterings and mournings, are sweet melody and powerful rhetoric in God's ear. Who are the men that have most of God's company? Who are they whom he doth most frequently visit? Are they not such as look upon themselves as the chiefest of sinners? These are they who are rapt up into the third heaven. None have so much of heaven upon earth as those that wonder that the earth doth not swallow them up, and that they are not in hell. But oh, saith the humble soul, God is the high and mighty God, and infinite in his holiness and justice; how then can such a creature as I ever expect that he should so much as cast his eyes upon me? Yes, sweet soul, such is the infinite condescension and goodness of God, that he will sooner look upon thee than another. And if you cannot credit my words, hear what he speaks himself: "Thus saith the high and lofty One that inhabiteth eternity, whose name is Holy; I dwell in the high and holy place, with him also that is of a contrite and humble spirit, to revive the spirit of the humble, and to revive the heart of the contrite ones," Isa. lvii. 15. The thoughts of God's majesty, eternity, and holiness may, and with good reason too, awe that soul that hath low thoughts of itself. Every sinner hath cause enough to cry out with astonishment, Will God look upon such a vile sinful wretch as I am? Will he that is infinite in holiness take any notice of me, except to show his displeasure against me? What shall I do? Sure such a creature as I cannot without a miracle have a smile from God. God may indeed look upon me in his wrath, and vex me in his sore displeasure; God may justly look me into hell; but that he should look upon me in kindness, or take any special notice of me in love, that would be a wonder indeed. What, God dwell with me! Yes, with thee, if thou hast but high thoughts of him, and low thoughts of thyself; the meaner thou thinkest of thyself, the greater worth he sees in thee. God will not only look upon thee, nor will he only knock at thy door, and call at thy house, or give thee a transitory visit, but he will come and dwell with thee. Now, dwelling speaks a continued abode with one; and thus God will continue with the humble; never remove from them, for any considerable time, till eternity hath an end, till himself and the soul cease to be, which will be never. God will not be a stranger to humble souls, but he will come to them, and bring that along with him that shall make him and them welcome too. God never comes to his friends but he brings good cheer along with him. When the soul gives God the best entertainment, it is all at his cost—his bread, his fatlings, his wine, his oil, his cordials, his rich dainties. Where God comes he will keep a noble house, and there shall be mirth and rich cheer in good store. "Thus saith the Lord, The heaven is my throne, and the earth is my footstool: where is the house that ye build unto me? and where is the place of my rest? For all those things hath mine hand made, and all those things hath been, saith the Lord: but to this man will I look, even to him that is poor, and of a contrite spirit, and trembleth at my word," Isa. lxvi. 1, 2. God seems to have low thoughts of heaven itself in comparison of an humble soul. This is the palace where this great King will keep his court, this is the place of his rest. God is not so much delighted and pleased in any of his brave seats as in this of an humble heart; here he dwelleth most commonly; this was the great purchase of his own Son; this was the masterpiece of his power and goodness; this was the project of infinite wisdom and counsel. "What shall I do to be saved?" is a language that makes hell in a rage, and heaven to rejoice. God is never so well pleased as when he beholds the beauty of his own grace shining in a poor, lost, self-debasing creature. The spouse is adorned with humility when Christ gives her that visit, Cant. i. 4. God hath far more kindness for one that lies under a sense of his own vileness, that thinks himself unworthy to tread upon God's earth, or to breathe in his air, than for the most confident-righteous Pharisee in the world. Such an humble soul will be much in admiring God, and will set a high price upon his kindness. A look, a smile, a visit! Oh, how welcome are they to those poor trembling ones! Wherefore God doth with frequency and love visit them; he knows that he never can be unwelcome to such; they will count it the highest honour, that the Most High should come in to them in their low condition. Wherefore, if you desire to have any intimate acquaintance with God, labour to be more and more sensible of your own unworthiness, study your heart and nature well, and be more curious in the observance of the baseness and treachery of your own soul; endeavour to have as mean thoughts of yourself as Paul had, who did not stick to call himself the chiefest of sinners. Humble yourselves before the Lord, and he will exalt you; he that is little in his own eye is great in God's. When was it that Jacob met with God, but when he had been humbling himself? as you may read at your leisure, Gen. xxxii. There is many a professor that holds out many a year in a course of external performances, and yet never knows what it is to have any intimate acquaintance or converse with God: whereas I am persuaded, if the business were thoroughly examined, it would be found that they were never made deeply sensible of their undone state out of Christ, never understood the desperate depravedness of their hearts and nature; that they never lay under any lively sense of their separation from, and enmity against, God, and they were never brought off from their own righteousness, and saw themselves poor, beggarly, starved creatures; and in this condition came to buy wine and milk without money and without price. But this humility is an excellent grace, it makes the soul fit for the richest enjoyments of God, and to do God the greatest service. Were it possible that God should converse much with a proud man, he would make a strange use of it; he would steal God's crown, and put it upon his own head; but God would not endure proud angels near him, and can it be expected that he should take proud men in their places? The more any one grows in grace and acquaintance with God, the more he sees his own unworthiness, the more he admires free grace. Why me, Lord? why me? will be the language of those who converse with God: and while they are thus admiring God, and laying themselves low, he comes again with his soul-ravishing kindnesses; and thus by humility they are more acquainted with God, and being more acquainted with God, they are made more humble; and the one increaseth the other. Thus the humble soul is raised higher and higher, till he come to an eternal possession of God in the highest heavens. When an humble saint lives, as it were, in heaven upon earth, he scarce thinks himself worthy to live upon the earth. When any one speaks well of him, and admires the grace of God in him, he looks upon himself as an unprofitable servant, and he durst not assume the least glory to himself: Not unto me, not unto me, but unto the Lord be the praise given. Who am I, poor wretch? Oh did you but know what a heart I have, did you but see the workings of my thoughts, could you but tell how things are, indeed you would rather admire God's patience than man's excellency! This he speaks, not that he is worse than others, but because he hath a more spiritual sense of his state than others have. Neither doth he speak thus in proud policy, thinking to make others have a better esteem of him for his humility, but he doth really feel the pressure of that filthiness of sin which makes him thus groan out these complaints. The reason why God doth converse most with the humble, is because they will be most thankful, and most fruitful, and make the wisest improvement of his favours. Wherefore, if you value the comfort of a spiritual life, if you desire communion with God, if you would have a heaven upon earth, endeavour to get an humble heart. To walk humbly and to walk with God go together

DIRECTION III.

If you would be acquainted with God, you must visit him often, be much at his house, knock at his door many times in a day, and resolve to continue knocking till he open; and if he do not come presently, wait for him; you would do as much for your prince, and, it may be, to a meaner person. We cannot expect to be acquainted with them that we will not come near. It is to no purpose for that man to speak of acquaintance with God, who never speaks to him, comes to him, or inquires after him. Neither will a slight visit or two, in a transitory complimental manner, serve the turn; a man may do this, and yet not be said to be acquainted with God. A stranger may come once to your house who was never there before, and never intends to come again; and I believe you will scarce write such a one down amongst your special friends and intimate acquaintance. So in spirituals: for acquaintance and converse with God are no such slight things as the world commonly takes them to be. If you would make anything of this great work of getting acquaintance with God, you must not jest in it, you must give God many solemn and set visits, and carry yourself with all the observance and respect to him that you can for your soul. This is that which keeps many thousands strangers from the life of grace and intimate acquaintance with God, because they know not what those more peculiar visits of God mean; they understand not what it is to draw nigh to God in secret; they come not to him with those more spiritual acts of religion; they pray, it may be, in their families, and, it may be, that but seldom, (but, by the way, never let such pretend to the knowledge of God, who call not upon him in their families,) but what they do, it is but in a poor formal perfunctory manner, between sleep and awake; and will you call this acquaintance with God? Will you call this an act of adoration and spiritual worship? Is it to bow down a while before God, and to read and speak a few words, and there's an end? Their work is over, their task is done, and they are glad of it. But now, such as these do not come into God's chambers; they come to his house, as I may so say, but they regard not whether he be at home, whether they speak to God, and have an answer from God or no. They call indeed, but desire not much to be heard; they knock, but are not very careful to stay till the door be opened. But alas, alas, such as these cannot tell what it is to enjoy communion with God. They have got, it may be, into some course of external performances, by reason of the example of their superiors, education, or by being under the sound of the gospel, and from some force that natural conscience doth put upon them, which will not be content except something be done. But such as these may not be said to visit God in that manner that I would persuade them to who would be acquainted with God; for all this they stand a great way off from God, and may be termed strangers and foreigners. How seldom are they upon their knees in secret! How rare a thing is it for them, with Isaac, to go into the field to meditate! They visit their farms, they visit their flocks, they visit their swine, they go often to visit their sottish drunken companions, whilst God and Christ, their Bible, their closet, their hearts, are forgotten, and seldom or never visited. And is this true kindness to one's self? Is it any wisdom to slight such a Friend as God would be to us, and to make so much of such sorry companions? Oh stupid and dull souls! Oh what do we mean, so strangely to forget ourselves! For who is like to get by it, God or we, when we come and feed at his table, and spend upon his cost? Oh, little do people think what they might enjoy, would they purposely set themselves to meet with God, and go to his house with a strong resolution not to come away from him till they have seen him, or heard from him. Now the great duties in which the soul may be said to visit God in, and in which God doth many times give out much of himself to the soul, are these:—

1. Solemn meditation.
2. Secret prayer.
3. Fasting.
4. Community of experiences, and communion with the saints.
5. The Lord's supper.

First, Meditation. When the soul doth fix itself upon the thoughts of some spiritual and divine object, such as the love of God in Christ, the glory of another world, &c., this is, as it were, going out to meet the Lord, and to take a walk with our Beloved; this is the getting up to Mount Pisgah, to take a survey of that goodly land. When the soul doth, as it were, bathe itself in the contemplation of Christ's beauty, and labours to enamour itself more and more with his love, and to throw itself, as I may so say, into that ocean of divine goodness, it will scarce leave till it be wound up to the highest pitch of admiration of that infinite boundless love which should do such glorious things for so rebellious and unthankful a wretch as that is. Oh, what manner of love is this! Oh that I were sick of love! Oh that I might die sick of love! Oh that I were once in the embraces of my dearest Lord and Husband! Oh that I could do nothing else day and night, but praise, love, and admire this infinite boundless love! And did Christ indeed offer up his life for my sin? Did he not think his precious heart-blood too dear for me? And shall I think my heart-love too dear for him? What, for me, Lord, who am the **chiefest of sinners**! Here, here is kindness with a witness!

Stand still, O my soul, and admire; stand looking upon this lovely sight till thou art all on fire. These are pure flames, here thou needest not to fear to exceed; widen thy desires, let thy affections run without control. More fire still; blow hard, it doth yet but smoke. Oh for some coals from the altar! Oh for more fire, more fuel! Oh that my heart were vehemently inflamed in the strongest love to Him who still deserves a thousand times more! Help me, all ye angels, to bless and adore His marvellous loving-kindness. Christ is a Friend to publicans and sinners indeed, or such a one as I had never been on this side of hell. Oh love, love, love! What shall I render unto the Lord? Oh that men would bless the Lord for his goodness, and for his wonderful works to the children of men! Oh, what meanest thou, O my soul, that thou art yet so cold! Awake, awake, psaltery and harp! I myself will awake and praise, admire and love thee, O my God, whose love to my soul is beyond expression. And thus, while the soul is musing, the fire begins to burn; while the spouse is thinking of her glorious Husband, he knocks at the door, she draws the latch, and he comes in, smelling of myrrh, aloes, and cassia; he comes and kisses the soul with the kisses of his lips; his love is better than wine; he comes and takes the soul into his arms. Oh the sweet pleasure of divine love, infinitely transcending all carnal affections! Oh the joy that is at this meeting, far surpassing human apprehension! Oh the sweet entertainment that God and the soul give each other at such a time! I appeal to the experience of those that have been much exercised in this great duty of meditation; if they have been in good earnest in the work, I am confident they can say something to this point. What sayest thou, O Christian, who art used to imitate Isaac? Didst thou never meet with another guess companion than Rebekah? As he met with a wife, so hast thou met with thy Husband? When thou hast been in the field, or closet, at this work, hath not Christ then taken you by the hand, and led you into his garden, and made you to taste of his pleasant fruits? Hath he not brought you into his banqueting-house, and brought out some of his choicest dainties? Are not those flagons more full of spirit, more cordial and refreshing than wine? Oh, little do any but those who have tried it think what a life they might lead, if they would with seriousness engage in this duty! Speak, O ye gracious ones, that make conscience of this soul-ravishing duty; speak, I beseech you, and do not smother the kindnesses of God to you; speak, and let him have the praise. It may be, by your venturing your experience, hundreds may be encouraged to set upon the same work, and hundreds may also have the same experiences. What do you say? Have you not found the benefit of this duty? Did you never find meditation a sweet work? Was it worth your while or no to sequester yourselves a while from the world to talk with your Beloved? Did you ever repent you of your labour, and think your time lost? And have you not been able to say, that at such and such a time, when you were in the mount, that it was good being there? Could you not have been almost content to have left the dearest relations, and to have quitted your interest in all creature-comforts, so you might have had fuller enjoyments of God? Could you not have been contented to pass from contemplation to vision and fruition? Why, speak then, for the Lord's sake, and for the sake of precious souls, and keep not such a thing as this is in; let your unexperienced neighbours know what a soul-ravishing and soul-raising duty meditation is. Let me ask you who read these lines, did you ever try what there was in this duty of meditation? I suppose, if you converse much with such books as speak of communion with God, you cannot but desire something of it, and I am persuaded you have sometimes wept since you began to read this book, to think how little you experience; I believe you would be glad, with all your soul, to know what it is to be acquainted with God, and to have such a Friend as I have been speaking of. Why, let me ask you again, did you ever try what meditation is? (You may read much of the excellency of this duty, and directions about it, in Mr. Baxter's "Saints' Everlasting Rest.") Did you ever get out of the world, and intensely fix your heart and thoughts upon any of the glorious attributes of God? Did you ever set before your eyes his love in Christ? If not, oh try and fall to this work seriously and speedily, and you shall soon find the sweetness of it; you will soon say that you lost many a good meeting, many a dainty bit for want of going for it. A carnal worldly heart, I must confess, may possibly spoil this duty, as all others, and grow formal in it, and be weary of it, and cast it off, (though, let me put in this: I believe it's marvellous rare for a hypocrite to have anything to do in such a secret duty as this is,) but if they were true to the interest of their own souls in the management of this work, I am confident they would be every day more and more in love with this duty. For I am persuaded that when the soul is in good earnest, nay, I can speak it positively, there is no duty doth so much raise and warm the soul; there is no duty wherein the people of God enjoy his sweet company more than in this. This opens the treasures of God's kindness; this takes his love-tokens, and presents them to the view of the soul; this unlocks the cabinets, and fetches out those precious jewels; by this the soul doth, as it were, talk with its Beloved; and in this Christ doth, as it were, take the soul by the hand, and lead it into his palace, and shows it all those glorious things which it shall shortly have in its possession for ever. And how can this choose but engage the soul to express its gratitude to the height in answer to such love? And when the soul is in this frame, Christ will not be behindhand with her, no love shall be lost between them. If the spouse walk out to look for her Beloved, she shall find him before she hath done.

Second, Another duty by which the soul doth visit God in a special manner, is secret prayer; by this the soul knocks, and God is quick of hearing, and none of his friends shall wait without doors so long as to catch cold. By this the soul doth, as it were, storm heaven; by this it gets into the presence-chamber, and presents its requests. In this duty a Christian doth, as it were, return the key of heaven's doors, and by this he unlocks the door of his own soul; and so there is free access on both sides; the soul visits God, and God visits the soul, and this creates an intimacy. The poor wounded creature opens his wounds, and then the great

Physician comes with the balm of Gilead. When Jacob is thus weeping and praying alone, he meets with God, he meets a blessing, he wrestles, he conquers. This duty of secret prayer, and that other of meditation, are two fattening duties, by which the souls of believers come to God's table, and eat and drink of strengthening food; and for want of these, many poor souls are thin. Oh why do Christians, why do professors maintain no fairer correspondence with God in such duties wherein he doth manifest himself more than ordinarily to the soul? The reason of this may be because God accounts himself more highly honoured, and more truly loved by them who are much in these, than by others. By this a man doth, as it were, honour the goodness of God, in that it shows it worth the while to steal out of the world, and to leave the best company on earth to go to God. He honours the truth of God, by being earnest for what God hath promised, though it be unseen; he honours the omnisciency of God, by contenting himself with his eye and his ear alone; he sanctifies his omnipresence, by believing that his God can hear him, and be with him into what corner soever he creeps. I might be large in speaking of the excellencies of this duty, but I refer it rather to another place. But I would not be mistaken in what I have delivered, as if I would by this exclude family prayer; no, far be it from me; for God in this doth many times exceedingly refresh his. But because a man cannot possibly judge so well of himself by public prayer, as he can by secret; and hypocrisy and pride do not usually so much attend secret duty as more public; it's possible in more public duty, that a man may be much raised, and be very warm and high in his expressions, and almost ravish the hearts of his hearers, whereas he may be all that while acted only by a proud heart, and, for aught I know, the devil himself may help a man thus to pray sometimes. This I am confident of, he is not afraid of such prayers as these, which tend so much to the hardening of a sinner, and make him believe that his heart is warmed with communion with God, when, as it is possible, it is nothing but a secret self-pleasing, that those that joined with him might think very highly of him, as one that was passing spiritual in his performances. Oh the heart of man is deep and desperately full of deceit! But now, there is none of this temptation in secret closet prayer, and there a soul may be more particular in its complaints and petitions, more earnest in pleading with God, and may use such expostulations, postures, and gestures, such intermissions and groanings, such pauses as would be very unfit for more public duty. Wherefore I lay somewhat the more stress upon this duty of secret prayer. But this I say again, where one of them is practised conscientiously, the other will not be neglected. I might add the practice and experience of God's children to enforce this duty. David would never have been at it so oft at midnight, if he had got nothing at all by it. Peter would scarce have forgot to eat when he was hungry, except he had met with a bit in a corner to stay his stomach.

Third, Fasting, especially private fasting, is another duty wherein God meets the soul and the soul visits God. This is, as it were, execution-day, the day when the soul brings out all the enemies of God to be crucified; this is the day wherein the idols are searched for, brought out, and buried, or ground to powder; and these are things which God will come to see with much delight. By this the soul is, as it were, adorned, her deformities done away, and she is trimmed up to meet her Beloved. When a saint fasts from sin, and abstains from sensual pleasures, then it is many times feasted by God and refreshed with spiritual enjoyments.

Fourth, Another season wherein God meets the soul, and the soul is visited by God is, when Christians are met together to communicate experiences, or to discourse together about the great things of God. What though most of the world are ashamed to own religion when it is out of fashion! What though but few dare meet together to speak of God's goodness, and to praise him and call upon his name! Why, Christ says, though there be but two or three of them, he will make the number one the more, he will be in the midst of them. And though they dare but whisper, it may be, and their meetings to observe God and do good to one another may be prohibited by the public magistrate, and consequently what they do in this kind must be done in a great deal of hazard, yet the people of God stand not long disputing, they know what to do in this case; yet they would be wise in it too. Not to dare the magistrate, and to do what they do to confront the authority, but in the uprightness of their souls they desire to meet together to worship God according to his own will. Yet for all this, though they manage their business with never so much secrecy, God will take notice of them; he hearkens and hears, and a book of remembrance is written for them that call oft upon his name, and God will make them up among his jewels. But I shall have occasion to speak of something to this purpose afterwards, and therefore I pass it over the more briefly.

Another time wherein the Lord is pleased to discover much intimacy and endeared affection to his people, is in the sacrament of the Lord's supper. This is the great passover; and it cannot be unwelcome news to the poor Israelites, to hear of redemption from worse than Egyptian bondage, instead of being burdened with barbarous task-masters, to be made free, rich, and honourable, and to see the strength of the enemy laid in the dust. It is not for nothing that this passover is to be had in everlasting remembrance. If I should appeal to the people of God that have kept this solemn feast, and ask them how their hearts were affected, do they not all bow their heads and hearts, and adore that goodness that should save, feed, and feast them, and punish, kill, and damn others? Are there not thousands that can tell you, that Christ's flesh is bread indeed, and his blood drink indeed? No provision so great, no banquet so sweet, so noble; no entertainment comparable to that which the princely Jesus giveth to his spouse in that ordinance! The King brings her into the banqueting-house, and his banner over her is love; she is then made to understand that the kisses of his lips do breathe life, and that his visits at such a time usually leave behind them more special testimonies of the largeness of his heart, the loveliness of his nature, and of his matchless excellency. Speak, Christian, what dost thou say to this? Canst thou not subscribe to this?

Art thou not able to say, that then thou hast tasted and seen? Couldst thou not then go out and invite all the poor starved hungry souls in the world, to come, and see, and taste? Art thou not able to say, Come, and I will tell you what Christ hath done for my soul? Let me ask that saint who hath been feasted many a time and oft, what he thought of his entertainment. Were you not made welcome? Was not the joy of the Lord your strength? Was not the provision that the world entertains its friends with, but mean, coarse, unsavoury, compared with it? Which was best,—the husk, or the bread and fatted calf, the garlic and onions, or the manna, the milk and honey? 'Tis not without cause that the faces of some do shine; their looks speak their face none of the meanest, and their activity is not a disparagement to their Keeper. Inquire further, and you shall be informed, if their experience be not too big to be clothed in words, how oft have some of Christ's favourites, after they have dined with their Lord, been led forth into the garden to walk; and, oh the delightful shades that they have sat under! At another time, Christ, not Satan, hath carried them, as it were, in his arms and bosom, and set them upon the pinnacle of the temple, not to make them giddy, and hazard their fall, but to let them understand how much he had preferred them before others, and as long as they are upon that great Corner-stone, no storms can shake, in Christ's arms no fear of falling. At another time, the soul hath been carried into the mount of God, and there it hath seen Christ transfigured, and beheld so much brightness, glory, and majesty in him, that hath reflected a glory upon itself, and even transfigured the soul, that it's scarce like itself, and there it could say, It's good being here; and then Christ hath bid the soul lift up its eyes and look up to the heavens, look round from one side to the other, and look beyond the visible heavens, by faith, to the seat of the blessed. Well, all this is thine, to thee will I give it, I purchased it, I have paid for it, and 'tis thine; and live like one that is worth more than a world; live up to your estate; expect that shortly I should set you in the possession of all. And as for the world, look down upon that; if it be worth the accepting, so much of it as is good for thee thou shalt have also. Oh, did weak Christians but know what strength, joy, and comfort this ordinance doth afford, I believe they would not be so hardly persuaded to come when they are invited! Did they but understand how sweet, how wholesome, how dainty the dishes are which wisdom prepares; could they but conceive what satisfaction and fulness there is for the empty, what joy and solace for the mourning and disconsolate, what strength and quickening for the weak, I am ready to think that they would scarce be so long absent from the Lord's table. But think not that every one that sits down is made so welcome, or that Christ gives his dainties to strangers or enemies; many may come and receive, and not only feed upon a piece of bread, and drink two or three spoonfuls of wine; and really, if this were all the provision that a saint were to have, it were scarce worth so solemn an invitation. It's possible to come thither to eat and drink your own damnation, and, instead of an affectionate treatment, to be dismissed with a "Friend, how comest thou hither, not having on the wedding-garment?" Yet the sensible, hungry, burdened souls, notwithstanding all their fears, may come, nay, they must, and it's little less than giving assent to Satan's calumnies, which he raiseth against Christ and his ways, to forbear; it's too ungrateful a contempt of one of the excellent cordials which the great Physician hath provided for the recovering and strengthening of his poor swooning patients; and, in a word, it's too like being foolishly fond of our sin and sorrow, when we refuse the comfortable appointment which the goodness and wisdom of a Father, the love and tenderness of a Husband, and the sweetness of the Holy Spirit, doth so freely offer, persuade, and command. The Spirit saith, Come, and the Bridegroom saith, Come, and why should not he that is athirst come thankfully, humbly, speedily? Well now, poor weary soul, what hast thou to say against the excellency of rest? Poor sick soul, what fault canst thou find with ease, health, and strength? Poor guilty soul, that lookest upon thyself as next to condemned, what harm would a pardon, and the public sealing of it, do thee? Who would think that man hungry that had rather eat ashes than bread? Who would judge that person thirsty that had rather drink gall, tears, and wormwood, than the clear refreshing streams that come from that rock, the Lord Christ? Will you never believe that Christ invites you? Look into the note that he hath sent out his servants with. Whose name do I read there? Who are the persons that are invited? Of what rank and quality? Are they the great ones of the world? Are they the learned? Are they the proud and self-conceited Pharisees? Why, I find none of these in the writing. Who are they, then, that may come with confidence to draw water out of these wells of consolation? The poor in spirit, the hungry, the sick, the wounded, the lost; these are pools of Bethesda, where the angels of the covenant do oft descend and move the waters; and where is it fitter for the impotent to lie, than there where they cannot miss of a doctor, a visit, or cure? What do you think of this, poor heart? Are they but flourishes? Do I speak, or doth Christ? And if he say it, who can disannul it? Will he, can he be worse than his word? I know he is usually better, but never short of his promise. Will you credit the experiences of Christians? Have they not seen, have they not known, have they not felt, yea, have not all their spiritual senses been exercised and refreshed at that time when the King hath been at his table? One is ready to say, If ever I could have left the world at a minute's warning, and have stept immediately into eternity, it was then when mine eyes beheld the King in his beauty, when he held out his golden sceptre unto me, and took me into his embraces. Yea, when the ministers of Christ presented me with the jewels and bracelets, and asked me whether I would go with them to Christ, my soul made a speedy and thankful reply, My heart and love are his, and his will I be for ever. Oh that I were once safe is his arms! Oh that I might live with him, and never part! Oh, when shall it be? Come, Lord Jesus, come quickly. I remember I have heard it reported of that reverend and holy man of God, Mr. Alleine, (who lived at as high a rate as most on this side perfection and glory,) that he was, before he died, in very rare seraphic raptures of joy and love, so that he could not choose but burst out into unusual expressions of praise, such as these: "Ten thousand praises to the King of saints for the freeness and riches of his grace to my poor soul; let every corner of heaven ring with hallelujahs; let all the angels help me to praise the incomparable, lovely, and glorious Jesus! Oh the joys that he feasts my soul with! Who would not be Christ's servant! Never did I feel such transcendent, pure, divine joys, except at the Lord's table; and then indeed I have been oft so raised in spirit, that my nature, except sustained by a miracle, could scarce bear a greater weight of comfort. Oh the unspeakable, vast, satisfying pleasures that Christ in that ordinance doth afford some of his sometimes!" I have heard another dear brother say, that for some years together, he scarce ever failed of some notable token of love at that great ordinance. But I would not, instead of comforting and encouraging the poor saint, bring him into greater fears and despondings. Judge not, therefore, that this is the portion of all God's children, nor of any, at all times to have such large discoveries as these. Heaven is reserved for heaven; some have a single mess, some a double, some five times more than their brethren. Let all be thankful if the great Joseph, instead of a prison, give a feast, and in it make himself known to us to be our Brother; let us love him, admire his condescension, and be ready to wonder that he doth so much for us, rather than repine that he doth more for others. If thou hast some drawings, and longings, and mournings after Christ, and a deep sense of thy hardness, unbelief, and worldliness, be thankful; it may be this is more wholesome entertainment, and fitter for the present temper and constitution of thy soul, than those flagons of wine; perhaps they would fly up into thy head, and make thee giddy, proud, and wanton. If thou be but well wrought, poor, and hungry, thou wilt be thankful for a little; and a crumb that falls from the table to a humble soul, is better entertainment than it knows it deserves, or could, without a miracle of kindness, have expected. Mistake me not, as if I would have Christians sit down satisfied with little or no comfort at that ordinance; no, 'tis quite another design that I am carrying on; 'tis only a hint to quell ingratitude; my great work at present is to quicken diligence in preparation, and to raise the saint's valuation of that ordinance, and his expectations from Christ in it. I say again, Christ usually proportions his entertainment to the diligent, faithful, humble preparations of the soul to meet him; they that trim their lamps, and have oil in them, are most like to meet that Bridegroom with joy; he that hath on the wedding garment cannot miss of a welcome, and the good and faithful servant is most likely to have the Master's commendation, and to enter into his joy. But more or less, every sincere soul, at one time or another, will meet with refreshment at that supper; and amongst all the rare dishes that are served up, no question but some will be suitable, (if not all) to a hungry, spiritual stomach. I can scarce leave this sweet subject. The time draws nigh, and the servants are sent out to invite, and thou, O my soul, art one of the guests that are bidden. Hark, methinks I hear a royal proclamation, "Whosoever is athirst, let him come and drink of the waters of life freely." Methinks the silver trumpet of the gospel and divine love sounds a jubilee. Methinks the air echoes with a strange harmony, somewhat like that, Luke ii. 14, " Glory to God in the highest, and on earth peace, good will toward men." Do not the very heavens ring with these blessed words, A Saviour! a Saviour! a mighty Redeemer! a pardon! a pardon! liberty! liberty! a glorious liberty! And again the congregations of the saints and redeemed ones cry, Hallelujah! hallelujah! hallelujah! I had thought to have done, but the feast is so sweet, I must fall on again. Here is no surfeiting, the more I feed, the more hungry; and yet the more satisfied, the more delighted. Here is nothing but fulness; sweetness and love may be written upon every dish; the royal, noble, everlasting bounty may be proclaimed before every course. All the dismal bonds are thrown in and cancelled; all our debts forgiven and paid; the great Surety shows the acquittance long since granted in the court of heaven, now it's given in to the court of conscience. The bloody war is concluded by a happy and firm peace: God is no longer a Judge, an Enemy, but now the soul hears such words, Friend, Father, Husband. The challenges of law, conscience, and Satan, are now silenced, the indictments against the soul are all quashed; the soul may now walk at liberty, and fear no arrest. Who can lay anything to the charge of God's elect? It is Christ that justifies, who can condemn? Christ says it, swears it, seals it; it cannot but be true. Why art thou then cast down, poor soul, and why art thou disquieted? Christ hath made a blessed exchange with thee, he hath drank the bitter cup, and offers thee the sweet, which is spiced with grace and love; Christ hath purchased the crown for thee, and taken the cross to himself; he took the rags, and gives thee the robes; he became poor that thou mayst become rich; he emptied himself that thou mayst be filled; he was esteemed as nothing, that thou mightest from worse than nothing possess all things; and what now remains, but that, with the greatest gratitude, thou acceptest of Christ's offer, whensoever he invites thee to his table? What doth better become thee, than the fullest acceptance of the highest kindness, and a grateful closure with all the overtures of divine goodness? Oh happy are the people that are admitted to this intimacy! Happy are the souls that know the worth, the use of this ordinance, and make it their business wisely to improve it. Oh what an opportunity have such of Christ here! What request may they not then have granted! And when Christ is giving, what will he, what can he deny them who have his heart already! I have been the more large in this, because it was the particular request of one of my brethren, a reverend minister, that in the next edition I would not forget that ordinance in which God usually doth most signally discover his love to his people.

DIRECTION IV.

If you would get acquaintance with God, get Christ along with you, when you go to God. You are like to speed no way so soon as this way; nay, let me say, all that I have said before signifies nothing at all without this. There is no name under heaven by which we can be saved but by the name of Christ; and whosoever comes to the Father by him, he will in no wise cast out. God cannot deny his own Son anything, he can never forget that great undertaking of his, by which he glorified his Father's infinite justice and infinite love, and did him more honour than all the saints and angels in the world. His Son, the Lord Christ, hath such an interest in his Father, that he can as soon despise his own honour as refuse any request that is presented to him by his Son. If Christ come unto him, and say, Father, here is a poor sinner that I have undertaken for, and that flew to me for refuge, look upon him for my sake; why, the Father's arms are presently open; he will not reject his Son's petitions. The truth of it is, this is the greatest cause of the miscarriages of poor creatures, that go about to do that themselves, and by themselves, which they can never do alone. They go to God all alone, and no wonder than they meet with a frown; for there is no name under heaven by which a man can be saved but by the name of Christ; and out of Christ, God is a consuming fire; and there is but one Mediator, the Man Christ Jesus; and there is but one Advocate with the Father, Jesus Christ the righteous. That which Joseph said of Benjamin, God saith of Christ, Except you bring Benjamin along with you, you shall not see my face; Except you bring Christ along with you, you shall not see my face. There is a notable story which is commonly by divines applied to our present purpose, and that not without good reason: it is concerning a law among the Molossians, where whosoever came to the king with his son in his arms should be accepted into favour, let his fault be what it might. So let a man be what he will before, yet if he come to God in Christ, he cannot be thrust away. Oh therefore, if thou wouldst have any countenance from God, beg for a Christ to bear thee company into the presence of God. I will tell you this for your comfort. Christ hath a loving design in his heart to do such offices of kindness for poor malefactors that understand something of their danger. If you see yourself lost for want of reconciliation with God, Christ stands ready to lead you into his Father's house. Oh did you but know how willing he is to bring undone lost penitents to God, it would make your heart leap within you for joy. Behold how oft he asks after you. What doth that sinner mean to ruin himself? I would with all my heart bring him out of all those perplexities, and undertake to make God and him friends, if he would be but ruled by me; and upon this account he sends up and down many hundreds of his ministers to tell sinners as much, that they may not be undone everlastingly. Doth not wisdom call? Doth not Christ plead the case, and expostulate with sinners? And who would not, that hath any understanding at all of his state out of Christ, with all possible thankfulness be encouraged to accept of his kindness? Christ hath done as much as this comes to already for many millions, and his Father never said to him, Son, why do you trouble yourself and me with so many of these wretched creatures? let them alone to take their course. Where did God ever express himself in this manner? Did he ever take it unkindly that his Son should every day bring such guests to his house, and be continually begging one boon or other for them, or putting up some petitions upon their account, or pleading with his Father for them when they do offend? Is God displeased at such work as this? Is he not as willing to receive such as his Son is to bring them? and both Father and Son more willing to save the sinner than he is to be saved? Oh kindness! Christ loves the sinner better than he loves himself! And as I said before, so I say again, the Father doth not grudge anything that Christ gives or doth for poor sinners. The righteousness of Christ is that wedding-garment in which we may sit at the King's table, and are welcome; these are the robes of our elder Brother, in which we cannot miss of our Father's blessing, Oh how many poor creatures have walked in the dark many years, because they have not been brought off from themselves, but have sought that by themselves which is to be sought only by Christ; because they have looked for that in the law which is to be found only in the gospel! And no wonder their business went on so slowly, when they went the quite contrary way to work. When any come to God without Christ, they come, like Simon Magus, with their own money in their hand to buy a great commodity, which is not to be purchased with such kind of coin. If you come to God through Christ, you may come with boldness to the throne of grace; but if you come without him, you do but come with madness upon the point of the flaming sword.

DIRECTION V.

If you would be acquainted with God, come much where he is wont to be, frequent his house, lie always at the doors of wisdom, engage much in his ordinances. This was that course which David took when he wanted God's company; away he goes to the house of God; and, oh what earnestness doth he use, when the doors of the Lord's tabernacle were shut, to get them open again! What moans doth he make, when he was for some time sequestered by his enemies from the enjoyment of God in his public ordinances! "As the hart pants after the water-brooks, so did his soul pant after God, the living God." Oh, when should he appear before him? When should he again behold the out-goings of God in his sanctuary, as sometimes he had? " How amiable are thy tabernacles," saith he, " O Lord God of hosts! And one thing have I desired, and that will I seek after, that I may dwell in thy house, and see thee, and inquire in thy tabernacle," Ps. xlii.; Ps. xlviii.; Ps. xxvii. 4. He thought God was like to be found nowhere so soon as at his own house; he was sure he was never from home. David can never forget what usage and entertainment he was wont to have there, and that this great Friend was used to have a standing table, an open house; and that when his guests were set, he would come and bid them welcome: " Eat, O friends, drink, yea, drink abundantly, O beloved." See then that you get into that part of God's house where he doth most frequently come. Get under the most powerful ministry. Oh hear the word with all the reverence, attention, and affection that you can for your soul! Miss not any opportunities that God puts into your hand, lest that should be the time in which you might have met with God. Lie at the pool of Bethesda, and wait for the moving of the waters. Set yourselves in the house of God, and remember, though you see not God, that he is always present in all places, but he is there more especially present, where his people meet together to attend upon him in his own ordinances. Wherefore, when you come to hear the word, set yourself as in the presence of God, and hear as for your life and soul. "Set your hearts unto all the words which I testify among you this day; for it is not a vain thing for you, it is your life," Deut. xxxii. 46, 47. "Hearken diligently unto me, and eat ye that which is good, and let your soul delight itself in fatness. Incline your ear, and come unto me; hear, and your soul shall live: and I will make an everlasting covenant with you, even the sure mercies of David," Isa. lv. 2, 3. He that hath ears to hear, let him hear what the mighty Jehovah is speaking to his soul. Wherefore I say it again, Set yourself as in the very immediate presence of God; and when you hear a word that you are very nearly concerned in, put up such a short ejaculation as this: Now Lord, strike this hard heart of mine; now Lord, come in, I beseech thee; oh that this word might be the key which might open my heart for the King of glory to come in! Oh command thy loving-kindness this day to break into my soul! Oh that this might be the day in which salvation might come unto my house! Oh that this might be the man that might be my spiritual father, that this might be the messenger, one among a thousand, that may bring me good tidings! Oh that this might be the sentence, that this might be the hour of love! Oh that this might be the day that I may have in everlasting remembrance! Oh that I might presently, without any more delay, set out for Canaan! Cry out, with as much earnestness as that poor man did who brought his possessed child before Christ, O Lord, I have brought my unbelieving heart before thee to cure; it exposes me a thousand times to unspeakable hazards; but, Lord, if thou wilt but speak the word, it shall be dispossessed: I would believe; Lord, help my unbelief. I have brought my hard heart before thee; Lord, soften it, and let me not go from time to time with these dreadful diseases hanging about me, to infect and undo myself and others. Oh melt me, O Lord, melt me, and let me have such a look from thee as Peter once had, which made him go out and weep bitterly! But I shall speak a little more of this nature under another direction.

DIRECTION VI.

If you would be acquainted with God, you must get acquainted with some of his friends; and they will do all they can, and be glad of it too, to help you to be acquainted with him; they will not spare to give you their utmost assistance in this great business. And when they shall hear you asking what you shall do to know God, they are glad at their heart, and will not be at quiet till they have got you home with them to their Father's house; they watch for your soul, and no greater joy than to help forward such a work as this, than to be employed any way in the service of your souls. They are glad when they hear any saying, Let us go to the house of the Lord, and asking the way to Zion with their faces thitherward. Oh! Christian society, good company, is of exceeding use; one good servant in a house, the whole family may fare the better for him. Laban and Potiphar, though ignorant enough in spirituals, could not but observe this, that the Lord blessed their families for the sake of one godly servant. I do not speak this only with respect to temporals, because of that diligence and faithfulness in their places that religion will put them upon; but with respect to spirituals: they will be dropping something that may tend to the awakening and convincing of their sleepy, unbelieving, ignorant companions; they have an inward principle which puts them upon communicating what grace they have received; they know, the more they impart to others, the more they shall have themselves; they have a compassion for souls, and would fain have as many as they can along with them to heaven; they will be teaching little children to pray, and instilling something, that the very babes may set forth God's praises, and they will be pleading with God for them. But this only by the by. Now, if those that are gracious endeavour what they can to bring in those that are open enemies, how much more will they be ready to give all the help they can to you that earnestly desire it! Now, when any one comes to this pass, that he sees a difference between the godly and the wicked, and to say that the righteous is more excellent than his neighbour, and to have an earnest desire to associate himself with them, it is a very great sign that God hath an intention to do such a soul good. Wherefore, if you would be brought to the knowledge of God, go speedily to them that know him well; and they will tell you great things of him, and how they came first acquainted with him, and how this acquaintance hath been kept; they will tell you where they first met him, they will give you to understand that at such and such a time, when they little thought of God, they were strangely brought acquainted with him. When they came (out of fashion or curiosity, or to laugh at him that taught them, or it may be to pick some quarrel with him) to hear such a man, they were made to see what they never took any great notice of before, that they were in an undone condition by nature, and that except Christ would pity them, there was no remedy, but to hell they must go; whereas before they thought themselves as safe as could be. But then they saw that it was no light matter to be out of Christ, and aliens from the commonwealth of Israel. After this they were made to understand something of Christ's undertaking for poor lost sinners, and they heard of his exceeding willingness to receive the chiefest of sinners; and that then they began to see an excellency in his love and goodness, and to be somewhat more taken with the kindness of Christ than ever they were before, and they felt some longings after the precious Jesus: oh that they had but a Christ for their souls! And that after this they were, by the Spirit of God, in some measure enabled to cast themselves at the feet of Christ for mercy, and that upon his own terms, knowing that if mercy came not that way to them, they must sink for ever; and that upon this act of recumbency, after they had for some time waited upon God in the way of his ordinances, they began to taste and relish the things of God, and at last they met him whom their souls loved. Inquire of them, I say, and they will talk thus to you, and tell you also that there was a time wherein they were foolish, disobedient, and unto every good work reprobate, and miserably neglectful of their souls; that they did not at all mind their eternal welfare, but made light of Christ, made a mock of sin, and made nothing of eternal damnation. And they will direct and encourage you also. Let me tell you, they have an interest in God, and their prayers for you may be more advantageous than you are aware of. Yet I would not that you should make Christs of the saints, nor forget what is the work of the Mediator alone. Saints are to be valued, but Christ is to be valued infinitely more. Get acquainted with some warm, rare, experienced Christian, and make him your bosom friend, and observe him, and you shall see much of the beauty of religion shining in him, and you shall see how cheerfully and comfortably he walks; now ask him what his practice is, and go you and do likewise. Have a care of harbouring ill thoughts of the people of God, or, for the sake of one hypocrite, of censuring a thousand sincere Christians. Judge you whether this be just and equal doing. How would you like it, if one that bears some relation to you should do some vile abominable thing, and bring himself to an untimely end, and people should say the whole family is like him, though it may be you are grieved to the very heart that such a thing should be done by any in the world, much more by any that bears any kind of relation to yourself? I tell you, as contemptibly as the world speaks of the godly, they are not such odious creatures as they are represented to be. The saints are not troublers, but peace-makers; they love to make peace between man and man, and, what in them lies, also between God and man. Your converse with such as fear the Lord will make you like them, at least they will endeavour as much. He spoke no untruth who said that "company is of an assimilating nature. A living coal laid to a heap of dead ones may kindle them all; but they are more like, except it be blown up, to put the live one quite out." (Ar. Epict. l. iii. c. 16.) "Therefore," saith the same author, "you must be very cautious of your company." It is storied of Socrates, that he had a rare art of making his familiar friends of his mind. Some active Christians take great pains to make their familiars of Christ's mind. "He that walketh with wise men shall be wise: but a companion of fools shall be destroyed," Prov. xiii. 20. "The tongue of the just is as choice silver: the heart of the wicked is little worth. The lips of the righteous feed many: but fools die for want of wisdom. The lips of the righteous know what is acceptable: but the mouth of the wicked speaketh frowardness," Prov. x. 20, 21, 32. Such as these will do what they can to make you out of love with sin, and in love with God. Such as these will, from their own experience, be setting forth the goodness of God, and tell you that which may stand you in stead as long as you live; it may be they may tell you, that when God began first to work upon their soul, he was pleased to make use of the particular application, and the spiritual conversation of such a Christian relation; and when God came in with comfort, and spake peace, such a one led them to such a promise, which was like a cordial to their fainting soul. When they were abroad, (they will tell you,) and were necessitated to the company of them who were strangers to the life of religion, and were at such a time troubled with horrible temptations, that they were in a wilderness-condition, and thought that never any that walked heavenward could be in the like state; but now, when they got acquainted with the people of God, they found, that as face answered face in a glass, so their experience and the experience of many of the dear children of God were exactly alike; and that that which they thought none in the world could parallel, they find that most of the Christians they meet with know as well as themselves, and at the first hearing, are able to go on with the story before them; so that they have sometimes wondered how any one living should know their hearts and thoughts so well, to whom they did not communicate them. I think it not altogether impertinent here to insert an observation of mine own. I remember, when I was once speaking concerning the duty of Christians in relation to their unconverted friends, and urging them upon doing what they could for God and souls, in the places where God hath set them: in speaking to this subject, I said, that there was not the meanest Christian but might be an instrument of the conversion of a soul. Upon this, I rehearsed a couple of experiences that I had of two persons, strangers one to the other, who gave this account of their conversion; they were upon the matter both alike, and therefore I shall tell but one of them, which take as follows: There was a poor, civil, yet very carnal creature, a servant in a religious family, who did from his soul abhor the spiritual conversation of those in the family, insomuch that he was resolved to run away from his service, he was so weary of such doings. But one night, hearing a strange sound somewhere, he arose out of his bed, and went to listen what was the matter: upon which, he heard one distinctly praying on the other side of the wall; he, still hearkening, heard one praying very earnestly for him, (who did not know but that he might be asleep,) and opening the condition of his soul so particularly, and with so much tenderness, that he was wonderfully awakened, to think that one that he hated should so much love him and pity his soul, and to consider how it was possible any one in the world should know his thoughts so well as that person did who prayed for him. Upon this he began to be very much startled to think of his condition, concluding thus, Surely I am in a lamentable state, and they see it, or else they would never do as they do; they are praying for me when I am asleep, they love me when I hate them. Upon this the man was very much troubled, and his trouble daily increased, till he was forced to open his condition to the person who had been praying for him, who was a poor maid-servant: upon which the work of regeneration was carried on very sweetly, and the man became an excellent Christian; whereas the instrument that God used in this great work was but a poor servant. Now, when I rehearsed this thing, which was the condition of two, as I said before, a third person stood by, (whom I never saw in my life before,) who fell a-sweating for trouble that any of his friends should tell such a thing of him to me, and thought I had meant himself in all the particulars, though I heard not a word of the man before in my life. This by the by. I could not but hint this for the encouragement of parents to get their children into families that are really religious, and to encourage all to associate themselves to such as fear the Lord. You see by what hath been spoken, that acquaintance with the people of God may be of great use for the bringing the soul acquainted with God.

DIRECTION VII.

If you would be acquainted with God, entertain all the messengers that he sends to you kindly. When God calls, answer, and when he sends any of his servants to you, bid them welcome; let the feet of those who bring glad tidings be beautiful in your eye; do not think much if they deal plainly and roundly with you; know that it is out of love to your souls, (God is their witness;) they see that your condition requires it, and that a man in your state is not to be jested with. The Lord knows that they take little pleasure in grieving people; they do it that you may rejoice for ever; they watch for your souls, and therefore you must account them worthy of double honour. But of all the messengers that God sends, have the greatest care of dealing unkindly with and grieving his Spirit; when you have any motions upon your soul by the Spirit, labour to cherish them with all the care and tenderness that you can: turn not convictions away with, I am not at leisure; or, I will hear you of these things when I have a more convenient season: but as soon as you find your heart begin to relent, cry out unto the Lord, and say, O Lord, I beseech thee, carry on thy work effectually upon my soul. Oh that I may have thorough work! Oh let not these convictions wear off from my soul, till they end in a real conversion! Oh let me not prove but a half-Christian! Anything in the world, Lord, so that I may but be made a Christian in good earnest! Oh let me not return with the dog to his vomit, and with the sow that is washed to her wallowing in the mire! Deliver me, O God, from sinning away these things, and getting into a cold world, and from shaking off all, lest I prove worse than ever, and my latter end be more miserable than my beginning. Labour to be very curious in the taking notice of God's absence or presence; and when you find your soul raised in any duty, and your heart somewhat drawn out after God, then be sure to own God's goodness, and bless the Lord for it; record his kindness, forget not his mercy, pass not over such great things in silence. Little do men think what a hazard they run when they quench the motions of God's Spirit. You may read in Cant. v. how dearly the spouse had like to have paid for such an unkindness. What, shall God send his Spirit to visit you? Shall the infinite Majesty so far condescend as to knock at your door, and will not you open? Why then, you may thank yourselves if he never knock more. But if you will now open to him, he will come in to you, and sup with you, and you shall sup with him.

DIRECTION VIII.

Seek his acquaintance most earnestly, if you would have it. Oh, why do men and women jest with matters of the greatest weight and importance in the world! What do people mean, to play with their souls, the wrath of God, and damnation! O sinners, have you nothing else to play with? no lower matters to sport with? Believe it, sirs, heaven and glory are not got with sitting still with our hands in our pockets. We think it worth the while to rise early, and to sit up late, to get an earthly estate; we count it no foolish thing for a man to be very diligent about his worldly affairs. The poor countryman ploughs and sows, harrows, weeds, reaps, inns, thrashes, and a great deal more, before he can eat his bread; and shall we look for a rich crop, and do nothing at all but eat, and drink, and sleep? Is this the way to be rich? Is this the way to be happy for ever? If you intend to do anything in religion to any purpose, you must buckle to your business at another guess rate than most of the professors of the world do: you must take as much pains about your souls as men do about their bodies or estates. Is there any comparison between the soul and the body, between a worldly estate and a heavenly inheritance? Hath a man more reason to look after tricking up his body that must die, or look after the adorning of his soul that must live somewhere for ever? Which are matters of the greatest consequence, eating and drinking, pampering the flesh, and taking our pleasure; or looking after life, salvation, and eternal joy? Do you think that the scripture saith in vain, that "we must strive to enter in at the strait gate?" Is it a bare seeking that will serve the turn? Will a "Lord, have mercy upon me," and bowing the knee, do as well as the greatest seriousness and diligence in the world? Do you think that God will be put off with the skin and garbage instead of sacrifice, with the shell instead of the kernel, with chaff instead of the corn? Doth not Christ say, that "Many shall seek to enter in, and shall not be able?" Oh, why do not lazy professors read the scriptures with trembling? Let all those that are angry with us for putting them upon making religion their business, and using all diligence "to make their calling and election sure," read that one scripture over again, "Strive to enter in at the strait gate: for many, I say unto you, will seek to enter in, and shall not be able," Luke xiii. 24. It was Christ who spoke that word. If we tell you of the danger of a formal religion, you will soon fall upon us as enemies to your peace, and those who impose too much strictness upon you. We therefore do here produce our commission for what we say; or rather, we desire you but to read yourselves what Christ spoke, as touching this matter. Oh! it might justly make a Christian's heart ache, to think how many thousands of professors will be disowned by Christ in that day, who will make many fair pleas for themselves, and pretend a great deal of acquaintance with him. Consider, I beseech you, here is no fear of excess; never any man in the world that was too solicitous about his salvation, never any man took too much pains for heaven. Awake, O sleeper, what meanest thou? Arise, and call upon thy God! If you make anything of the loss of a soul, look about you; if you think the wrath to come considerable, be serious; if you would not be burnt by the fire of his indignation, you must take hold of his strength and make peace with him, and God will be at peace with you,

Isa. xxvii. 5. It is not without cause that the prophet doth complain: "There is none that calleth upon thy name, that stirreth up himself to take hold of thee," Isa. lxiv. 7. One would think that that were strange. What, none call upon his name, when so many of them made so many prayers, as you have it in the first of Isaiah! What, did they nothing but look upon one another when they had their solemn assemblies? Did they say nothing to God when they came before him? Did they do nothing at all when they are said to seek him daily, when they seemed to delight in his way? Isa. lviii. Yet, in God's esteem, all this goes for nothing at all, this prayer is no prayer, this is only wording of it with God. But prayer is another kind of thing, it is the stirring up of the soul, and awakening all its strength to wrestle with God, to lay hold upon God, and to prevail with the Almighty. And where are such as these to be found? who is this that engages his heart in the service of God? It is one thing to engage the tongue, and another thing to engage the heart. Men come to pray with a common spirit, and are many times weary of the work before they have well begun it; what they do they do lifelessly. They can follow their worldly employments with life and delight. They have a male in their flock, but that's too good for God; a lame, blind, starved weak thing must serve his turn. And is this the way to have the blessing? Are such as these like to have any thanks for their kindness? Let them try how any of their friends would take such a present. Now, would you have the blessing of acquaintance with God, you must wrestle for it, and not let God go without it. You must be "fervent in spirit, serving the Lord;" you must "fight the good fight of faith, and lay hold on eternal life." You must grasp about Christ, as a man that is drowning would grasp anything that is thrown out to save him; you must use "all diligence to make your calling and election sure;" you "must work out your salvation with fear and trembling;" you must "seek for wisdom as for silver, and search for her as for hidden treasure. Then shall you understand the fear of the Lord, and find the knowledge of God." What excellent thing is there that is got without pains? Who ever came to be an exquisite curious artist in any skill whatever, that never served an apprenticeship to it, nor at the least gave his mind to it? Where is there a famous physician that never studied in his life? Who gets a victory by sleeping and carelessness? Who expects to have riches drop into his mouth when he goes all the ways that can be to make himself a beggar? Doth the husbandman look for a good crop without ploughing or sowing? Why then should we expect such great things as heaven, eternal happiness, and the favour of God, without looking after them? Whatsoever the lazy formal professor may say, the kingdom of heaven is not obtained thus. There must be running, watching, fighting, conquering, holding fast, holding out, and all little enough; it requires all the strength of thy soul to engage in this great work; it requires some resolution to do such a work as every Christian must do, or else his religion signifies little. Further, it calls for some time too; it is not a thing to be minded now and then, by the by, between sleep and awake, when the devil and the world have had as much service as they call for. Were it for your bodies that I am now pleading; were you like to get any great matter in the world by following my directions; could you be shown a way how to get a great estate, honours, and long life, I am verily persuaded a few words might prevail much. Why, if you will believe the word of God, I am telling you of other kind of things than these be, greater matters by far; and yet how little are men and women affected! as if we spoke but in jest always, when we spoke about things that did concern souls. How little time do men spend in their inquiry into these things! Ask Epictetus, (Ench. c. 63,) and he will tell you that it is a sign of a low soul to bestow much time upon the body and the thoughts of it, and little upon the soul; to be long eating, and long drinking, and long a-dressing, and short in prayer, short in the thoughts of the soul, and short in the service of God; and that it is a sign of a base degenerate spirit to be very curious about toys and inconsiderable trifles, and to be negligent about matters of the greatest importance, to slubber over the great works of religion with the greatest slightness. Remember, O man, thy great work is to take care of thy soul, to look after a Companion, a Friend for thy soul, to get food and clothing for thy soul, that it famish not with hunger and cold. To be indifferent in all externals is the greatest prudence; but to be indifferent about spirituals and eternals is the greatest madness. We are all soldiers, and must fight in such a war wherein we must never lay down our arms. The favour of God is worth the striving for, it is as much as heaven and glory are worth. If your estate or life lay at stake, would you not be willing to use all the interest you could to make the Judge your Friend? Would you go up and down laughing as if you had nothing to do? Would you eat and drink as merrily as ever, and say, It is but dying, it is but being a beggar, it is but the undoing of my wife and children? Would you not look upon a man that should argue at this rate to be little better than frantic? And, I pray, which is most considerable, the death of the body, or the death of the soul; the loss of a temporal, or the loss of an eternal inheritance? Most men's diligence in temporals will condemn their negligence in spirituals. Christ said, " Seek ye first the kingdom of heaven, and the righteousness thereof;" but most men say, I will seek first the earth, and the glory thereof; and if God will give me heaven and happiness after I have served the devil and the world as long as I can, I shall be contented to have it. No such matter; never expect it; God must sooner cease to be than to gratify you in this. Wherefore, do you think, did David follow his work so closely? Why did all those noble worthies in the church of old take so much pains? Why should they not much stick to venture estates and lives too? Will you condemn them all as guilty of too much curiosity and unnecessary preciseness? Do you think their labour was in vain? Are all those disappointed who willingly parted with present things for future things? I must tell you, if you expect to sit down with Abraham, Isaac, and Jacob in the kingdom of heaven, you must do as they did. Heaven will not be obtained now upon any lower terms than then. Your souls are as precious as theirs, and heaven will be as well worth your minding as theirs, and God will look upon you as well as upon them, if you will value his favour as they did. Never look to have God give you that which you will not thank him for. What do you say after all this? Will you sit down before your work is done? Open thine eyes, and consider what thou hast to do, and then tell me if it be not the greatest folly imaginable to be slight in these affairs. Oh, how canst thou eat, or drink, or sleep, whilst thou hast such a great work to do which is undone? Oh, give not sleep to thine eyes, or slumber to thine eyelids, but deliver thyself from the hand of the hunter, and as a bird from the hand of a fowler! "Go to the ant, thou sluggard: consider her ways, and be wise; which having no guide, overseer, or ruler, provideth her meat in the summer, and gathereth her meat in the harvest." How long wilt thou sleep, O sluggard? When wilt thou arise out of thy sleep? "Yet a little sleep, a little slumber, a little folding of the hands to sleep: so shall thy poverty come as one that travailleth, and thy want as an armed man." And will you now labour to get acquaintance with God, as you would to get food for your body? Will you endeavour as much to make sure of his love, as you would to make sure of a pardon, in case of the forfeiture of your life? If so, we have some hopes the work may have some considerable issue.

DIRECTION IX.

If you would be acquainted with God, be much in expostulating the case with God, in urging those arguments which the Scripture doth afford you in such a case. Take with you words, and come unto the Lord, and spread your requests before him, and say, O Lord, thou hast sent thy servants the ministers, and hast invited me to come unto thee, and thou hast offered peace and reconciliation, and to be acquainted with me. O God, I desire, from my soul, to come upon thy call, and would fain be acquainted with thee. I see myself in an undone state while I am a stranger to thee. But, O Lord, I have a cursed base heart that keeps me back from thee, and I cannot tell what in the world to do. O Lord, I beseech thee, help thy poor creature to come unto thee, lead me by the hand, let thy goodness and love constrain me, conquer me by thy kindness; come, Lord, into my soul, and let me see thy face, and look upon thee till I am in love with thee. Oh why art thou as a stranger to me? Wilt thou forsake me for ever? Shall I be one of those thine enemies that shall be slain before thy face? Shall I be one of those that shall dwell with everlasting burnings? O Lord, pity, pity, pity, for Christ's sake, a poor creature that would fain love thee, and be acquainted with thee. I am convinced that I must be damned without thee, and come to thee of myself I cannot. Oh draw me! Oh carry me! Oh compel me, constrain me, make me willing in the day of thy power! I cannot get loose, my heart is too hard for me, my lusts are too strong for me, my temptations are too many for me to conquer of myself. O Lord, help me. Turn me, and I shall be turned. Pluck my feet out of the snare, or I shall be utterly destroyed for ever. Forgive mine iniquity, make me a clean heart, make me thy servant. Tell God that thou hast heard of his goodness and mercy, and that the King of Israel is a merciful King, and that it is his nature to pity. Say to him, Oh, I am a poor undone creature, and wilt thou send me away without mercy? will the God of grace send me away without grace? Hast thou not called me, O God? Thy servants tell me so. O Lord, speak, and give me ears to hear; O Lord, I am come in upon thy merciful proclamation, and I desire to lay myself at thy feet; mercy, Lord, mercy upon what terms thou pleasest. Didst thou not say in thy word, "Ho, every one that thirsteth, come, and buy wine and milk without money and without price?" Have not thy servants pleaded with me to come? and hast thou not sent for me? Oh! a blessing a blessing for me, even for me! O my Father, hast thou not a blessing for me? Shall I be sent away as I came? O Lord, I come at thy word! Do not say unto me, Beg me out of my sight. I cannot go, I will not go. Whither shall I go from thee, for thou hast the words of eternal life? Though I cannot say, Be just to me a saint, yet I will say, Be merciful to me a sinner. Plead the blood of Christ; you may safely say, that if there be not enough in Christ to save you, you do not desire salvation: for in him there is all fulness. You may plead your own absolute necessity. Tell God that if ever poor creature in the world had need of mercy, you have; tell him that you are resolved not to be content without his love. You may plead his promise, in which he hath said that "he will take away the heart of stone, and give a heart of flesh; and that he will put his fear in our hearts, and write his laws in our inward parts." You may plead also the power of God, whereby he is able to subdue all things unto himself; and many such like arguments you may find in many places in the Scripture. But because I have touched upon this before, I shall pass this by.

DIRECTION X.

If you would be acquainted with God, look after it speedily; defer not a moment; your enemy is marching on apace; you may be surprised; your soul is hasting on upon its eternal estate; your glass is almost run; there are but a few sands behind: therefore seek the Lord while he may be found, and call upon him while he is near; erelong it will be too late; wherefore what thou dost, do quickly. What is the voice both of Scripture and Providence? Doth not the word of God say, *Now*, and commend the present time above all. Acquaint *now* thyself with him. Remember *now* thy Creator. Turn *now* unto the Lord. Let a poor heathen shame you into greater speed in this necessary work. I shall translate his words into English: "How long," saith he, "will you defer the looking after the best things? How long will you abuse your reason? Have you not heard such precepts which you ought to agree to, and which you seemed very well to like? What kind of teacher is it that you stay for? For whose coming do you defer, before you will mend and turn? You are come now to years of discretion, (if I should say you were not, you would be angry;) if you will neglect and delay, and add one delay to another, if you will add one put-off to another, and make one resolution and purpose after another, and set one day after another, in which you will think of these things, consider that all this will do you no good; for all your resolutions and promises, for all that I see, you are like to die a common man; therefore now live as a perfect growing man, and follow that which is most excellent unalterably. If anything of difficulty intervene, remember that now is the time for you to show what respect you have for your God and your soul. Remember the goal is not far off, and that now you must not falter, and that as you demean yourself now, it may be you may be happy or miserable while you have a being." (Epict. En. c. 75.) This is the language of that excellent moralist. I add, What is it, O sinner, that thou stayest for? Is it for the day of judgment? Would you be taught by flames the worth of time? You may then indeed learn; but, believe it, your knowledge and learning will do you little good; you may then learn what it is to be miserable, but you cannot learn how to get out of it; you will know what you have lost, but you will never know how to repair your losses. How many thousands of them who have set a day in which they would return and repent, have set, and set, and set it again, and what with one thing or other they could not be at leisure to repent till they came to hell; and there indeed they have leisure enough to repent, and they do repent too, if hell-repentance would do anything. I believe that all that come there do repent and believe too, more than they did while they were alive; but then it's too late. They are now in those dreadful flames. Many of them thought, it may be, of repenting before they died as well as you, and did just as you do. Oh that you would understand yourselves before your state be like theirs! How infinitely doth it concern you to improve time, and to comply with the present tenders of mercy that are made to you; for erelong it may be too late for you too. Oh! know this therefore, that now thy God makes you a gracious offer of pardon; and if you refuse now, this may be the last time, this may be the very cast for eternity. God may say before to-morrow, "This night thy soul shall be required of thee." Go to, therefore, you that talk of trading for the great things of eternity, I do not know when, thirty or forty years hence. Do you not know that your life is but a blast? When your breath goes out of your nostrils, you are not sure that you shall draw it in again. What then do you mean to talk of delay? Have you not stayed long enough already? Consider, man, what thou dost. He that saith he will be good to-morrow, saith he will be wicked to-day. And what if God should say, Thou shalt have the pleasure of sin to-day, and the sorrow of sin to-morrow! Thou shalt be hardened to-day, and damned to-morrow! If your house were on fire, you would scarce say, I will go and sleep four or five hours, and then I will rise and call my neighbours to help to quench it. If your child were drowning, you would scarce say, I must needs stay till I have drank a flagon or two more, and about half an hour hence it may be, I may go and see whether I can get a boat to help him out. If you were condemned to die to-morrow, you would scarce say, I will have music, and sack, and good company all night, and then I will send a messenger, if I can get one to ride a hundred miles, to try whether he can get a pardon for me. Yet thus, for all the world, dost thou do in the great affairs of thy immortal soul. "Oh the folly of man," saith Seneca, "who thinks to begin to live, when a thousand to one but he will be dead and rotten!" I may say, oh the madness of sinners, who make account to be looking after heaven then when it's likely their souls may be in hell! Judge now whether this be wisdom. Now you think time one of the poorest commodities in the world; it's a very drug which lies upon your hand; a day or two, a week, a year is no great matter with you: but believe it, the case will be altered with a witness erelong. Seneca wondered when he heard some asking one of his friends to spend two or three weeks with them, and saw how easily the request was granted, as if they asked as little as nothing when they asked time of him: "Thus," saith he, "one of the most precious things in the world is thrown away as little worth." When you come to lie upon your death-bed, we shall have you have other thoughts of time: then, a world if you had it, for one of those hours that you could not tell how to spend. You now study how to rob yourself of your precious time; you invent pastimes, not considering how swiftly time flies, and how much you will prize it before long. Oh remember, nobody can give you a moment of that time when you want it, that you are now so prodigal of. When time is past, if you would give a world to recall it, it could not be. If you would give thousands for the renewing of this lease, it would be refused. Therefore, live quickly. Man's time runs away first. "*Optima quæquæ dies miseris mortalibus ævi prima fugit.*" (Seneca.) And then my author comments very bravely upon the whole verse

I think that proverb, though it be an Italian one, is worth our remembering, " He that will lodge well at night must set out betimes in the morning." That which keeps us from living to-day is the thoughts of living to-morrow, so that we lose this day while we expect the next. Commenius, speaking of the tiger, saith, " That when he hears the sound of the trumpet, he tears and bites himself." This will be the work of the merciless tigers of the world, that spend their time (in which they should be providing for eternity) in hunting God's people and taking their pleasures, and, it may be, think to be a little more mild before they die; but of a sudden the trumpet sounds, Away, away; and oh, then, what a lamentable taking are they in! How do they wish for time again, or that they had spent that which they had better! Wicked men never know the worth of time till they come to a death-bed, or a while after. Oh then, they that made nothing of spending thirty or forty years would lay down all they are worth for one year, one month, one day, one hour, but it's then too late. Oh how do they gnash their teeth! With what horror do they think of past mercies and future miseries! Men fear generally that Death will come sooner than they would have him; they bewail that their lives are short at the longest; whereas, if men would wisely husband that time which God hath given them, it would be long enough. Oh, happy is that man that hath done his great work before his sun is set! Oh foolish men, that complain of God making their lives so short, and complain not at all of themselves for making them ten times shorter! For most men live not at all the life of religion, and may be called dead. Others have a name to live, and yet are little better than the forner. Most that live spiritually begin their life after they have been many years dead; and though we sit and condemn others as guilty of great imprudence in these affairs, yet how do we at the same time justify them, by being as profusely expensive of precious time as they! Oh, where's the man almost to be found that doth improve time to as good advantage as he should? Among other symptoms of a fool, this is none of the least, "to be always beginning to live." What an unhandsome sight is it to see an old man learning his letters! Oh remember, man, thou hast a great work to do! Oh remember thy precious time runs away with an unspeakable swiftness! What do you mean, to sit with your hands in your bosom? Look about thee, O sinner, 'tis not time-a-day for you to be sleeping or playing; methinks a man in your condition should be up and doing with all the diligence that you could for your soul, and labouring "to make your calling and election sure." Methinks we should hear you asking what you shall do to get a pardon for your sins, to get God reconciled to you. Methinks you should be inquiring what you should do to redeem your time, and to spend every moment of it so to the best advantage, as that you may appear cheerfully before your Master at night. That I may enforce this weighty direction, I shall propound a few serious questions to you.

Quest. 1. Do you think that these things are necessary, or are they not? If they are necessary, why do you not mind them speedily? If they are not necessary, do not look after them at all.

Quest. 2. Do you expect to be in a better capacity to look after these things hereafter? Do you hope for more strength when you are worn out with sin and age, when your back begins to bend, and your joints to shake? Do you think you shall be more at leisure when your work will be much increased? Know this, that sin grows upon you daily, it preys upon your vitals. He that is not fit to-day will be less fit to-morrow. As for leisure, I must confess you may have leisure enough in another world to think of these things. But I wish you well to consider whether it be greater wisdom to repent in this world or in another. I would be loath to be repenting in another; it's sad weeping indeed there where tears shall never be dried up. I have told you oft that God saith, To-day, and it is both wickedly and foolishly done of man to say, To-morrow. I must tell you but so, that it is a dreadful hazard that every delaying sinner doth run. It is a question whether God may not deny his grace, stop the preacher's mouth, stop his ears, and stop your breath. And where are you then with your To-morrow? Delays in these affairs always cost dear; they have cost many thousands dear already, and if you make no more haste than you have done, they will cost you dear too.

Quest. 3. When would you get acquainted with God?—when he hath shut up his door? When would you run his race?—when you have lost your legs, or can but creep with crutches? Is that the best time to do your work in when it is next to impossible to do it?

Quest. 4. Who deserves best at your hands,—the devil, the world, and the flesh, or God? Resolve me this, I pray. Whom do you call your master? Whom have you most reason to make haste for?

Quest. 5. How would you take it, if any of them who depend upon you should serve you as you serve God?

Quest. 6. Do you think you can make too much haste? Who is afraid of being rich too soon? Although a man may with reason good enough be afraid of that which may make his happiness far more uncertain, and his miseries more intolerable. Who fears to make too much haste when his prince sends for him with speed? Oh that men did but know who it is that calls them, and whither they are going, and what they have to do, when they come to their journey's end!

Quest. 7. Are you sure you shall live till you are an hour older? You are strong and healthful, it may be, but did you never hear that such have died with a very little warning? Have you never known a man well one hour, and dead the next? If you have not, I tell you of one now that was very well one moment and dead the next, myself being an eyewitness of it. It's possible there may be but one small moment between a strong working healthful man and a breathless corpse.

Quest. 8. What do you think will become of you, I ask again, if you put off till it be too late?

Quest. 9. What would you do if you were sure you should die, or the day of judgment come before you were a week older?

Quest. 10. Do you think to get acquainted with God in another world, when you do not mind him here? Will God, think you, own them hereafter that disown him here? Will he know them in heaven who would not know him upon the earth?

DIRECTION XI.

If you would be acquainted with God, take heed of those things which keep God and man at a distance, and make the Lord take no pleasure in us. In general, take heed of all sin. "Wash you, make you clean; put away the evil of your doings from before mine eyes; cease to do evil; learn to do well; seek judgment, relieve the oppressed, judge the fatherless, plead for the widow. Come now, and let us reason together, saith the Lord," Is. i. 16–18. You must wash your hands in innocence if you intend to compass his altar, to sit down at his table. In Ps. ci. David is exceedingly desirous of God's company, and he cries out, "Oh when wilt thou come unto me?" He thinks long to have a visit from his old Friend; he would gladly walk with him. Now what course doth he take to get God's company? Why, he goes the best way to work in the world. He will set no wicked thing before his eyes. He knows it is to no purpose for him to expect much of God's company, while he doth entertain his greatest enemies; therefore he turns them out of doors. "I hate," saith he, "the work of them that turn aside; it shall not cleave to me." And that God may dwell with him, and make his house, as well as his heart, a temple for himself, he will not suffer a wicked person to live in it; he will have none in his family but such as shall be ready to serve God and bid this his great Friend welcome.

But more particularly, if you would have much of God's

company, and be intimately acquainted with him, take heed more especially of those particular sins which make God most estrange himself from us. As,

1. Take heed of pride. That was the sin which made the first breach between the creature and the Creator, the sin that sunk the angels; that made God and them, who were very good friends once, to be bitter enemies; this hath made the breach infinite, the feud everlasting, the wound incurable; and this made the first quarrel between God and man. When man thinks himself too good to be but a man, he must be a god; he quickly is too bad to be a man, he is but one remove from the devil. To be a favourite of his Prince is not enough, except he may step into the throne; it's therefore high time for his Prince to remove such from his presence to a prison, from the court to a dungeon. It was pride that cast Adam out of paradise; and do you think that that sin is now less hateful to God, and less dangerous to man than it was five thousand years ago? Did it then spend all its poison? and can it now do no harm? Do you believe that God will take that into his bosom now that formerly he abhorred to look upon? Now sin hath increased its strength and deformity, and heightened its enmity against the infinite majesty of the holy Jehovah, shall his hatred against it decrease? Will he be more willing to accompany proud aspiring rebels now than then? No such matter: God is still as holy as ever, and hates all sin, especially pride, as much as ever. Do you think that it is for nothing that the word of God speaks so much against this sin? Can it be that the Holy Ghost would say, that "Every one that is proud is an abomination to the Lord," Prov. xvi. 5, except God did indeed hate them? Why should God threaten such so much, if he took any pleasure in their society? Though hand join in hand, yet the proud shall not go unpunished. Now we call the proud happy, but shall we call them so when the day of the Lord shall burn as fire, and all the proud shall be as stubble? And the day that cometh shall burn them up, saith the Lord, and it shall leave them neither root nor branch. When the Lord shall tread down the wicked,

and they shall be like ashes under his feet. Mal. iii. 15; iv. 1, 3. There is not one proud man in heaven, I am sure; nor a proud man upon the earth, that shall have much of God's acquaintance. And let me say, he that sets himself above God, (for that's the pride I mean,) whilst he stands in that state, must never expect that God should look upon him with any kindness. Heaven and hell will as soon be agreed, as God and such a one shall be united. The proud now overlook others that are their betters, and scorn their Maker; but shortly they shall be paid in their own coin, they shall be scorned too. If all the proud Nimrods, Pharaohs, and Belshazzars in the world should enter into a league, and combine against the Almighty, and say they will cast away his cords from them, and that they will never debase their noble spirit so low as to stoop to his commands; yet none of them all shall go unpunished: they they shall be like stubble before the devouring flames, and like chaff before a mighty whirlwind: God is not afraid of their big looks. Prov. xxi. 4; vi. 17; xv. 25; Isa. ii. 12; Luke i. 51; James iv. 6. God will clothe himself with vengeance, and the mighty Jehovah will gird his weapon upon his thigh, and march out in fury and indignation, and draw his glittering sword, and resist the proud, and teach them what it is to bid defiance to the Lord of hosts. We shall soon see who shall be uppermost, God or they. And when the proud sinner lies conquered at his feet, how doth he with infinite scorn look upon him, and say, Behold, the man is become like one of us! This 'tis for man to attempt the dethroning of the Almighty! But it may be, most may think themselves little concerned in that which I now speak; wherefore I must add this one word. Be it known unto thee, O man, whosoever thou art, that thinkest thou hast no pride, I am sure thou art one of those that are in the black roll, which have proclaimed war against heaven; thou art the man that shall never be acquainted with God whilst thou art in that mind. It may be thou mayst speak peace to thyself for all this, and flatter thyself as if God and thou were friends: but, let me tell thee, I come with heavy tidings in my mouth to thee: if thou turn not he will whet his sword; he hath bent his bow, and made it ready, he hath prepared for thee the instruments of death; the day of thy calamity is near; the dreadful Jehovah is upon his march; and if you ask me whether there be no peace for thee, I answer as Jehu did to Jehoram, What peace, O haughty sinner, so long as the pride of thy heart is so great, and thy rebellions against thy Maker so many! There is no peace, saith my God, to the wicked. Wherefore, as you value your soul, as you tender your everlasting salvation, and desire to be owned by the Lord in the day of your distress, take heed of pride. Go quickly, and humble yourself, and make sure your Friend; labour to pull down every high thought and every proud imagination, and let your arrogant spirit bow before the mighty God; there is no way will do but this, as you have already heard. You must set the crown upon the Lord's head, you must lay yourself at his feet, and lick the very dust. Your betters have done so before you, and have thought it their honour to lie at the feet of Christ; this they looked upon (and with good reason too) as the first step to preferment. If, therefore, you would be acquainted with God, take heed of pride.

2. Take heed of a worldly mind. What concord is there between earth and heaven? What agreement between God and the world? What delight can his holiness take in him who had rather be wallowing in the mud and treading of clay than bathing himself in divine contemplation; that thinks it higher preferment to sit by his bags of gold, than to stand in the presence of his God; a greater happiness to be rich than to be holy; that had much better be in a fair, market, or exchange, gettng money, than with his God, getting pardon, grace, and heaven? How pregnant is the Scripture of proofs for the evidencing of this truth! To name one or two of a hundred: "To be carnally minded is enmity against God: for it is not subject to the law of God, neither indeed can be," Rom. viii. 7. What do you say to this Scripture? Those who walk with God live in the world, and yet they live above the world; they all look for a city that hath foundations, whose Builder and Maker

is God. It was not for nothing that the apostle John laid so strict a charge upon those whom he wrote to, "That they should not love the world, nor the things of the world. If any man love the world, the love of the Father is not in him," 1 John ii. 15. Whence is it that so few great ones go to heaven, and that it is next to impossible for such to be saved? Is it not because they have chosen mammon for their friend, rather than God? He hath their heart, their love, their time, their service, and they have little to spare for God, and therefore God hath but a little happiness, a little heaven, a short glory for them; they shall have but a little of his sweet company, little acquaintance with him. Why doth James speak so terribly to the rich men, and bid them go and weep and howl? Was it not because their riches were like to undo them? Did the wealthy man in the parable live ever the longer for his riches, or fare ever the better for his greatness, when he came into another world? There is no question but he might have more flatteries; there is no doubt but he hath more worldly friends; but bring me a man upon the earth that lets his heart without control fly upon the world, cleaves to it, and takes it to be his best friend, that knows God, that's acquainted with his Maker, that prizeth his Redeemer. It was a wise man who said that it's absolutely impossible to mind externals and internals, this world and another, with earnestness, at the same time: but it was Wisdom itself who said, that "No servant can serve two masters: for either he will hate the one, and love the other; or else he will hold to the one, and despise the other. Ye cannot serve God and mammon," Matt. vi. 24.

3. Take heed of hypocrisy. Who are the persons that God doth denounce his dreadful threatenings against? Are they not such as honour him with their lips, when their hearts are far from him? With what abhorrence doth he look upon such, and all that they do! Isa. i. They never bring their heart to visit God with, and therefore they have little reason to expect that he should bring his dainties to entertain them with.

4. If you would be acquainted with God, take heed of

being acquainted with wicked company. We read that many wicked men have fared the better for the company of the godly; but we scarce ever heard that any godly man ever fared the better for being in the company of the wicked, except they went on God's errand amongst them. This is clear in the case of Lot, who first lost his goods, and was made a captive by being in Sodom; and though they were restored to him again for a while, (one would have thought that should have been a fair warning how he came again into such company,) yet because that would not do, a while after you may read how dear Lot paid for dwelling in Sodom. Poor man! he lost all that he had, and was fain to fly away without either flocks or herds, and little more than his clothes on his back, and, that which was more sad, to leave some of his own dear relations behind him, roasting in those dismal flames. Whereas had he never come to Sodom, or, upon the sight of their wickedness, speedily left them, it had been much better with him in many respects. Jehoshaphat fared never the better for joining in affinity with his wicked neighbours, it had like to have cost him his life. But were it only loss of temporals that a man hazarded by such society, the danger were not so considerable; but the peril is greater than this; for by it they make God stand at a distance; they must never look to have such company and God's company both together; I mean, when they do unnecessarily or delightfully converse with such. If, therefore, you intend to be acquainted with God, you must not have them always in your company whom he hates, and who hate him, and will labour all they can to cool your affections towards him. "Wherefore, be ye not unequally yoked with unbelievers: for what fellowship hath righteousness with unrighteousness? and what communion hath light with darkness? and what concord hath Christ with Belial? or what part hath he that believeth with an infidel? and what agreement hath the temple of God with idols? for ye are the temple of the living God; as God hath said, I will dwell in them, and walk in them; and I will be their God, and they shall be my people. Wherefore come out from among them, and be ye separate, saith the Lord, and touch not the unclean thing; and I will receive you, and will be a Father unto you, and ye shall be my sons and daughters, saith the Lord Almighty," 2 Cor. vi. 14–18. But I would not here be mistaken, as if I would commend an ungodly proud separation from all that are not just of our mind; or as if a man ought to have nothing at all to do with wicked men. No, no, every one ought to do what he can in his place for the good of souls. Oh that Christians would thus converse more with their poor, ignorant, carnal, Christless neighbours! Oh that they would thus be more acquainted with the wicked, and then they should have never the less of God's company, but the more. But it is unnecessary delightfully associating ourselves with them that I mean, especially such of them that will stifle every spiritual discourse, and divert you from anything that tends to the promoting of the interest of religion; and such as have frequently expressed their detestation of the way of holiness, and make but a mock at your serious counsels, stop their ears to wholesome advice, or make some indecent reflections upon the strict profession of godliness; such as labour to make you believe that all religion but that which will consist with their wickedness is but a fancy. As for such as those, abhor their company, fly from them as those that have the plague; the marks of death are upon them, and you may write "Lord, have mercy upon us" upon their doors, but go not in, lest you be infected.

5. If you would be acquainted with God, take heed of unbelief. Unbelief will make your soul depart from God, and God quite to depart from your soul. This, this is one of those dreadful and God-estranging sins which leads on whole legions against the Almighty; this is that bold daring sin which gives truth itself the lie, and saith that the word of God is false, his promises airy, his threatenings but a wind. But know this, O sinner, such a wind they be, that will rise to a dreadful storm, and tear your strong confidence up by the roots, and blow it into hell, if you make no more of it than you do.

6. If you would be acquainted with God, beware of sensuality. To be sensual and devilish are near akin. To be

lovers of pleasure and haters of God are usually concomitants; in a word, to fare deliciously every day and to be despised of God are no strange things. But I waive the further prosecution of these things, because they are so largely and excellently handled already by so many of our brave worthies. See Mr. Baxter's "Saints' Everlasting Rest," and Mr. Alleine's "Vindiciæ Pietatis."

DIRECTION XII.

If you would be acquainted with God, resolvedly and freely give up yourself to him, and enter into a most solemn covenant with him. And here I shall make bold with that reverend author whom Mr. Alleine makes mention of in his "Vindiciæ Pietatis," and present you again with that excellent form, with the preparatories to it, which I have lately met with in the forementioned author. After your most serious addresses to God, and after a deliberate consideration of the terms of this covenant, and after a thorough search of your own heart, whether you either have already or can now freely make such a closure with God in Christ as you have been exhorted to, and when you have composed your spirits into the most serious frame possible, suitable to a transaction of so high a nature, lay hold upon the covenant, and rely upon his promise of giving grace and strength whereby you may be enabled to perform your promise. Resolve, in the next place, to be faithful; having engaged your hearts, and opened your mouths, and subscribed with your hands to the Lord, resolve in his strength never to go back. And being thus prepared, and some convenient time being set apart for the purpose, set upon the work, and in the most solemn manner possible, as if the Lord were visibly present before your eyes, fall down on your knees, and spreading forth your hands towards heaven, open your hearts to the Lord in these or the like words:—

"O most dreadful God, for the passion of thy Son, I beseech thee, accept of thy poor prodigal, now prostrating himself at thy door. I have fallen from thee by mine iniquity, and am by nature a son of death, and a thousandfold more the child of hell by my wicked practice; but of thine infinite grace thou hast promised mercy to me in Christ, if I will but turn to thee with all my heart. Therefore, upon the call of the Gospel, I am now come in, and, throwing down my weapons, submit myself to thy mercy. And because thou requirest, as the condition of my peace with thee, that I should put away mine idols, and be at defiance with all thine enemies, with whom I acknowledge I have wickedly sided against thee; I here, from the bottom of my heart, renounce them all, freely covenanting with thee, not to allow myself in any known sin, but conscientiously to use all the means that I know thou hast prescribed for the death and utter destruction of all my corruptions. And whereas I have formerly inordinately and idolatrously let out my affections upon the world, I do here resign my heart to thee that madest it; humbly protesting before thy glorious Majesty, that it is the firm resolution of my heart; and that I do unfeignedly desire grace from thee, that when thou shalt call me hereunto, I may practise this my resolution, through thy assistance, to forsake all that is dear unto me in this world, rather than to turn from thee to the ways of sin; and that I will watch against all its temptations, whether of prosperity or adversity, lest they should withdraw my heart from thee; beseeching thee also to help me against the temptations of Satan, to whose suggestions I resolve, by thy grace, never to yield myself a servant. And because mine own righteousness is but monstrous rags, I renounce all confidence therein, and acknowledge that I am of myself a hopeless, helpless, undone creature, without righteousness or strength. And forasmuch as thou hast of thy bottomless mercy offered most graciously to me, wretched sinner, to be again my God through Christ, if I would accept of thee, I call heaven and earth to record this day, that I do here solemnly avouch thee for the Lord my God, and with all possible veneration, bowing the neck of my soul under the feet of thy most sacred Majesty, I do here take thee, the Lord Jehovah, Father, Son, and Holy Ghost, for my portion and chief good, and do give up myself, body and soul, for thy servant, promising and vowing to serve thee in holiness and righteousness all the days of my life.

"And since thou hast appointed the Lord Jesus Christ the only means of coming unto thee, I do here, upon the bended knees of my soul, accept of him as the only new and living way by which sinners may have access to thee; and do here solemnly join myself in a marriage-covenant to him.

"O blessed Jesus, I come to thee hungry and hardly bestead, poor, and wretched, and miserable, and blind, and naked, a most loathsome, polluted wretch, a guilty, condemned malefactor, unworthy for ever to wash the feet of the servants of my Lord, much more to be solemnly married to the King of Glory; but since such is thine unparalleled love, I do here, with all my power, accept thee for my Head and Husband, for better for worse, for richer for poorer, for all times and conditions, to love, and honour, and obey thee before all others, and this to the death. I embrace thee in all thy offices, I renounce mine own worthiness, and do here avow thee to be the Lord my righteousness; I renounce mine own wisdom, and do here take thee for mine only Guide; I renounce mine own will, and take thy will for my law.

"And since thou hast told me that I must suffer if I will reign, I do here covenant with thee, to take my lot as it falls with thee, and, by thy grace assisting, to run all hazards with thee, verily supposing that neither life nor death shall part between thee and me.

"And because thou hast been pleased to give me thy holy law as the rule of my life, and the way in which I should walk to thy kingdom, I do here willingly put my neck under thy yoke, and set my shoulders to thy burden, and subscribing to all thy laws, as holy, just, and true, I solemnly take them as the rule of my words, thoughts, and actions; promising that, though my flesh contradict and rebel, yet I will endeavour to order and govern my whole life according to thy direction, and will not allow myself in neglect of anything that I know to be my duty.

"Only because, through the frailty of my flesh, I am subject to many failings, I am bold humbly to protest, that unhallowed miscarriages, contrary to the settled bent and resolution of my heart, shall not make void this covenant; for so thou hast said.

"Now, Almighty God, Searcher of hearts, thou knowest that I make this covenant with thee this day without any known guile or reservation, beseeching thee, that if thou espiest any flaw or falsehood herein, thou wouldst discover it to me, and help me to do it aright.

"And now, glory be to thee, O the Father, whom I shall be bold, from this day forward, to look upon as my God and Father, that ever thou shouldst find out such a way for the recovery of undone sinners. Glory be to thee, O God the Son, who hast loved me, and washed me from my sins in thine own blood, and art now become my Saviour and Redeemer. Glory be to thee, O God the Holy Ghost, who, by the finger of thine almighty power, hast turned about my heart from sin to God.

"O dreadful Jehovah, the Lord God omnipotent, Father, Son, and Holy Ghost, thou art now become my covenant-Friend, and I, through thine infinite grace, am become thy covenant-servant. Amen. So be it. And the covenant which I have made on earth, let it be ratified in heaven."

THE CONCLUSION.

And now my work is done, I must leave you; and whether I shall ever speak to you, or see you, or write to you again while the world stands, I know not. My body is frail, and I am a poor dying man, and before it be long, my mouth will be more stopped than it is, and yours too. And therefore it's high time for us to look about us. As for my part, I have, with all the seriousness that I could for my soul, spoken to you about the great and weighty affairs of your souls and eternity. I again call heaven and earth to witness that I have set life and death before you; I have, in the name of my great Master, been wooing you to accept of his Son for your Lord and Husband; himself for your God, Father, and

Friend. I have told you what the Lord doth require of them that would be in covenant with him. I have given you a rude description of Him whom I would have you acquainted with. I have told you of some of the glorious effects of acquaintance with God. I have told you of the danger of being a stranger to God. I have told you how thankfully some have closed with these offers, and how well they like their choice. I have further shown you what a peaceable state you shall be in, immediately upon your spiritual alliance with this great and noble Friend. I have told you also of some further benefit and good that will come unto you upon your acquaintance with God. I have given you to understand how desirous the Lord is, notwithstanding all that is past, to forget and forgive, and to receive you into favour, if you will in good earnest return to him with speed. I have again and again propounded this match to you, and told you as much as I could well do in so short a time. I have stayed a great while for an answer. I have put the business forward all that possibly I could; because I see how foolishly and madly you make light of those advantageous offers that are made to you. I have again and again pleaded with you, as if I were ready to starve, and begging an alms of you; nay, if it had been for my very life, I could not have spoken with more earnestness. I have expostulated the case with you, and asked you several weighty questions, and you have not, you cannot, answer any one of them, but you must condemn yourself, and by your own confession, you have nothing in the world to say against the excellency of this Friend. And therefore you must either speedily come in upon the invitation, and close with those gracious overtures that are made to you, or you must, without any reason in the world, (yourself being judge,) cast yourself away. And in hopes that all that have heard me will not be so mad as to make light of these things, but be asking, with some seriousness, that great question, How shall I do to get acquainted with God? how shall I do to get a Friend for my soul? what shall I do to be saved? I have laid down some directions for those that are unfeignedly desirous to be reconciled to God. I have told them that they must labour to be thoroughly acquainted with that strangeness and enmity that is in their hearts against God, and of the unspeakable danger of their being strangers to God. I have further directed them that would be acquainted with God to labour to get humble hearts. I have advised that they visit him often, if they would be intimately acquainted with him; and that not in a transitory way, but to make a solemn, set visit of it, and to be sure that they do not forget to get Christ along with them. I counselled them also to be much in those places where he is wont to walk, and to get intimately acquainted with some of them that know him very well, and will do their best to get them to be acquainted with him. I have told you that if you would be acquainted with God, you must kindly entertain and make much of any messengers that come from him to you; and if men would make sure work, I desired them, as they loved their souls, that they would follow this great business with the greatest earnestness and seriousness in the world; and that what they do they would do speedily. I informed you what arguments the Scripture puts into our mouths, which we may urge, at the throne of grace. I entreated you, for your soul's sake, to take heed of those things which kept God and man unacquainted; as, namely, all sin in general, but more particularly pride, worldly-mindedness, hypocrisy, delight in wicked company, unbelief, and sensuality. Lastly, I direct all such as would be at peace with God to give up themselves to him resolvedly and freely in a solemn covenant.

And have I been beating the air all this while? What will ye do after all this? What shall become of all these sermons? Dare any of you all still be contented to be unacquainted with God? Can you be very well satisfied, after you have heard of such a Friend, to be a stranger to him? Can any of you look upon your state as safe while God is your Enemy? Oh, how shall I leave you with hearts full of enmity against your Maker! Alas, alas, poor hearts! You look very merrily, as bad a condition as you are in; but did you but know how near you are to everlasting burnings, I believe it would put a damp upon your spirits, and spoil your mirth. Oh, how shall I leave that poor sinner that stands as a person altogether unconcerned, whereas Death stands ready for his commission, to fetch him away before God! And where are you then? Oh where are you then, if you come before God as a stranger? Oh what shall I do for you? What shall I say to you, to prevail with you? Oh, what arguments will persuade you? Oh, how shall we part? Brethren, my heart's desire is that you may all be saved. Oh that you may all know, in this your day, the things of your peace! Oh that I could mingle all my words with tears! Oh pity, pity, for the Lord's sake, pity your precious souls! Oh, come not here to ask counsel of God, and then go away, and take the counsel of the devil. And what, will you yet make light of all the tenders of the Gospel? Are peace, pardon, reconciliation, and acquaintance with God still nothing with you? Will you, for all this, take up with a lifeless religion, and never mind a more spiritual, intimate converse with God? As the Lord liveth, thou speakest that word against the life of thy soul. But if thou wilt go on, and despise God, who can help it? I have told thee, and told thee again, what the end of these things will be. Well, once more, I ask thee, in the name of God, Wilt thou have God for thy Friend or no? that is, Wilt thou love him above all the world? Wilt thou accept him for thy Lord and Husband? Wilt thou be ruled absolutely by him? Wilt thou lay down thy weapons, and turn on God's side, and fight under his banner? Wilt thou have holiness here, and happiness hereafter? One would think this is a question that one need not be long resolving. Come, come away, for the Lord's sake, for your precious soul's sake; as you would be owned at the day of judgment, as you would rejoice when most of the world shall be filled with unspeakable horror and perplexity, as you would not hear that heart-rending word from the mouth of the Judge, "Depart, I know you not," come away, I beseech you! Come away! Oh ye, my dear friends, the cloud hangs over the world, and erelong it will fall with a vengeance. Oh, come out of Sodom, linger not, for the Lord's sake, lest the dint of that storm fall upon you. Fire! fire! fire! Awake! awake! awake! The fire is kindled. What meanest thou, O sinner? If thou sleepest a little longer in that bed of security, thou art a dead man, thou wilt be awakened of horror, when thou shalt know thy danger, but not know how to avoid it. And do you still stay? Make haste! Oh make haste! Your glass is almost out, your time almost spent, and death is hastening apace upon you. I speak it again, make haste! come away! I cannot, I cannot hold my peace! How can I endure to see the ruin of thy soul, and say nothing! Oh follow those directions which I have given thee out of the Scripture! Seek the Lord while he may be found, and with all possible speed, seriousness, and gratitude, accept of his kindness, while you may. Methinks some of your hearts seem to be affected; methinks your countenances speak you to have some thoughts of returning; some of you look like persons almost resolved to set upon this great work: oh that it may not be almost, but altogether! Speak in such language as this to your own souls. What meanest thou, O my soul, thus to stand disputing? Is this a time for thee to stand still, as if thou hadst nothing to do? Hark how the King of Glory calls! Hark how his messengers invite thee! Consider how long they have stood waiting for thee! And shall they go away without thee? O foolish heart and unwise, wilt thou answer all these gracious offers with a flat denial? or that which is little better, wilt thou put off all God's messengers with some sorry excuses? Awake, O my soul, and look about thee! How canst thou refuse when mercy calls? How canst thou deny when kindness itself asks, entreats, beseeches thee? Awake! for shame! up and put on thy wedding-garments! Oh that this mind might be in thee always! Oh that thou wert up and ready! And then happy were the day wherein thou wert born; then happy were the day that ever thou heardst of a Christ, of acquaintance with God, and reconciliation with thy Maker. Oh then, how glorious shouldst thou be for ever! I rejoice to see the day of thy marriage coming; when thy Lord and Husband shall bring thee home in the greatest state, and in infinite glory, to his own house, where thou shalt sit like a queen for ever and ever. Behold his harbingers are coming! Behold how many messengers the Lord hath sent to prepare his way! Awake, O Zion, and put on thy beautiful garments! Rise up, O royal bride, and put on thy princely robes! Clothe thee with the sun, and put the moon under thy feet. Go out and meet the King, thy Husband. Behold, O Jacob, the waggons of Joseph are coming! Behold, O daughter of Zion, the chariots, the chariots of thy King and Husband are coming! They are coming! Oh why doth not thy heart leap within thee? Oh why do not thy spirits even faint for gladness? Why dost thou not say, It is enough, I will go out and meet my Lord before I die? When will the sun be up? When will the day break? When, oh when will the shadows fly away? I will get me up to the mountains of myrrh, to the hills of frankincense. I am travelling for Zion, my face is towards Jerusalem. Who will ascend the holy hill with me? Who will bear me company to my Husband's house? Let us go up to the Lord's house. Come away, the sun is risen, the shadows are flying away; thousands are gone already. Let Barzillai and Chimham, old and young too, go along with the King to Jerusalem. Come from the highways and hedges, come with your wedding-garments; come quickly, and he will make you welcome. The King hath sent to invite us to a feast, a feast of fat things, of wines on the lees, well refined. Come, for the table is spread, all things are ready, and his servants stay for us. And will God entertain such creatures as we are? And will the Lord open his doors to such loathsome beggars? Will the Father receive such prodigals? Return then unto thy rest, O my soul, for the Lord will deal bountifully with thee. Who is he that I see coming in the field? Who is this that comes from the wilderness? that comes to meet us? Hark! methinks I hear the trumpet sounding! Hark! What's the matter? How do the mountains echo! How doth the air ring again! What noise is that which I hear? What glorious train is that which I see? Whence do they come, and whither do they go? It is my Master's Son, dear soul, thy Lord and Husband, with his royal attendants. Behold he comes! He comes apace! leaping upon the hills, skipping upon the mountains. He is coming! He is coming! He is even at the door! Erelong thou shalt see the mountains covered with chariots and horses of fire; the earth will tremble and shake; the heavens and the earth will be all on a flaming fire; the King of Glory will come, riding upon the wings of the wind, accompanied with millions of his saints and angels. He is coming, he is at the door! Go, veil thy face; alight and meet thy Husband. He will bring thee into his Father's palace, and thou shalt be his wife, and he will love thee for ever; and thou shalt remember thy widowhood no more. Even so, come, Lord Jesus; come quickly. Amen. Amen.

OTHER PURITAN CLASSIC TITLES

In addition to *Heaven upon Earth* we are happy to offer the following Puritan Classic Reprints.

The Redeemer's Tears Wept Over Lost Souls by John Howe is subtitled: A PURITAN VIEW OF OUR LORD'S WEEPING OVER JERUSALEM. According to Dr. Joel Beeke, "This is Howe's most searching and compelling book for wooing a sinner to Christ. He stresses the responsibility of man within the framework of divine sovereignty. It makes for a compelling read."

A Commentary on the Epistle to the Hebrews by William Gouge is the MAGNUM OPUS of this gifted Puritan divine. This two volume work contains over 1120 pages of exegetical and expository brilliance. Spurgeon said, "We greatly prize Gouge." Peter Masters said, "The exegetical value of this commentary is enormous: every vital word in Hebrews is explained in a manner far superior to that which suffices for modern word studies. The expository value of the commentary is equally rich: every doctrine, theme and argument which is found in the Epistle being given its own heading and section. May the Lord greatly bless this magnificent help to many preachers of the Word in these needy times."

We also have plans to produce several more Puritan Classics in the months ahead, including:

A Body of Divinity: Being the Sum and Substance of the Christian Religion by Archbishop James Ussher. This massive volume has been out of print for over 300 years. "Publishing *The Body of Divinity* will help many in our generation to recover or reaffirm the faith of the Reformation--the greatest revival of true religion ever." – Dr. Mike Renihan

The Complete Works of Thomas Manton is a priceless set of 16 large volumes containing the very essence of the ministry of one of the greatest of the Puritans. "Though he is best known for his biblical chronology, I believe that his *Body of Divinity* is his most valuable legacy. This volume, long overdue to be reprinted, was once regarded as a classic in the field of Reformed systematic theology and deserves to be so regarded again." – Dr. Joel Beeke

Call us Toll Free at 1-877-666-9469
Send us an e-mail at sgcb@charter.net
Visit us on line at solid-ground-books.com

OTHER SGCB TITLES

In addition to *Heaven Upon Earth* we are happy to offer the following related titles:

A Pathway into the Psalter by William Binnie is a masterful study of the Book of Psalms by a master teacher. Spurgeon said, "A highly valuable work. Supplies a desideratum."

Psalms in Human History by Rowland Prothero is "a fascinating account of the varied ways in which the 150 Psalms have influenced, encouraged, challenged, and preserved God's people through the centuries. You will thank God for this book!"- David B. Calhoun

The Psalms in History and Biography by John Ker is a perfect compliment to *Psalms in Human History.*

Notes on Galatians by J. Gresham Machen is a precise and practical exposition of Paul's Epistle that opens up the glorious doctrine of justification by faith alone in Christ alone. It is very timely.

Biblical and Theological Studies by the professors of Princeton Seminary in 1912, at the centenary celebration of the Seminary. Articles are by men like Allis, Vos, Warfield, Machen, Wilson and many others.

Theology on Fire: Vols. 1 & 2 by J.A. Alexander is the two volumes of sermons by this brilliant scholar from Princeton Seminary.

A Shepherd's Heart by James W. Alexander is a volume of outstanding expository sermons from the pastoral ministry of one of the leading preachers of the 19th century.

Evangelical Truth by Archibald Alexander is a volume of practical sermons intended to be used for Family Worship.

The Lord of Glory by Benjamin B. Warfield is one of the best treatments of the doctrine of the Deity of Christ ever written. It is simply masterful.

The Power of God unto Salvation by Benjamin B. Warfield is the first book of sermons ever published of the expositions of this master-theologian.

The Scripture Guide by James W. Alexander is a helpful guide to lead young people and new converts into a deeper appreciation of the Word of God.

My Brother's Keeper by James W. Alexander is a book of letters he wrote to his 10 year old brother. It is full of sound advice on a wide variety of subjects.

Call us Toll Free at 1-877-666-9469
Send us an e-mail at sgcb@charter.net
Visit us on line at solid-ground-books.com

www.ingramcontent.com/pod-product-compliance
Lightning Source LLC
Chambersburg PA
CBHW020350170426
43200CB00005B/120